THE SUNDAY TIMES

Money Guide

Edited by Diana Wright

7/6

)06

HarperCollins*Publishers*

HarperCollins*Publishers*
Westerhill Road
Bishopbriggs
G64 2QT

The HarperCollins website address is www.harpercollins.co.uk

First published in 2004 by HarperCollins Publishers
Copyright © Times Newspapers Ltd 2004

ISBN 0-00-718138-8

The Sunday Times is a registered trademark of Times Newspapers Ltd

British Library Cataloguing in Publication Data
A catalogue record for this book is available from the British Library.

Typesetting and digital artwork by
Morgan Studios, Linlithgow

Printed and bound in Great Britain by
Clays Ltd, St Ives plc

Contents

Introduction   1

Section One: Savings   7

Section Two: Borrowing   29

Section Three: Investing   63

Section Four: Insurance   107

Section Five: Pensions and Retirement   139

Section Six: Tax and Tax Planning   185

Section Seven: Getting Advice and
Making Complaints   203

Appendix   215
Useful names, addresses and websites

Index   229

About the Authors

CHRISTOPHER GILCHRIST has been involved in the financial services industry since 1970. He has written for *The Sunday Times*, *Financial Times*, *Daily Telegraph* and *Daily Mail*. He is the author of several books on personal finance including *The Sunday Times Personal Finance Guide to Tax-Free Savings*. He has contributed extensively to radio and TV on personal finance and is the editorial director of the financial website Everyinvestor and a director of independent financial adviser Churchill Investments. He is the author of Sections One and Three.

KEVIN PRATT has been writing on insurance and personal finance issues for 20 years. After editing publications for insurance brokers and independent financial advisers, he became a full-time freelance journalist in 1992. He has since contributed regularly to *The Sunday Times*, *The Times*, *Financial Times*, *Daily Telegraph*, *The Scotsman*, *Yorkshire Post* and *Manchester Evening News*. He is the author of *The Sunday Times Guide to the Protection Game*. He wrote Section Four.

HELEN PRIDHAM became a journalist specialising in personal finance after gaining a degree in economics. She has more than 20 years' experience in the field and has written for *The Sunday Times*, *The Times*, *Money Observer* and *The Herald* in Glasgow. She is the author of several books on personal finance including *The Sunday Times Guide to Your Pension*. She has also won a number of awards and commendations for her work, including the 1999 Scottish Life Best Freelance Pensions Journalist of the Year. She is the co-author of Sections Two and Five and the author of Section Seven.

DIANA WRIGHT has been writing on personal finance issues since 1982. She was editor of *The Sunday Times* Money section for ten years to 1995 and since then has been a regular contributor to the paper as well as writing a number of books, including *The Sunday Times Personal Finance Guide: Retirement*. She has won numerous awards for writing on pensions, unit trusts, investment trusts and insurance, including the Association of British Insurers Lifetime Award for insurance journalism in 1998. She is the co-author of Sections Two and Five and the author of Section Six.

Introduction

You've bought this book because, I hope, you want to make the most of your money. So where do you start? Right at the beginning, of course. If you follow these ten simple steps, you should at least avoid many of the major traps and problems that, week after week, beset readers who write in to *The Sunday Times* problem page.

Basically it boils down to one question: who do you want to be in charge? Your money or you? Taking control of your financial affairs – being able to assess clearly where you are and foresee what you are going to need in the future – is half the battle. Understanding the big picture means you'll be able to make the most of the tax breaks that are going, to get better rates on your savings and to follow a calculated investment course which should, in the end, produce very decent rewards.

Nothing in life is certain, and the one thing this book cannot do is tell you where to invest for instant, risk-free riches. They don't exist. Anyone who tells you they do is probably after your money. In financial terms, there truly is no such thing as a free lunch, and if that comes as a disappointment, I'm sorry, but we all have to grow up sometime. Nevertheless – to continue the culinary metaphor – you do have a choice: you can pay over the odds for a practically inedible meal, or you can walk a bit further down the street and get fantastic food at an excellent price.

So use these steps as a checklist and be honest with yourself. Getting into the habit of looking after your money can be for some people a bit of a shock to the system, but once you make the effort you'll be surprised how little time it takes. If you are into making resolutions, make one now: once you've read this book, and spent some time getting things into good shape, devote half an hour a week from then on to looking after your money. It could turn out to be the most remunerative half-hour of your week.

Step one: Call your bank to account

Check your bank statement. It may sound blindingly obvious but how many of us actually do it? If you're not into internet banking, make sure you get statements every month. Some banks still send them out quarterly, which makes it hard to keep an eye on things, so insist on monthly. Make sure your regular standing orders and direct debits are going out each month, and don't go into the red – you'll only pile up needless bank charges.

How much interest are you getting on your current account? It's probably something like 0.1% if you're lucky. If you're prepared to spend the time, change your bank account to one that pays a better rate. Look at Section One for more details of bank accounts and how to change them. And if you have a mortgage, consider moving to an offset loan, which combines savings, possibly a current account and your mortgage all in one. It could save you money without any conscious effort on your part. Section Two will fill you in.

Step two: Build up your nest egg

Nobody can operate sensibly without a small stash of ready money to be used for emergencies or for extra spending such as holidays, clothes and Christmas presents. Yes, you can pile it onto your credit card and guarantee yourself an expensive time paying it back, but why should you? Do you want to enrich yourself – or the banks?

Whether you have £500 or £5,000 in your nest egg is going to depend on you. Some people feel happier with a good-sized chunk stashed away. Maybe it's their 'running away money' in case they want to move jobs in a hurry; maybe it's simply for the next holiday. You can leave it hanging around in your current account but it's much better to put it into a decent paying instant access account. Check out the best rates in *The Sunday Times* savings table, published weekly. If you need to build up your nest egg, make sure you put in a regular amount each month. If you're not sure of your resolve, set up a standing order or direct debit from your current account so it happens automatically. Section One gives you more details.

Step three: Tame the plastic in your life

Years ago, an early credit card advertisement promised to 'take the waiting out of wanting'. It sounds attractive, but the credit card issuers would say that, wouldn't they?

If you've got into a pile of debt on your plastic, look out for cheap rate balance transfer deals. But read the small print – they're not always as attractive as they seem. By all means go for special deals, for points or cash back related to the amount you spend on the card, but make sure you pay it back every month if you possibly can. That way you win, not the issuer. If you can't pay back the full amount, don't get into the habit of just paying the minimum. It's set deliberately low to maximise the amount of interest piling up on your statement. Section Two will tell you more.

Step four: Choose the right mortgage

Your mortgage is almost certainly the biggest debt in your life so make sure you pay the lowest possible amount of interest. That could mean going for a short-term fixed-rate loan or a discounted deal or you may find an offset mortgage suits you best. Don't just look at the monthly payments – think carefully about what you want out of the deal. If it's protection from future rising interest rates, go for a fixed rate. If it's the lowest possible payments in the short term, look at discounts – but remember you're going to have to meet bigger payments in later years. And if your priority is to repay the loan as soon as possible, look at offset and flexible mortgages. You'll find more about all of these in Section Two.

Maybe you've already got an endowment mortgage and consider yourself one of the victims of mis-selling. If so, do something about it. That may include making a complaint to the Financial Ombudsman Service and, depending on the circumstances, you may get compensation. But don't sit back. Now you know your endowment is not guaranteed to pay off the loan, it's up to you to work out how to handle that. Maybe you should change to a repayment basis or save extra sums elsewhere to meet the anticipated shortfall. The trouble-shooting pages at the end of Section Two will guide you through endowment problems.

Step five: Organise your insurance

Maybe it says something about our society that the only thing we are legally required to insure is our cars. But trying to do without insurance in other areas is crazy. You can save money by shopping around, and you can waste far more by not paying proper attention to the conditions attached. Find out more in Section Four.

And don't forget that the most important thing to insure may be yourself. If you have dependants, the first thing you need to think about is how they will cope financially if you die or become unable to work. Once again, it's all about getting in control and not letting chance events wreck everything.

Step six: Build up your long-term investments

Unless you're content with living more or less hand to mouth, you'll want – if you can – to build up some longer-term savings and investments. This may seem an impossible ambition, particularly if you're a student or bringing up a family and struggling with a large mortgage and maybe school fees as well. But unless you make the effort, at some stage, to get to grips with investment, you'll lose out – you won't be able to do all those things you promised yourself or maybe help your children to buy their first house.

Investing involves thinking about risk, what it means and how much you are prepared to take. There is no way you can eliminate risk from your financial life but there are ways to cut it down. Read about it all in Section Three.

Step seven: Maximise your pension

Maybe you enjoy your work so much you want to carry on until you drop; maybe you're confident someone is still going to want to pay you when you're aged 75 or 80. If so, you're probably extremely rare – and very lucky.

The rest of us have got to build up some other source of income to keep us going after paid work ends. Forget about relying on the state unless you're prepared to live more or less at subsistence level. So that means getting a pension plan. It doesn't have to be a tailor-made plan provided by your employer or a pension company. But given the tax breaks involved, and for many employees the extra subsidy from their companies, you'd be mad not to join such a scheme, even if it's only part of your overall financial planning.

Unfortunately, pension legislation is extremely complicated – and it is going through one of its periodic shake-ups, which means at the moment it's more complicated still. Also there have been some total disasters with pension schemes going bust, with dreadful consequences for the individuals involved. That said, for most people, a sensible pension plan is a hugely important part of an overall financial strategy. Section Five is where to find out about pensions and retirement.

Step eight: Keep tax to a minimum

Fail to get your tax return in on time and you start piling up penalties. The Inland Revenue pulls in around £85m a year from taxpayers too lazy, or maybe just too scared, to send their forms in by the deadline. And it makes many millions more in surcharges and interest on late payments. Getting your tax affairs under control is crucial if you want a comfortable financial life.

So what about evasion – and avoidance? Forget the first; it's the illegal one. You may not agree with everything that taxpayers' money is spent on, but if you try to evade tax you're short changing your fellow citizens and you could also be piling up some extremely nasty problems for yourself.

Tax avoidance is the acceptable one. It means using the rules, legally, to minimise the amount you pay. Some tax avoidance is incredibly simple, effectively free and essentially a 'no brainer'. Using an individual savings account (Isa) for your cash deposits is one obvious example. More contentious are the various schemes for avoiding inheritance tax: contentious because they can be expensive, while it is far from certain they will still work by the time you die. But by all means consider them. Section Six provides details.

Step nine: Get good advice

You don't have to take anyone's advice on your financial affairs. And it's fair to say that for some people who have done so, it has been to their detriment. Dubious products such as high income 'precipice bonds' (see page 101) have been foisted on a public who have been lured in by headline figures, baffled by fine print and ended up with huge losses. There seem to have been so many 'mis-selling' scandals recently that the financial advisory industry has a long way to go before it earns our respect.

But there are good financial advisers, and if you want to make the most of your money you could do well to find one and listen to his or her recommendations with an open and critical mind. The more you know yourself, the better you'll be able to judge the value of what they say. Find out how to spot the good advisers – and the bad – in Section Seven.

Step ten: Deal with any problems

Few of us get through life without some money problem or other. Maybe you've got a shortfall on your endowment, a high income bond that is set to lose you money or a pension that isn't performing. Or maybe it is something essentially simpler – a bank's call centre which won't listen to you or a 'customer care' department that couldn't care less.

The number one rule if you've got a problem is: don't ignore it and hope it will go away. Problems don't – the more you ignore them, the bigger they get.

Read Section Seven for good advice on how to make your voice heard, how to complain, and where, to get results. And how, if at all possible, to make sure you don't get into a mess in the first place.

Living with money in the 21st century

It's not an easy time for investors and savers – or indeed for borrowers. Maybe no time ever was – it just seems so with hindsight. Many of us make our financial decisions using basic assumptions which we have never articulated and which we may have inherited, tacitly, from our parents. The problem is, they could be years out of date.

Take the matter of inflation, for example. In the 1970s and 1980s, it reached 20% or more. That meant the wisest thing to do was borrow – you were paying less in interest than you were 'gaining' in inflation. So piling up huge debts you could hardly afford on your current income was positively beneficial. Especially, if you used the money to buy a property, whose real value kept pace (and more) with inflation, while your debt rapidly diminished in real terms. But by the late 1980s, the inflation rate plummeted and a generation of housebuyers, caught between rising interest rates, falling property prices and negligible pay rises, plunged into the nightmare of negative equity.

As we moved through the 1990s, returns from stock markets just kept going up. Owning company shares seemed a fast way to mega-profits. Investment companies were confident enough of the future to predict sky high returns for your regular savings into a pension plan. In those days, it seemed perfectly possible for your plan to grow by 10%, 12% or even more a year. So putting £100 a month into a pension appeared to provide a sure-fire guarantee of a rich old age. And then came the crash: and investments were worth less than half what they had been before.

Now think of the past few years. The rise and rise in property prices has helped many people to tens of thousands of pounds of paper profits as the value of their homes have risen – and if they had invested in buy-to-let properties, even more.

But is the property bandwagon about to run out of steam? If so, buyers who have borrowed heavily could find themselves in serious trouble.

The investor's road map

So what are we looking at for the next decade? It's good to start with a basic 'road map' reflecting the situation as it is today (rather than as it was five, ten or 20 years ago). I can't guarantee its total accuracy – no one could – but at least it should ensure you're not basing your decisions on judgments that are years out of date.

This road map uses the key notion of 'real' returns and interest rates. 'Real' returns are the only ones that matter – that is, returns after stripping out the effect of inflation.

◆ Inflation will remain relatively low, though it may be a touch higher than we have been used to.

◆ Borrowers will continue paying a real rate of interest, and unless their income rises markedly because of promotion, the value of their debts will only slowly decline as a proportion of their income.

◆ Real returns from low-risk savings – in other words, cash deposits – will be positive after inflation, at least for basic rate taxpayers, but very modest. Think in terms of 1% to 2%.

◆ Returns from assets such as stock markets and property are much harder to call. Much depends, of course, on the particular investments you choose. But unless you are especially fortunate in your choices, it is probably safe to look for a long-term annual return somewhere between the rate of price inflation and that of earnings inflation – or perhaps a touch more. That translates to a return of, say, 2% to 8% in nominal terms. In 'real' terms, for practical purposes, you should think of somewhere between 3% and 5% a year.

This, then, is the road map for making decisions from now on. The one thing you can be certain of is there will be unforeseen events and trends unfolding as the years go by. You will have to revisit your map frequently in the light of developments. But at least you can be reasonably confident you are starting off in the right direction.

1

Savings

In this section we will look at

Rainy day money

Choosing new accounts

Variable rate accounts

Short-term fixed-rate investments

Three types of savings plans

Isa allowances

The Child Trust Fund

Savings strategies

1

Savings

Getting small sums right can have a big payoff. Finding good accounts for your rainy day money and other savings is not as exciting as investing in penny shares. But getting the basics right in your personal finances will both save you money and make you money. It will also give you the confidence that you have your affairs well organised and under control.

Very few of us are saving enough for our future. So devoting serious thought to this and setting money aside for longer-term savings is a vital step in building financial security.

What are your savings for?

'Savings' covers two quite different things: lump sums you have already accumulated and want to keep in a good home, and the regular monthly amounts you put aside for the future. They have very different purposes, so this section has two parts:

◆ **Rainy day money** This will protect you if you lose your job and can't immediately get another one, if you face unexpected bills, or if you need to top up your income if you are unable to work through illness, or want to pay off short-term debt such as credit cards.

◆ **Accumulating capital out of regular contributions** Building up longer-term savings will give you a nest egg for the future to cover major expenses ranging from school or university fees to supplementing your pension provision.

How much rainy day money do you need?

While everyone needs some money available at short notice for emergencies or unexpected requirements, the amount depends on your personal situation and your responsibilities. For example, as a single person in your first job and living in a rented flat, an emergency fund equal to three months' expenditure will probably cover any cash needs you may have.

But a couple in their late 20s with two children and owning their own home and car will need more, both to cover the children's needs and the things that may go wrong with the boiler, roof or gearbox. Financial planners generally consider a sum equal to between three and six months' expenditure is adequate.

If you are self-employed, you could need more because you will not receive sick pay. Retired people will usually need less because their pension income is more secure than income from employment.

Until recently, most people used a branch-based bank or building society instant access account for their emergency fund, though the newer internet or internet/telephone accounts are also suitable since they all give access to thousands of cash machines. Today, most banks and building societies operate a tiered interest rate structure where the bigger the sum you invest, the higher the rate you get. A great many high street accounts pay rather poorly, but with a little shopping around you should be able to find an instant access account that offers a reasonable rate.

The benchmark rate

The benchmark interest rate for savings is the Bank of England's base rate . This is the rate at which the UK's central bank will lend money to banks that need it. The rate is reviewed every month and changes are widely reported in the media. Base rate is generally the lowest rate at which any bank will lend money to anyone. Typically, banks lend at a minimum of 2% to 3% above base. And they try to borrow money at below base rate – which means they will mostly pay less than this on their accounts.

However, there are usually some banks and building societies prepared to pay the equivalent of base rate or even a bit more. Small building societies, for instance, do not have the standing to borrow large sums from bigger banks to lend out on mortgages, so they have a greater need to pull in money from individual savers than Barclays or Lloyds TSB. Some banks that provide credit cards or other higher rate lending may be willing to pay more to savers. And many internet-only accounts can afford to pay more because they do not incur the costs of a branch network.

When the base rate rises or falls, most banks adjust their interest rates – but they do not have to move exactly in step. If it rises by 0.5%, it is quite common for some banks to raise their rates to savers by only 0.4% while others increase theirs by 0.6%.

The savings market is a busy, jostling place where banks with good accounts scream about them with big adverts. But the dark secret of all the banks is what happens to these accounts. The typical pattern is that a new account is launched with a great fanfare and pays a top-of-the-market rate. But each time the base rate changes, the bank raises its rate by less than this or reduces it by more, until savers are getting a poor deal. Most banks have dozens of old accounts that now pay derisory rates of interest.

This means you cannot afford to find a good account and simply park your money there. You need to review the rates on all your savings accounts regularly and be ready to switch to a better one if necessary. In the noisy warfare of the banks, all aiming at capturing the maximum number of prisoners, think of yourself as a guerrilla saver.

The most reliable source of up-to-date information on interest rates is the daily updated www.moneyfacts.co.uk. Many newspapers including *The Sunday Times* publish weekly 'best buy' tables.

Access to your emergency fund

Your emergency fund must be available to meet emergencies. So you should place it in a form that is easily accessible, preferably in an instant access account so you can withdraw it at any time without notice. If you live with a partner, your emergency fund should be in a joint account that either of you can access. This means individual savings accounts (Isas) are unsuitable for emergency funds. Isas have to be in the name of one individual and cannot be opened jointly. If you were ill and could not access your Isa, neither could your partner or anyone else.

Also, if you open one of the internet/telephone accounts as an emergency fund, be sure you both have the security codes needed for access. Banks discourage you from writing these down, but will you remember the vital information in an emergency? If not, store it – in disguised form – so you can look it up if you have to.

Beyond the rainy day

Many people like to have more cash on deposit than they genuinely need for emergencies. And most of us also use deposit accounts to accumulate the cash we need for purposes such as buying a house or car or paying for a holiday. You can, of course, have just one account that includes both your emergency fund and other money. But if you know you would be tempted to dip into the emergency pot, you may be better off keeping it separate.

If you do not require access to such an additional sum of money beyond what you need for emergencies, you can consider placing it in an account where you have to give notice before you can withdraw it. Notice accounts sometimes offer better rates than instant access. Typical notice periods are 30, 60, 90 and 120 days. But if you do not get a worthwhile addition to the interest rate for having to give the extra notice, it is not worth bothering.

Postal accounts can also offer premium rates. You can only make deposits and withdrawals by post and can only get a withdrawal in the form of a cheque you pay into your bank account. Telephone accounts have not entirely superseded postal accounts, so you may still find one that offers a good deal. But check the terms. Usually, with postal accounts you only get interest from the date a cheque you pay in is cleared, which can take up to four days. And you may cease to get interest from the date you pay a withdrawal cheque into your bank account – though it may be several days more before you have the cleared funds in your account. Postal accounts are designed for people who do not make many transfers in or out.

Telephone and internet banks also offer notice accounts and their rates tend to be higher than for branch-based accounts.

Opening new accounts

In principle opening a new account is straightforward but the recent tightening up of money laundering rules has sparked a wave of complaints. The rules, originally designed mainly to catch drug traffickers, have been adapted to make it harder for terrorists to move money around. To open a new bank account, you will now have to provide convincing proof of your identity in the form of passport, driving licence or Inland Revenue tax notification and proof of your address in the form of a recent utility bill, council tax bill, bank or mortgage statement. If for good reasons you do not have the necessary documents, banks are permitted to verify your identity from other sources, so if, as is often the case, counter staff say it isn't possible to proceed without the documents listed above, insist on seeing someone more senior.

Most of the UK-based banks have signed up to the Banking Code (www.bankingcode.org.uk) and are committed to providing a new bank with details of your standing orders and direct debits within three days of you making a request.

Comparing interest rates

In the UK, the rates for deposits are usually quoted gross, meaning before deduction of tax. But they may be quoted on two bases. The nominal rate is that applied to the account, while the annual effective rate (AER) takes into account the frequency of interest payments.

The nominal rate is not affected by whether you draw your interest or leave it. But if interest is paid more than once a year and left in the account, you will earn interest on interest and end the year with an even higher balance. The difference tends to be marginal – if you receive monthly interest, a nominal rate of 5% becomes an AER of 5.12% – but always compare accounts on the same basis to ensure you are getting a true comparison.

Tax on interest

UK banks and other organisations offering deposits must by law deduct tax from the interest before paying this to the account holder. The rate is 20%, and this is regarded as satisfying the account holder's liability to the basic rate of income tax, even though at the time of writing this is 22%. If you are liable to tax at only the lower rate of 10%, and have interest paid to you net, you can reclaim the 10% you have overpaid through your tax return.

To have interest paid without deduction of tax, you must sign form R85 declaring you are a non-taxpayer. It is available from any bank or building society. Parents may sign on behalf of children so their interest is not taxed. But if the interest a child gets from money given by parents is more than £100 a year gross, it will all be taxed as if it were the parent's income.

Banks based outside the UK are not subject to UK tax legislation and may offer accounts where no tax is deducted. In particular, many UK banks and building societies have subsidiaries in the Channel Islands or Isle of Man that offer gross interest paying accounts to UK residents.

Whether you receive interest gross or net, you are still bound by law to declare it on your tax return. And if you receive gross interest it is your legal responsibility to ask the Inland Revenue to send you a return and to declare the income. If you have not had tax deducted at source, you will be assessed for the amount due. In the case of higher rate taxpayers, the total liability will be the higher rate of tax less any tax paid by deduction at source.

Some National Savings accounts pay interest without deduction of tax at source but the interest is still taxable.

Variable interest accounts

UK banks and building societies offer a wide variety of accounts. The following pay variable rates of interest. The next section covers accounts paying fixed rates.

Children's accounts

These often offer better variable interest rates than can be secured on a small deposit in a normal instant access account. They may also offer other features, such as magazines, stickers, moneyboxes and savings clubs.

Club or treasurer accounts

These are designed for use by clubs and associations that are not registered charities. Typically, such associations do not need a normal bank current account because they do not have many payments into or out of their accounts and want to earn interest on their balances. For a comprehensive guide to these accounts see *Moneyfacts* magazine (see Appendix).

Instant access accounts

These permit withdrawal of capital without notice, though there is usually a restriction on how much can be withdrawn in cash on any one day. The interest may be credited yearly, half-yearly, quarterly, monthly or daily. With most accounts, the interest rate depends on the amount invested. Many can be opened with as little as £10 but the rate may be very low on deposits of under £1,000.

Internet accounts

These have to be set up over the internet. The initial transfer is made electronically from your current account and future transfers are to and from your current account. Interest rates are usually higher than on branch-based accounts.

Mini individual savings accounts

Isas come in two forms, mini and maxi. Most banks and building societies offer mini cash Isas into which you can invest up to £1,000 in each tax year (£3,000 in 2004-5). Regardless of your personal tax status, no tax is payable on the interest you earn in an Isa, whether you draw it out or leave it in the plan. Mini cash Isas usually offer instant access and a variable rate of interest which is frequently higher than for other types of account. If you have large sums to invest, though, it may well be to your advantage to open a maxi Isa rather than a mini (see Section Three).

Monthly income accounts

These may have a minimum notice period for withdrawal. The income is usually paid direct by bank transfer to your current account. There is often a minimum investment of £2,500 or more.

Notice accounts

Money can be withdrawn without penalty by giving the appropriate period of notice. Common terms are seven, 30, 60 and 90 days. If you wish to withdraw money without giving the requisite notice, you will lose interest, often the amount that would have been paid during the notice period. Minimum investments are usually £1,000 or more.

Postal accounts

Some building societies offer these accounts, where deposits and withdrawals can only be made by post. Interest rates are variable and may be higher than on instant access accounts, as are the minimum investments required.

Premium bonds

These are not a conventional investment. The amount of money paid out in prizes is a percentage of the total invested in the bonds and this will vary. But if you invest the maximum amount of £30,000, because most of the prizes are small you should receive a tax-free return equivalent to this rate – though you may have to hold the bonds for several years before your prizes average out at this level.

Telephone accounts

The initial deposit is made by cheque. You set up a direct debit arrangement with your current account and can then transfer money between it and your telephone account. You have to create a security code and every time you phone to make a transfer it is used to identify you. The interest rates paid may be variable or fixed and are usually very competitive. Only instructions by telephone will be accepted.

Fixed-rate accounts

If you have cash you know you will not need for a year or more, you can consider fixed-rate accounts as well. The key point here is that every fixed-rate account levies penalties if you change your mind and extract your cash early. So you must be confident that the money will stay there for the full term.

Logically, you would expect to get a higher rate for tying your money up for a set period and that the longer the period, the higher the rate should be. Most of the time, this is what happens, but when financial conditions are turbulent, variable rates can be higher than fixed.

Choosing a fixed-rate account is a more complex decision, because at the time you commit your money you cannot be certain you will get more interest than you would from a variable account. A fixed rate of, say, 5.5% may be on offer for a three-year period at a time when variable rates are only 4.25%, making the fixed rate seem attractive. But the variable rate may rise at any time. If it rises sharply soon after you have made your investment, you could obtain less interest over the three years in the fixed account than you could have in the variable account. Of course, if the variable rate fell to, say, 3% after you had made your fixed-rate investment at 5.5%, you would be sitting pretty.

This shows you have to consider the outlook for interest rates before committing yourself to fixed-rate investments. Much will hinge on the prospects for inflation: is there any reason to expect it to rise or fall? If inflation looks more likely to rise, a fixed-rate investment is unlikely to be profitable, because the Bank of England will have to raise short-term interest rates to restrain it.

Unfortunately the evidence shows even highly qualified economists' interest rate predictions are no better than random guesses. So you should not have too high an expectation of getting your own guesses right.

You also need to look at the possible downside as well as the upside. Maybe you will not make a big profit by fixing your return at 6% when variable rates are 4.25%. But suppose you are counting on getting a minimum rate of interest over the three-year period. If you invest at a variable rate you might not get it if rates fall sharply. Fixed-rate investment enables you to assure yourself of reasonable returns.

Longer-term and more complex forms of fixed-rate investment are covered in Section Three.

Short-term fixed-rate investments

Children's Bonus Bonds

Issued by National Savings & Investments, these tax-free bonds have a fixed rate of interest. The face value of the bond grows by a set amount over a five-year term. You can 'roll over' the bonds until the child is aged 21.

Escalator bonds

These are issued by building societies and pay a rate of interest that rises each year for a fixed period. A typical pattern would be to get 4% in year one, 4.5% in year two, 5% in year three and 6% in year four. An enticingly high rate is often paid in the last year, but this may be balanced by a below average one in the first year or two. Since these are fixed-rate accounts, once your money is committed you cannot usually get it back early, or if you can there is a significant penalty (except in the event of death). These bonds often have minimum investments of £1,000 or more.

Fixed-rate bonds

These bank or building society accounts pay a flat fixed rate of interest for a fixed period from one to five years. Early withdrawal may not be permitted, but if it is there will be a penalty. Minimum investments are upwards of £500.

Guaranteed growth bonds

Issued by insurance companies, these guarantee a fixed rate for a specified period, usually between two and five years. They pay out a lump sum at the end of the term. The return is usually treated as having borne income tax at the basic rate, so only higher rate taxpayers will have an additional liability. Non-taxpayers and those paying at 10% cannot reclaim the tax paid by the insurance company.

Guaranteed income bonds

These pay a fixed income for a specified term, usually two to five years. The tax treatment is the same as for guaranteed growth bonds.

Individual savings accounts

Many banks offer mini Isas with rates fixed for periods of two to five years. Some companies offer maxi Isas with a fixed rate of return for periods of up to five years. The returns are tax-free. Sometimes a rate of income is guaranteed, but at maturity you do not get all your capital back unless a stock market index is above a certain level (see 'precipice bonds' on page 101). Examine such plans carefully and be absolutely clear about what you might stand to lose.

National Savings Certificates

These grow in value at a fixed rate over a period of up to five years. The profits are tax-free. There is usually a limit on the amount you can invest.

National Savings Pensioners' Guaranteed Income Bonds

These pay a fixed rate of income over two or five years. The interest is paid gross but is taxable.

How much protection?

UK banks and building societies are covered by a compensation scheme that guarantees to repay 100% of the first £2,000 and 90% of the next £33,000 per individual, making a maximum entitlement of £31,700, in the unlikely event that they should go bust. Banks based outside the UK may be covered by other compensation schemes but you would be wise to deal only with large and reputable institutions.

Trouble-shooting guide

On the whole the UK money transmission network is highly reliable and efficient. But among its millions of daily transactions there are inevitably some errors. If you spot one on your account, notify the bank immediately and keep copies of everything, printing off any relevant internet pages. If the bank branch or division does not resolve the problem, direct your complaint to head office. If that fails, contact the Financial Ombudsman Service (see Appendix).

Why save rather than spend?

Regular saving requires strong motivation. Most people find it easier to spend money than save it. So why should you make the effort? The answer will be in the form of personal goals you want to achieve. Defining those goals more clearly will help you sustain the motivation you need. Those goals will be concerned either with short-term needs, such as having the money to mend the roof or go on holiday, or longer-term ones such as having enough to pay your child's university fees in 15 years' time or to top up your pension income.

Recognising the benefits of 'compound interest' should also help keep you motivated. Actually this is a misnomer because what we are concerned with is the effect of 'rolling up' both interest and capital growth. Albert Einstein famously described compounding as the eighth wonder of the world.

Consider the following: how much more would you have if you got a return of 7.5% a year rather than 5% on a regular saving of £100 per month over five years – at which point your total saving would be £6,000? The answer is that at 5% you would have £6,900 and at 7.5%, £7,400. The difference hardly seems worth bothering about.

Now make the same comparison over 20 years. Your total saving is now £24,000. At 5%, the accumulated sum would be £41,500 but at 7.5% it would be £56,100 – a difference that is certainly worth bothering about. In the 21st year, even if you put no more money into the account, the annual growth at 7.5% (£4,207) is more than double the annual return at 5% on £41,500 (£2,075). The longer the period, the more you will gain by securing a higher rate of return on your regular savings (see page 26).

The three types of savings plan

There are three basic types of savings plan: fixed, managed and stock market. Over the long term, stock market plans can be expected to produce the highest returns, but over periods of up to ten years they may do worse than the other types because of the periodic fluctuations in share prices. The table later in this section shows the results of different types of plan over different periods but, most important, it also shows the results to different end dates. This gives a good idea of the fluctuations in values seen in the past and there is no reason to expect the future to be any different.

If you expect your savings plan to run for ten years or more, there are strong arguments for putting at least some of the money into a stock market plan.

Fixed return plans

Few companies today offer regular savings plans that guarantee fixed returns, even though there is a demand for them. The reason is regulators now require all potential liabilities of a financial services company to be matched by adequate capital reserves. This makes offering fixed return guarantees so costly that companies cannot offer attractive returns on plans of this type.

A few companies have offered guaranteed fixed returns on plans running for a year or two. These may be a worthwhile alternative to saving at a variable rate in a deposit account.

Managed plans

Managed savings plans divide your money between different types of asset such as deposits, fixed-rate investments, property and shares. Most are designed to run for a minimum of ten years and aim to secure a higher return than you would get from a deposit account, but with less volatility in the capital value than applies with a pure stock market plan. These plans are of two types: with-profits and unit-linked, which have very different characteristics.

With-profits plans were the staple savings product in the UK for more than 50 years but over the past few years they have been radically altered. The changes resulted from three developments: the near insolvency of Equitable Life, the 2000-3 bear market and endowment mortgage shortfalls.

With-profits problems

Equitable Life was a highly respected mutual life assurance business that from 1970 attracted policyholders by paying high bonuses and claiming it paid no commission to salespeople. In fact, by the early 1990s, it had used up all its reserves by paying them out as bonuses. It had paid out bonuses greater than the returns it had earned on its investments and had insufficient capital to meet its liabilities to policyholders – facts confirmed by the Penrose Report into its affairs, published in early 2004, but not known at the time by policyholders or regulators.

The near failure of Equitable Life in 2001 led to a drastic tightening of the prudential regulation of life assurance companies by the Financial Services Authority.

The FSA's tightening of rules governing how much capital life assurance companies had to hold to meet their liabilities to policyholders coincided with the worst crash in share prices for more than 30 years, at a time when most life assurers held 60% or more of their with-profits funds in shares. Many were forced to sell shares at low prices to improve their reserves, and the result was deep cuts in bonus rates on almost every type of with-profits policy. On top of this, most companies also applied a market value reduction, which meant the benefits received by those cashing in their policies were cut by up to 20%.

The bonus cuts meant many policyholders who took out with-profits endowments in the 1980s to pay off their mortgages faced shortfalls. Because endowment premiums at that time were low, it was cheaper in terms of monthly repayments to have an interest-only mortgage and a with-profits endowment than to have a repayment mortgage, so these policies were very popular with home buyers. See Section Two for more on mortgages.

The premium rates for these endowments were set on the basis of annual returns of as much as 10% on the investments. While these returns had been achieved in the 1980s, in the new low inflation, low interest rate environment of the 1990s they became unrealistic.

Lower returns and bonus rates mean a typical policy expected to produce a payout of £50,000 in 2012 will now be projected to fall short by £15,000 or more. The actual shortfalls will only be known when policies mature, but the

2000-3 bonus cuts mean likely shortfalls have increased significantly for most endowment mortgages.

Of course, as interest rates fell in the 1990s, mortgage borrowers' payments on their interest-only mortgages also declined and if they had added a portion of this windfall to their regular savings, they would have no shortfall. However, few were advised to do so by the insurers. This, and the fact that many advisers recommending endowment mortgages made no mention of any possible shortfall, has given rise to widespread complaints of 'mis-selling'.

The Financial Ombudsman Service is handling tens of thousands of such complaints. If you believe you have a case for compensation – which will require evidence that the endowment mortgage was inappropriate to your circumstances at the time and/or that the risk was not explained – you should contact your insurer in the first instance to register a complaint. If you are unhappy with its response, you can take your complaint to the Financial Ombudsman Service. For more on endowment mortgage problems, see Section Two.

Reinventing with-profits

In 2002 the Sandler Report on long-term savings recommended the creation of a simpler set of financial products, the intention being that these could be sold to consumers with minimal advice and so have lower charges than existing products. In respect of with-profits, the report recommended the creation of a new 'transparent' structure in which the actual investment returns earned and the way these were allocated to policyholders would be clearly reported. The major insurers have incorporated much of this methodology in their latest with-profits policies, which means there is now a major distinction between old-style and new-style policies.

Essentially, in old-style policies insurers had and still have far more discretion over bonus rates. This may work to the advantage or disadvantage of old-style policyholders – much will depend on the pattern of future investment returns and on the rate at which people surrender their policies before maturity. On early surrender the policyholder forfeits part of the accumulated bonuses, which are therefore available to pay to those whose policies run to maturity. With new-style policies, early surrender penalties are much lower.

Assessing the merits of keeping a with-profits policy going, surrendering it or making it 'paid up' – paying no more premiums but leaving it in force – is extraordinarily difficult since it involves considerable crystal ball gazing. The future returns earned on the with-profits fund cannot be predicted with any certainty. There are companies (like Equitable) which have reduced the holding of shares in their with-profits funds to 30% or less, and over the long term it is clear their bonus rates are likely to be well below those of insurers with a higher percentage of their funds in shares.

However, if you are contemplating cashing in a life insurance policy, bear in mind that if your health has deteriorated, you will pay above the normal premium rates for any new life cover. Also, if you plan to cash in a with-profits policy, it is always worth getting a quote from one of the dealers in second-hand life policies. You can sell the policy, via one of these dealers, to an investor who will continue to pay the premiums and get the maturity value. Often you will get more from selling than surrendering it to the life assurance company.

Rather than approaching an individual endowment policy dealer, you can use a broker service such as the one operated by Newcastle Building Society, which will shop around to get the best price for you, or contact the Association of Policy Market Makers (see Appendix).

Future with-profits

The new-style with-profits plans give policyholders more safeguards and security but also lower returns. Old-style policies often produced annual returns over the long term equivalent to or greater than those from stock market plans (see table on page 26), despite the fact with-profits funds typically invested only 60% to 70% of their money in shares. Such high returns are very unlikely with new-style policies.

Many insurers' new-style with-profits funds have little more than 50% of their money in shares. If, as is likely, shares produce the highest annual returns over the long term, you should expect new-style with-profits payouts to be lower than those from stock market plans over periods of ten years or more.

However, if you need to encash your savings plan at a definite date, a with-profits plan involves less risk of the kind of downward fluctuation you can see in the table.

With-profits policies have other advantages too. Their payouts, after ten years, are free of all UK tax, though the insurer itself pays tax on income and capital gains, and policies can easily be placed in trust, which makes them useful in estate planning.

Managed unit-linked savings plans

The difficulties of the insurers have led investment managers to launch unit-linked plans with some of the features of with-profits. The cash-in value of these plans is simply the value of the units that have been purchased with contributions. Managers of these plans attempt to limit the volatility of cash-in values in two ways:

◆ They spread money between fixed-interest investments, property and shares and adjust the proportions to try to lower risk, sometimes providing limited guarantees that the price cannot decline by more than a set percentage.

◆ They offer 'lifestyle' plans where you specify the encashment date and over the period to that date, they progressively switch a larger proportion of your fund out of shares and into safer investments such as fixed-interest.

It is too early to judge the success of the lifestyle plans but given the long-term data, you should expect final payouts will on average be lower than those that maintain a 100% exposure to shares.

Is it worth giving up some of the returns from shares to obtain an element of capital security with one of these managed plans? Only you can answer this, but the key point is that if you don't need to have the money on a specific date and can wait for any decline in share prices to be reversed, the case for the managed plan is much weaker.

Stock market plans

All the long-term studies show that shares produce higher returns than other types of financial asset (see page 69) and in the UK, shares have produced higher returns than property over most periods of ten years or more. This often puzzles people who have made big gains in property but it is simply the effect of gearing. If you buy a £100,000 property with a £75,000 mortgage, and the value rises to £125,000, you have not made a 25% gain but a 100% gain – you have benefited from the 'gearing' provided by the loan. Over any 25-year period since 1900, you would have made far more money buying £100,000 worth of shares with a £75,000 loan than you would have in residential property.

Managers of unit trusts, open-ended investment companies (Oeics) and investment trusts all offer regular savings plans. All these funds are collective investments in which investors own units or shares in the fund. For more information on these funds see Section Three.

It is clearly impossible to foresee what will happen to the economy and business over a period of 15 or 20 years. So there are large risks in selecting specialist funds that invest in only one type of share or industry. The two types of fund best suited to long-term regular saving are:

◆ **An index-tracker fund** These replicate a stock market index – in the UK, either the FTSE 100 Index of the largest 100 companies or the more representative FTSE All-Share index which has more than 700 constituents. These funds have low charges and are a buy-and-forget choice since they automatically reflect the current stock market favourites.

◆ **An internationally investing investment trust** These usually have around half their money in the UK with the rest in the US, Europe and Japan, so you are buying a small slice of the world.

These regular savings schemes are much more flexible than with-profits plans. Usually, you can stop contributions and start again without penalty and add lump sums if you wish. You can also withdraw all or part of the value of your plan at any time. Costs vary – with index trackers annual charges should be no more than 1%, while many investment trust schemes charge 0.5% to 1% a year.

Mix and match option

Many regular savings plans have a £50 or £100 per month minimum. If you save more than the minimum, you can choose to put contributions into two different funds. If you want to avoid paperwork, set up your savings plan with a fund supermarket, since you can have regular savings going into several funds but get just one valuation and set of paperwork. You can also switch funds easily without having to cancel one plan and start another. Fund supermarkets are covered in Section Three.

If you start a plan with one of the two types above, you could choose something more adventurous for your second fund – such as a UK smaller companies fund or a biotechnology or natural resources fund.

Make use of the Isa allowance

You are allowed to invest up to £5,000 each year in a maxi Isa (£7,000 in 2004-5). If you have no plans to use this allowance for lump sum investments, it can make sense to use it for regular savings. Under current legislation the tax exemption for Isas lasts until 2009.

As far as shares are concerned, if you are a basic rate taxpayer you get no income tax benefit from holding shares in the tax-exempt Isa (see page 102). If you pay tax at the higher rate, you avoid any extra income tax charge on dividends by holding shares in an Isa.

Investments held in an Isa are free of capital gains tax. This may not at first seem a big advantage: so long as your annual gains are less than £8,200 (2004-5), you will pay nothing on gains on taxable investments. But if you save a sizeable sum over the years, you could become subject to CGT – and if this happened when your personal tax rate had risen to the higher rate, it could prove costly since gains are charged at your highest marginal rate.

Many people use their investments to generate a top-up income in retirement. This usually means switching capital from shares to fixed-interest investments that generate a higher income – and income from these, unlike shares, is completely tax-free in an Isa, which means at least a saving of the 20% income tax you would otherwise pay.

To give yourself most flexibility, choose a 'self-select' Isa with a fund supermarket (see Section Three) that allows you to select and alter the funds in your plan. You should pay no extra for this.

Friendly society plans

Friendly societies are permitted to run tax-sheltered savings schemes with low minimum and maximum investments. Some are of the with-profits type while others are unit-linked. Some plans have high costs and charges which wipe out the value of the tax concessions, so study the small print closely. The plans have a minimum term of ten years and there may be penalties for early encashment. If you do make a profit it may be subject to tax if you cash in early.

Some of these plans are marketed as ways to build up a nest egg for children. But the only advantage they offer over a unit trust savings plan is the low monthly saving. Every child has their own tax allowance and if your child cashes in a unit trust savings plan that is theoretically taxable, if they are a non-taxpayer they will escape tax.

The Child Trust Fund

A new arrival on the savings scene, the Child Trust Fund (CTF) launches in April 2005. The government will place £250 in the CTF for each child born after September 2002 (£500 if household income is below the Child Tax Credit threshold). Each child can have only one CTF account and parents and other relatives may contribute a further £1,200 a year to accumulate tax-free for the child's benefit. The government has said it will make an additional payment into the CTF on the child's seventh birthday. All the proceeds from the account will be paid out on the child's 18th birthday.

As mentioned above, the tax exemption of the account is insignificant. The dividends from UK shares are paid net and tax cannot be reclaimed, so the same dividends are received in a CTF or Isa as would be received directly by a standard rate taxpayer. Given the annual exemption of £8,200, moreover, few children will ever become liable to capital gains tax. The CTF will have advantages, though:

◆ **Lockaway** The money will not be accessible under any circumstances before age 18. Though you can achieve this result by setting up a trust, most normal savings and investment schemes in practice give children access to their capital sooner than this.
◆ **Charges** These are likely to be lower than on many regular savings schemes, with a maximum of 1.5% a year.

Since the savings term will be more than 15 years, the natural choice is a plan investing entirely in shares – though you may like to have the option of being able to switch to a less risky fund in the last few years. The default option, however, will be a 'stakeholder' fund in which less than 100% will be invested in shares and the managers will switch a progressively larger proportion from shares to other assets from age 13 onwards. Provided you are prepared to review the plan yourself at regular intervals, opting for an all-share fund could prove more rewarding.

Savings strategy

Use one of the simple web calculators (www.e-gismos.com/savings.asp, www.webcalculator.co.uk/financial) to help you plan your long-term savings. If you are accumulating capital to generate a future income, assume you will get a 5% yield – in other words, you will need a capital sum 20 times greater than the income you want.

Long-term savings plans linked to equities are the easy way to grow rich slowly. Set up your plan or plans and add to them whenever you can. Use different types of plan and choose funds managed by different managers, or investing in different areas, to spread the risk. Once you have a basic plan in place, preferably one linked to a very widely spread general fund, consider a more volatile type for your next plan: one linked to emerging markets, say, or smaller companies.

Use the flexibility of the Isa, unit trust or investment trust savings plans. Instead of feeling gloomy when prices fall, be courageous and add whatever lump sums you can afford. On a long-term view, this is almost certain to pay off.

The tax exemptions of the Isa under existing legislation will end in 2009. By then there will be so many Isa savers it seems unlikely that any political party would risk voters' wrath by abolishing the tax breaks, so they could end up being extended indefinitely.

As long as Isas have these tax breaks, you will be better off keeping your money in one. When it comes to taking money out of savings plans, you will therefore usually do best to draw from taxable plans and leave your tax-free Isa untouched.

Past results from different types of savings plan

Maturity values of £50 per month plan

Term in years	10	15	20	25
Maturity date: February 2000				
With-profits	£10,000	£21,800	£47,250	£101,490
UK equity income	£10,520	£21,690	£60,350	n/a
International general	£12,990	£29,560	£79,130	n/a
Maturity date: September 2001				
With-profits	£9,410	£20,690	£43,810	£93,880
UK equity income	£9,230	£18,140	£46,700	£111,800
International general	£9,820	£21,150	£51,070	£132,940
Maturity date: August 2002				
With-profits	£8,550	£18,440	£38,070	£82,490
UK equity income	£7,720	£15,990	£37,600	£91,700
International general	£7,580	£17,240	£38,070	£101,420
Maturity date: February 2004				
With-profits	£7,240	£14,900	£29,570	£61,490
UK equity income	£7,500	£15,800	£32,400	£85,800
Global growth*	£7,500	£18,800	£31,800	£85,100

Capital sum accumulated from £50 per month

	10	15	20	25
An annual return of 5%	£7,900	£13,500	£20,800	£30,000
An annual return of 7.5%	£9,100	£16,800	£28,100	£44,500
An annual return of 10%	£10,500	£21,100	£38,700	£67,500
An annual return of 12.5%	£12,100	£26,800	£54,100	£104,900

Sources: Money Management With-Profits Surveys; Standard & Poor's, unit and investment trust performance. Figures are averages for each type of fund. Unit trust data, bid price to bid price with all income reinvested. Investment trust data, mid price to mid price with all income reinvested. *Formerly international general

Trouble-shooting guide

Several websites and fund supermarkets provide information about funds and may even publish recommended fund lists, but this does not count as advice. Unless you obtain specific, personal advice from an individual you will be transacting on an 'execution-only' basis and will have to take responsibility for your own decisions. If you want advice, ask for it and expect to pay about £80 to £120 an hour.

The better qualified an adviser, the better advice you will get. Be wary of counter staff in high street banks and building societies. Most simply push their firm's products. Independent financial advisers are a more reliable source of advice.

If you buy funds direct from a fund management group, you may pay more than if you buy via a fund supermarket, because you will not get the discounts provided by the supermarket.

Always check your plan statements – managers will usually be quick to sort out any administration errors.

See Appendix for sources of fund performance information.

2

Borrowing

In this section we will look at

How the credit system works

How to get the best credit deal

Solving debt problems

Choosing the right mortgage

The costs of buying and selling property

Equity release schemes

Buy-to-let mortgages

Endowment problems

2

Borrowing

Borrowing has become the norm. Students do it to get through university, car buyers do it, retired people do it to release equity from their homes. The great majority of us have credit cards not only so we can have credit on tap but for convenience as well.

There is nothing wrong with borrowing. Most of us could never afford to buy a house if we didn't. But repaying debt should also be a top priority. So it is very important to borrow as cost effectively as possible and, above all else, to keep your borrowing under control rather than let it control you. If you have spare cash, paying off debt – especially where high interest rates are involved – should take precedence over just about everything else. In this chapter we will be helping you get the best out of your borrowing by looking at:

◆ **How the credit system works** We explain what happens when you ask for credit.
◆ **The pros and cons of different sorts of credit** Which to go for and which to avoid.
◆ **Where you can get the best mortgage deal** How to get value for money whether you are a first-time buyer, want to remortgage or buy to let.
◆ **Unlocking the value of your home through equity release** Taking capital out your home is becoming increasingly popular but it is not without its pitfalls.
◆ **What to do when you have debt problems** Keep your cool, we can help guide you through your difficulties.

Credit where credit is due

Offers of credit are constantly tumbling onto our doormats and it is hard to set foot on the high street without being offered some form of borrowing or other. But despite their marketing efforts, lenders will normally want to check you are a good risk before they give you any money. They will want to find out whether you are likely to pay back what you owe.

Knowing how they assess your creditworthiness can be important, especially if you are turned down, although you may not be able to do much about it if they do refuse. Lenders cannot be forced to give credit but you can ask them to reconsider if they have their facts wrong.

Credit scoring

Many lenders use credit scoring when deciding who to lend to. This is a points system based on the contents of your application. A variety of factors will be taken into account such as your age and occupation, whether you own or rent your home and how long you have lived at your address or had your current bank account. The points are added up to arrive at your total credit score. If it is over the lender's pass mark, your application will be accepted.

But it may not be an all-or-nothing decision. Some personal loan and credit card companies will use your credit score to determine the rate of interest they will charge you – the better your rating the less you will have to pay. Credit card companies may also refer to it when setting your borrowing limit.

Credit reference agencies

As well as credit scoring you on the basis of your application, your lender may contact a credit reference agency. The agency itself won't actually assess whether you are creditworthy. It is the lender which decides this on the basis of the information provided. This will include whether you are on the electoral roll in order to confirm your current address. The agency will also provide details of your existing credit commitments – supplied to it by other lenders – and any problems you have had with these, such as whether you have made late payments, exceeded your credit limits or defaulted on previous agreements. Any county court judgments against you will be noted too.

Information stays on record for six years. Details of other credit searches are also logged and kept on file for one or two years. If you have made several applications for credit recently, this may count against you even if you were just testing the water and haven't actually taken out the other loans or cards. Until the end of 2004, your file will also include similar details for other people living at your address as part of your family. However, from then, it will only include details of those with whom you are 'financially connected', such as someone with whom you share a bank account or credit arrangement.

What to do if you are turned down

This can be annoying and embarrassing especially if you have no idea why you have been refused. There is no legal obligation for lenders to tell you why this has happened, though as a matter of good practice they should give the broad reason. If it is on the basis of credit scoring, bear in mind lenders each have their own system and some have stricter criteria than others, so you may be accepted by one and rejected by another.

If you are refused on the basis of information supplied by a credit reference agency, the lender should tell you which one it used. You can then request a copy of your file to check the information is correct. You will need to send the agency £2 and state your full name, date of birth and any previous names and your addresses for the past six years. It must send your file within seven days. You can also apply online but this will cost more.

If there is a mistake on your file, ask the agency to correct it, giving details and any evidence you have to show it is wrong. If the agency decides not to correct it, you can send a notice of correction of up to 200 words to be added to your file. If you find a mistake on one file, it is probably a good idea to check with the other agencies as it may appear elsewhere too. If details of other people who live at your address appear on your file, you can also ask for them to be removed if you are not financially associated.

The three credit reference agencies are Equifax (0870 010 0583, www.equifax.co.uk), Experian (0870 241 6212, www.experian.co.uk) and Callcredit (0870 060 1414, www.callcredit.co.uk).

To ensure your credit file makes you look as creditworthy as possible, make sure you are on the electoral roll and keep up to date with any existing credit arrangements. If you have had problems in the past, try to get them sorted out as quickly as possible – the longer you can put between a previous problem and your next application for credit the better.

Ironically, if you have not borrowed before you may find it as hard to get credit as if you had a poor record. This is because you have no history to show how you have coped with debt. In these circumstances, the best place to go may be your own bank. Once you have established a credit record you can go elsewhere for a better deal.

Identity theft

One way in which your credit record could be damaged is by identity theft. This is when someone pretending to be you runs up credit card or other debts in your name. The first you are likely to know about this is when mystery items appear on your credit card bill or withdrawals on your bank statement that you did not make. You will then have to persuade your card issuer or bank that it was not you who ordered the goods or made the withdrawals.

One way fraudsters may get hold of your details is by cloning your credit card, so try not to let it out of your sight when making payments. Another is by searching through rubbish to find old credit card slips or bank statements. To avoid falling victim in this way, shred or tear these up before disposing of them.

Are you sure you want credit?

Even if you have no problem raising credit, think carefully about the commitment you are taking on before going ahead. Ask yourself:

◆ Could I wait and save for what I need instead of borrowing?

◆ How much more will the item cost if I borrow to pay for it? For example, borrowing at an APR of 10% over ten years will mean paying back 50% more than you have borrowed.

◆ What can I realistically afford in monthly repayments?

◆ Do I really want to have to sacrifice future income over a lengthy period to meet the repayments?

◆ If my repayments are not fixed, how will I cope if interest rates rise and my repayments increase?

◆ Should I take out insurance to cover my repayments in case my income drops if I am unable to work due to sickness or redundancy? This is probably worthwhile for a mortgage or secured loan, as you risk losing your home if you do not keep up repayments, but bear in mind that you will not be covered for any pre-existing illnesses.

Getting a cheap deal

The main yardstick for comparing the cost of different credit and loan deals is the annual percentage rate of interest or APR. This is not a perfect solution, particularly when it comes to credit cards as different companies use different methods of calculating their APRs. But it is the best tool there is at present when looking around for a cheap deal.

Generally, the lower the APR, the lower the cost of the credit. But the actual amount of interest you have to pay will also depend on the repayment period. A three-year loan at a 10% APR may sound a lot cheaper than paying a 20% APR over one year but the amount of interest you pay will be considerably more, as the ready reckoner opposite illustrates. To find out the cost of borrowing other amounts at various rates, see the payment calculator on the Office of Fair Trading's website (www.oft.gov.uk).

Loan ready reckoner

Total cost of a £1,000 loan at different interest rates over different periods

APR	Length of loan					
	1 yr	3 yrs	5 yrs	10 yrs	15 yrs	20 yrs
5%	£1,027	£1,077	£1,129	£1,266	£1,413	£1,569
10%	£1,053	£1,154	£1,262	£1,557	£1,887	£2,248
15%	£1,078	£1,231	£1,398	£1,867	£2,404	£2,995
20%	£1,102	£1,308	£1,536	£2,191	£2,947	£3,773
25%	£1,126	£1,385	£1,675	£2,523	£3,502	£4,557
30%	£1,149	£1,461	£1,815	£2,860	£4,058	£5,333

Figures assume repayments made by equal monthly instalments.
Source: Office of Fair Trading

Weighing up your credit options

Most forms of credit have their advantages as well as their disadvantages. Some can meet certain needs better than others. But with all of them, costs can vary widely, so it is always important to shop around to get the best deal possible. If you want a credit card or personal loan, for example, don't just try your own bank – look for the provider offering the most competitive APR. Nowadays, it is much easier to find cheap deals as many national newspapers include 'best buy' tables of loans and credit cards in their personal finance sections. The internet is also a good tool. One particularly useful site is www.moneyfacts.co.uk.

Overdrafts

Most current account holders go into the red from time to time but overdrafts should only be used for short-term credit and then with your bank's permission. Only students or graduates with special interest-free facilities can afford them longer term. For the rest of us, overdrafts tend to be relatively expensive. Even a few days of being overdrawn can cost you dear if you don't ask your bank first. Not only will you have to pay a high rate of interest, usually over 25%, but you will also be charged an unauthorised overdraft fee of up to £30.

If you think you are likely to overdraw, ask for an authorised overdraft facility. Normally this is arranged free of charge and you pay a lower rate of interest. But rates on authorised overdrafts also vary considerably, so this may be a good time to consider moving your current account.

◆ **What not to do** Sometimes people who are regularly overdrawn are tempted to use another loan to clear their overdraft. This is generally a bad idea. If you are overdrawn at the end of every month, this is not so much a sign you require credit but that you are living beyond your means. You really need to sit down and work out a balanced budget.

◆ **Other snags** Consider the timing of any direct debits or standing orders that might cause you to go into the red or get bounced if you are overdrawn. If you are earning interest on your current account balance it is best to time these as late in the month as possible, but for budgeting purposes setting them at the beginning of the month may be better because you will know how much you have left to spend.

Credit cards

Borrowing on credit cards has become one of the most popular forms of credit in the UK. The amount of debt on cards is increasing all the time. During 2003, we borrowed nearly £48bn in this way. Fortunately, there is plenty of competition between card providers but finding the cheapest deal is not always easy. The main factor determining your choice of credit card should be how you use it and how good you are at organising your finances. See if one of the following profiles applies to you:

◆ **You never pay off your balance in full and are a financial bargain hunter** Look out for a card which charges little or no interest for the first six months or so. The best deals give the introductory rate not just on your balance transfer but on new purchases as well. When the introductory period is over, switch to another one offering a similar deal.

◆ **You never pay off your balance in full and tend to be financially disorganised** If you don't want the bother of switching cards every six months, look for one which combines a low introductory rate on balance transfers and new purchases with a low follow-on rate.

◆ **You usually pay off your balance in full** Look for a card with a competitive rate of interest combined with cashback rewards, but make sure you follow the rules so you don't forfeit the benefit (see below).

◆ **You always pay off your balance in full** You don't have to worry about the interest rate on outstanding balances, so look for the card with the best cashback rewards or, if you are feeling charitable, a donation card. Most cashback cards pay you 0.5% of your purchases but with some it is 1%. The money is normally paid once a year but beware – with some you may forfeit your whole year's cashback if you miss a single monthly payment or exceed your credit limit just once. You may also miss out on your cash if you close your account part way through a year. Donation cards pay money to your chosen charity instead.

◆ **You like to use your card on holiday, including to withdraw cash** Choose a card with a low foreign usage charge and cash withdrawal fee.

Whatever type of card user you are, there are certain things you should never do.

◆ **What not to do** Don't just pay the minimum amount every month on your credit card, otherwise it will take donkey's years to clear the balance and you will end up paying loads of interest. Don't pay your credit card bills late or exceed your credit limit either, or you will be charged an extra £20 to £25. You can make sure you always pay on time by setting up a direct debit.

◆ **Other snags** Avoid setting up direct debit-type bill payments from your card to other providers as you may not be able to stop them in future. Only the company taking the payments can cancel these instructions and if it is an overseas company which does not react to your cancellation request, you could have problems. Even if you cancel your credit card account, you can still be billed for the payments.

Gold, platinum or black cards

These are upmarket credit cards which require holders to have a minimum income of £20,000 to £25,000. Apart from the 'status' they confer on their holders, they offer various perks, mainly travel related, but as a form of borrowing they are no more competitive than ordinary cards.

Store cards

You may be offered a generous discount on your first purchases with these cards but thereafter they offer few advantages. In fact, unless you are very disciplined and pay off your balance in full every month, you should not touch store cards with a bargepole. They are a very expensive way of borrowing, charging interest rates that are typically around double those on ordinary credit cards.

Personal loans

With a personal loan you borrow a fixed sum over an agreed period and the repayments are usually fixed too, so you know exactly how much to budget for. There are two types – secured and unsecured:

◆ **Secured** These loans are aimed at homeowners who can provide their homes as security. But your first options should be an unsecured loan or an increase in your main mortgage. Secured loans should only be considered as a last resort, particularly if you are in any doubt about your ability to keep up your repayments. If this happens, the lender will be able to demand repossession of your home to recoup its loan even if you are up-to-date with your mortgage repayments.

   Secured loans may not be as cheap as they are made to look either. Payments are normally spread over longer periods than for unsecured loans and you may be sold expensive loan protection insurance.

◆ **Unsecured** Most personal loans nowadays are unsecured and, provided you are considered creditworthy, you should have no problem arranging one. The increasing availability of loans has created competition among lenders which has helped bring rates down. Don't make the mistake of many consumers and go to your bank or building society for a loan (unless you encounter problems elsewhere) before checking out what rates are available from other lenders. Supermarkets, motoring organisations and other institutions also offer loans nowadays. Bear in mind the rates are normally tiered, so some lenders may be more competitive for some amounts than others. Some will also adjust the interest rate according to your credit rating (see page 32). When you compare rates make sure you compare like with like.

Whatever type of loan you go for, there are certain things you should avoid.

◆ **What not to do** Forgetting to check out the early repayment terms on any loan you take out can cost you dear. Even if you don't expect to have enough money to pay it off early, you may want to switch to a cheaper lender in future. Secured loans can be particularly expensive to redeem early, but with unsecured loans there may be also be a penalty, typically of two months' interest. Look for loans without penalties as this will give you more flexibility.

Car loans

Many people take out loans to buy cars. If you are offered a specialist car-related loan always compare the cost with the best personal loan rates, as you may actually get a better deal that way.

◆ **Low or zero percent finance** Car manufacturers often provide these deals to tempt new buyers. They usually run at low rates for the first year or two but shoot up thereafter. If you need to spread your payments beyond the reduced rate period, you may be better off with an ordinary personal loan.

◆ **Deferred car purchase loans** These loans, also known as personal contract purchase schemes, were originally offered by manufacturers but you can now get them from other lenders so it's worth shopping around. They work in slightly different ways but the basic idea is that, to keep the cost down, you do not borrow the full purchase price of the car. Instead, a contract is fixed for a period of between one and four years and your loan is based on the difference between the present price of the car and its 'guaranteed future value' at the end of the contract.

When the contract ends you can either return the car and pay no more (assuming reasonable wear and tear and mileage, otherwise there may be penalties to pay), get a new vehicle and start the process again, or pay the outstanding balance and keep the car. Bear in mind you will not own the car at end of the initial term. These schemes can be attractive, though, if you like to have a new car every two or three years.

Credit unions

One way of gaining access to low-cost loans is to join a credit union. These are financial co-operatives set up and run by people with some form of bond. For example, they may be members of the same club or profession or they may live or work in the same area. Members who save regularly can obtain cheap loans. The amounts you can borrow will be based on your savings record and ability to pay, rather than a formal credit record. This makes them particularly useful for people who have had problems obtaining credit from more conventional lenders. To find out if there is a credit union you can join or how to start one yourself, contact the Association of British Credit Unions (0161 832 3694, www.abcul.org).

Trouble-shooting guide

Dealing with too much debt

Getting into debt is simple; getting out of it can be a different matter. It is very easy to underestimate the burden of debt repayment, and if interest rates rise and push up your repayments, it becomes even more difficult. If you find your debts are getting too much for you, it is time to take a long hard look at your financial situation. Here are some things you should and shouldn't do. Some are pretty obvious but worth pointing out nonetheless.

◆ Consider whether you can clear your debt by cashing in some savings. There is little point having savings when you owe money, as the cost of the debt will invariably outweigh the returns you are earning on your savings.

◆ Most of us are prepared to go on diets from time to time, so why not go on a money diet? Examine your lifestyle and budget for ways in which you could spend less and use these savings to pay off your debts a bit faster.

◆ Think about ways you could boost your income and use that money to help pay your debts. Could you, for example, do some overtime, take a casual job or let out a spare room to a lodger?

◆ If you have expensive forms of credit such as store card balances, try to shift them to cheaper forms such as an ordinary credit card with a low introductory rate.

◆ Consider asking your family for help.

◆ If you are finding it impossible to meet your repayments, write to your creditors, starting with your mortgage company, explaining your problems and suggesting how much you can afford to pay them – they will normally prefer you to pay a little than nothing at all.

◆ If your creditors are unwilling to accept a compromise or you need help in sorting out your problems, contact your local Citizens' Advice Bureau (details in the phone book, www.citizensadvice.org.uk), the National Debtline (0808 808 4000, www.nationaldebtline.co.uk) or the Consumer Credit Counselling Service (0800 138 1111, www.cccs.co.uk).

◆ Don't take out secured loans to pay off unsecured debt as you could put your home at risk.

◆ Don't use your credit or store cards anymore.

◆ Don't go to a credit repair company which charges fees to sort out credit problems – it could leave you with a worse credit record than you had before.

◆ Don't panic – there are plenty of organisations willing to help you resolve your problems (see above).

Bankruptcy and individual voluntary arrangements

Declaring yourself bankrupt may seem an easy way of wiping the debt slate clean, especially since a recent change in the law has made it possible to be discharged from bankruptcy after just one year instead of the previous three. But it is not as simple as all that and should still be considered a last resort, as it can cause you considerable problems even after discharge.

An alternative to be considered first is an individual voluntary arrangement (IVA) which involves you approaching your creditors with an offer of how much you can afford to repay. Providing at least three-quarters agree, you will usually have five years to repay your debts. Insolvency practitioners can advise you on how to make these arrangements.

If you opt for full-blown bankruptcy, it can damage your reputation and your career prospects. You will have to pass details of all your financial affairs to an official receiver. You will be unable to use your bank, building society or credit card accounts and may have to go to court. Unless you have dependants, you could lose your home. You will only be able to keep work-related and basic personal possessions, with everything else sold by the receiver and the proceeds used to pay the costs of your bankruptcy and then your creditors. Part of your income can also be used for up to three years for this, and even after you are discharged you may have problems, particularly in getting credit or a mortgage.

Still, it may be tempting for students with heavy debts and few assets to opt for bankruptcy. However, the government is making sure one debt students will not be able to get out of this way is money owed to the Student Loans Company

For more information about IVAs and bankruptcy, contact the National Debtline (see page 39).

Choosing a mortgage and buying a home

Just about everyone wants to own their own home. It doesn't just make financial sense; for most people, it feels like emotional sense as well. Getting the right mortgage and fighting your way through the cumbersome buying process is a chore. And for first-time buyers, the prospect is made more daunting in many parts of the UK as house prices have well outstripped the growth in their incomes. Add the burden of student debt, which more people are facing, and the dream of home-owning can recede even further into the distance.

Despite the numerous opinions of 'experts' that property prices are about to level off, maybe even fall – expressed with great conviction over the past couple of years – there has been little sign of it yet. It will happen one day; anyone looking to buy now has to acknowledge that possibility. And interest rates will rise, one day, maybe soon. So it's vital to do the sums before you buy and make sure you can afford to continue paying your mortgage at higher rates.

The table below shows monthly mortgage payments at various rates of interest. It will, hopefully, be a long time before rates hit 10% again, but they might reach 7% or even 8% in the next few years.

The monthly cost of a £100,000 mortgage over 25 years

Interest rate	Monthly cost	
	Repayment	Interest-only
4%	£527.83	£333.33
5%	£591.27	£416.67
6%	£651.89	£500.00
7%	£715.09	£583.34
8%	£780.66	£666.67
9%	£848.39	£750.00
10%	£918.07	£833.33

Source: Halifax

How much can you borrow?

The key question, especially for first-time buyers, is how much they can borrow. Lenders use two yardsticks: a multiple based on the amount of the borrower's income and a maximum based on the value of the property.

Income

The 'normal' multiple offered by mainstream lenders is 3.5 to four times your annual income. Couples may be offered the choice of 3.5 times the higher income plus once the second or maybe 2.75 to three times joint incomes.

It is reasonably easy to get a bigger loan than this: but you will probably have to show you are in a secure job and have a decent credit history and credit rating. If you can prove this, you may be able to get a loan of four or five times your income; more if you can persuade parents, for example, to offer a guarantee (see page 49).

But remember, the fact that you can borrow this amount doesn't mean it will be easy to repay if interest rates rise. If you do need such a big loan, using a mortgage broker should help you find the best deals.

Property value

Lenders will only lend a proportion of the property's value. You will get the best mortgage rate if you can put down a decent deposit. The bigger the deposit, the more choice: a 10% deposit will give you access to some good deals, and with 25% or more, you will have the widest possible. Many lenders will go up to 95% of property values, some to 100%. It will cost you more to borrow such a high proportion though (see pages 46-47).

Fixed or variable rate

There are usually scores, sometimes hundreds, of different mortgage deals on offer at any one time. They include:

◆ **Fixed rates** These can be short or long term, with or without penalties for early repayment.
◆ **Capped rates** The rate can fall if interest rates in general move down but cannot rise beyond a pre-fixed level.
◆ **Discounted variable rates** The discount will last anything from a few months to several years.
◆ **Standard variable rates** These move in line with interest rates generally.
Each has its advantages and disadvantages.

Fixed and capped rates

These are usually priced slightly higher than the best discounted rates, especially if it looks like the next move in interest rates is going to be up rather than down. You are paying for certainty, in effect protection against rising rates. Two to five-year fixes are most common and most popular with borrowers.

The government wants to encourage borrowers to move to much longer-term fixed rates – lasting maybe ten or even 25 years, as is usual in America. This, it thinks, will make the housing market less volatile and lead to fewer problems for homebuyers if rates rise. The drawback is the cost: borrowers like to go for the cheapest monthly payments in the short term and long-term fixes cost more.

Whatever the term, there is the gamble that variable rates might fall below the fixed rate, leaving borrowers marooned on an expensive rate. Nearly all deals have early redemption penalties which come into force if you repay the whole or even part of the loan. Some deals allow you to repay a limited amount of capital each year without penalties. Some have a sliding scale of penalties, with lower rates applying the longer you have held the mortgage. If you decide on a fixed or capped loan, it's essential to understand the implications of the penalty structure.

Capped loans are usually priced a little higher than fixed rates and may not always be the bargain they seem; it all depends what the capped rate is linked to. If it is the lender's standard variable rate, you may find even if interest rates in general fall, your capped rate will not.

Discounted variable rates

These deals usually offer the lowest monthly payments at the outset, which makes them very attractive to borrowers who are pushing themselves to the limit. It's the small print that is important. You are often tied in at the end of the discount period and have to spend the next few years paying the lender's standard variable rate – and it can work out expensive in the long run. Escaping the deal means paying additional penalties.

Standard variable rates

No one should voluntarily choose a standard variable rate loan, as this is usually the most expensive deal of all, offering no protection from rising rates but often no 'sweetener' either.

Cashbacks

Some lenders provide cashbacks – lump sums – to new borrowers. They are highly tempting for first-time buyers, for instance, who need to furnish their new home but have precious little cash. The amount of cashback is likely to be between 5% and 10% of the total loan. There is always a drawback with these deals: they are usually only available with higher rate deals and have tough redemption penalties if you want to get out in the early years. There is often a one-year penalty for each 1% of cash back. So if you're getting a 5% cashback, you will face penalties for remortgaging within the first five years.

Mortgage term

It is so common for lenders to set up loans on the basis of a 25-year term, many borrowers don't realise they don't have to stick to this. In general, lenders are unwilling to set up a loan beyond normal retirement age and there are often additional constraints on long leasehold flats. Typically, lenders want the mortgage to expire while there are still 25 or 30 years to run on the lease. These days, flat owners have rights to extend the term of their lease or buy the freehold, making lease length less important (see pages 54-55). If you're buying a flat with a short-term lease, lenders may offer a short-term, interest-only loan to start with, while you sort out an extension of the leasehold or freehold purchase, then you can go for a longer-term repayment deal.

Choosing a shorter term increases the monthly payments but means the overall cost of the loan is lower, as the table shows.

£100,000 repayment mortgage at an interest rate of 5.75%

Term	Monthly payment	Total interest paid
10 years	£1,098	£30,916
15 years	£830	£48,404
20 years	£702	£67,078
25 years	£629	£86,840
30 years	£584	£107,577

Source: Halifax

Flexible offset and current account mortgages

Most borrowers choose 'conventional' mortgages which are basically a self-contained package, separate from the rest of their financial life. But it is also possible to choose a 'flexible' product which gives you more control over how fast you repay the loan and allows you to dovetail it into the rest of your finances.

Flexible loans allow borrowers to overpay, underpay, take payment holidays and even borrow back what they have previously overpaid. Some are tied into a bank current account and savings account: the principle is you have one 'pot' of money where savings, credit card debt, personal loans and the mortgage are all tied together and offset against each other.

Flexible mortgages require a different attitude to borrowing and won't suit those who like to keep their borrowings and savings in watertight compartments. But they can be extremely efficient. Anyone who has a reasonable amount of cash saved in a deposit account, for example, while also paying a mortgage or interest on their credit card is losing out. They may be getting only 2% or 3% on their savings after tax while paying 5% or 6% on their mortgage and perhaps 15% or more on the credit card.

Self-employed people can do especially well out of a flexible loan. They pay income tax in lump sums, twice a year. Meanwhile, the money saved towards the tax can be used to reduce the loan temporarily, saving interest. If you choose one linked to a current account, you will make savings by virtue of the money that comes into your account on payday and is spent throughout the following month, as the box shows.

James has a flexible mortgage of £100,000, set up for 25 years, which is linked to his current account. He earns a salary of £35,000, all of which he spends, in equal stages, throughout the month. He makes no specific overpayments, but thanks to the temporary overpayments made from his salary each month, the loan is paid off five months early, saving total interest of £3,566.

Interest rate assumed throughout: 5.2%
Source: The One Account

Choosing a flexible mortgage

Flexible loans are nearly always on a variable rate and rarely offer the best deals. So think twice before taking one out. If all you really want is the freedom to repay the loan early, a conventional mortgage might be just as good if you are prepared make specific arrangements to repay capital during penalty-free periods and if you're happy to remortgage every few years to make sure you're on the best deal possible.

But if you're convinced you will use all the flexible features to your advantage – if you're self-employed, for instance, with a fluctuating income, or are planning a career break in the future – a flexible loan could come up trumps.

There are scores of these loans on offer from various lenders and some are more flexible than others. These are the points to consider:
◆ Does it offer full current account facilities?
◆ Does it have links to savings accounts?
◆ Does it allow overpayments and is there a minimum?
◆ Does it allow regular underpayments and in what circumstances?
◆ Can you draw out lump sums and, again, in what circumstances?
◆ Can you take payment holidays?
Some lenders let you agree a 'loan facility' at the outset, based on a percentage of the property's value. You don't have to borrow the full amount initially but can draw on it as required, for instance to fund home improvements or school fees. The maximum loan is usually 95% of the property's value. But be wary of agreeing a facility you are unlikely to use fully as you may be charged a higher interest rate. Other lenders only let you borrow back amounts you have already overpaid.

Remortgaging and the rate tarts

If you take out a flexible mortgage, the idea is you stick with it for the life of the loan, because it will adapt to your changing circumstances. But if you go for an ordinary mortgage, the likelihood is you will choose a special deal, either a discount or fix, which ties you in for maybe two to five years. At the end of this, and any penalty period, you are free to remortgage. Increasing numbers of people are doing just that rather than sticking with their original lender at their standard variable rate. Mortgage lenders grumble that such borrowers are 'rate tarts', but they only have themselves to blame as they persist in offering better terms to new borrowers than to existing customers.

Remortgaging costs money. There will be a fresh valuation fee, legal fees and probably an arrangement fee as well. And it takes time. It is always worth asking your current lender, as you approach the end of the term of your special deal, what offer it can make to you to stay. The very best rate may be reserved for new customers, but you could still do better than the standard variable rate. And if you don't ask, you won't necessarily get.

The hidden costs of high percentage loans

Many lenders charge an extra fee if you borrow more than 90% of your property value. The old name for this charge was a mortgage indemnity guarantee (MIG) but that has largely been dropped because it gave borrowers the impression they benefited from some sort of guarantee on the repayments. Far from it – lenders benefit, if you fail to keep up repayments, but borrowers pay for it. These days, the charge has more anodyne names such as 'higher loan to value fee' or 'additional mortgage security fee'. There are two ways lenders can make this charge. They can ask for a one-off sum from the borrower or load the interest rate.

One-off payments

The way these payments are worked out is a bit convoluted. Once your borrowing trips over 90%, you pay a percentage of the total amount borrowed over 75% of the property's value. A typical rate these days is 7.5%. So, for example, if you are buying a flat worth £100,000 and borrowing £91,000 to do so, the fee will be 7.5% of £16,000, or £1,200. But if you borrow only £90,000, there will be no charge at all. It's clearly nonsense to pay £1,200 for the privilege of borrowing £1,000, so check the sums before you agree and if necessary beg or borrow the extra from someone else such as your parents. Even putting the extra on your credit card and paying it off over a year or two could be cheaper.

If you have to pay the fee, lenders are usually happy to add it to the mortgage so at least you don't have to find the money up front. That still doesn't make it a good deal, however.

You can get caught out if the lender downvalues the property from the price you have agreed to pay. If you agreed to pay £100,000 and need a 90% loan, you may think you're free of the MIG. But if the lender values the property at £99,000, your loan becomes 90.9% of the value and you're caught. Lenders won't necessarily point this out to you – they'll simply include the MIG fee in your monthly payments and hope you won't notice.

If you know you are going to need a high percentage loan, it could be worth going to a mortgage broker. The best deals, as mentioned above, are usually only offered to people looking for a lower percentage. A broker may be able to organise a split loan – the best mortgage deal plus a separate top-up from another source.

Self-certified and fast-track mortgages

Most lenders want proof of your income before they are prepared to lend. What happens if you don't want to, or can't, produce this? You may, for example, have recently become self-employed or set up a business where you cannot predict what your income will be. The answer is a self-certified loan, where you simply tell the lender what you are earning and it does not ask for proof. It sounds too good to be true, so you can be sure there is a drawback. Typically, the mortgage rate will be between 0.5% and 1% higher than on a standard loan and there is much less choice in the way of discounted and fixed rates.

The industry has started to worry that self-certified mortgages encourage people to claim much higher incomes than they have. They end up with a bigger loan than they can comfortably repay, which in turn might lead to arrears and, in the worst case, repossession. If you're tempted to lie about the level of your income, don't: it is a criminal offence.

Self-certified loans tend to be the province of specialist lenders; high street banks and building societies offer what they call fast-track or streamlined loans, where proof of income is not necessarily required, although lenders usually reserve the right to check later. They can be a good option for self-employed people who cannot produce proof of their income and for those whose job provides them with bonuses, overtime or commission. With an ordinary mortgage, lenders usually only count half of such non-guaranteed payments as income when working out the maximum you can borrow. A fast-track loan will let you count the lot and they tend to offer better rates than a full-blown self-certified mortgage.

Impaired credit loans

A number of lenders specialise in lending to people with bad credit records, including people with county court judgments (CCJs) against them. Once again, interest rates will be much higher than on standard loans.

This type of loan can usually only be arranged through a mortgage broker.

There may be extenuating circumstances as to why you have built up a bad credit record and a good mortgage broker may be able to persuade a lender you are not as bad as your credit record paints you – and so get you a getter deal. Read pages 32-33 on credit records and how to make the best of them.

If you do have to get an impaired credit loan, check how easy it will be to remortgage once you have built up a decent credit record. Some arrangements make it very expensive to change.

Borrowing for home improvements

The simplest and cheapest way of borrowing money to finance home improvements is to add it to your mortgage, assuming you have enough equity in your home. If you have stayed with the same lender for years, use this as an opportunity to check out the competition and be prepared to remortgage elsewhere for a better rate. Even if you stay with the same lender, you will most likely have to pay for a fresh valuation on the property. If you don't want to increase your long-term debt, you could go for a shorter-term personal loan instead.

Adding value

Many home improvements add little to the value of the property in terms of its sale price: installing a state-of-the-art kitchen costing many thousands of pounds may make the house more saleable, if your taste coincides with your buyer's, but you are unlikely to recoup the whole cost.

The best 'investment' in property is routine maintenance work, keeping it wind and weather tight. After that, installing central heating or adding a garage will add value, but loft conversions and extensions may not add much, especially if they have not been carried out well. New windows in a style inappropriate to the age of the property could actually decrease its value, as will the infamous stone cladding.

First-time buyers

Property prices in many parts of the UK have risen so far that first-time buyers are finding it almost impossible to borrow enough for even the smallest flat. In London, you need an income of at least £70,000 to get a big enough mortgage for a typical flat – way out of reach of many people, even when two incomes are combined. Not surprisingly, the proportion of buyers in the housing market who are first-timers had, by the spring of 2004, fallen to its lowest level for 30 years. But there are still ways to get yourself onto the property ladder.

Get a deposit

Being able to produce a good-sized deposit – say, £10,000 to £25,000 – helps in two ways. It means you can borrow more – maybe 4.5 times income rather than

3.8 – and you will probably have access to better mortgage deals at lower rates. But building up that deposit, when in all likelihood you are paying heavily in rent, is another matter.

Many parents now recognise they will have to help their children if they are to have a hope of buying. If they don't have the capital themselves, they might consider remortgaging their own property and raising the cash that way. A word of warning here: if you decide you would like to pay your parents interest on that sum, think twice and certainly don't make a formal arrangement to do so, as they would be obliged to declare the income to the Inland Revenue and pay tax on it.

Get your parents to guarantee your loan

This allows you to borrow more than the normal income multiple your salary would entitle you too, but it does depend on your parents having sufficient income to support not only their own mortgage but also the full amount of your loan – even though it is you who actually pays the mortgage. Some special deals aimed at newly qualified professionals and recent graduates will allow parents to guarantee only the part of the loan the child cannot cover, which gets round this problem – although technically, the parent could still be liable for the whole loan.

Go for shared ownership

Shared ownership schemes are run by housing associations. They allow you to buy a proportion of your property and pay rent on the rest. If your income rises, you can buy another tranche, though you will have to pay the current market price. When you sell, you have to offer the property to the association first and only if it turns you down can you sell on the open market.

Use the Key Homebuy scheme

If you are a 'key worker' – a nurse, doctor or teacher, for example – you can use the government-backed Key Homebuy scheme. This lends buyers enough for a decent deposit – an average of £20,000 – and you don't have to pay interest. The drawback is that when you move, the amount repaid will reflect the current property price. So if prices rise after you have moved in, there will be a hefty charge waiting for you when you sell. On the other hand, if property prices fall, the amount you must repay will also fall.

How to repay your mortgage

There are two basic ways to repay a mortgage:
◆ **Pay off capital as you go**   In other words, a repayment mortgage.
◆ **Take out an interest-only loan and start a separate savings vehicle**   This could be an endowment policy, pension or unit trust savings scheme to build up capital, which can be used to repay the loan at some point in the future.

The repayment mortgage is the most obvious and straightforward way of repaying a loan. As long as you stick to the monthly payments required, the loan is guaranteed to be paid off after a set number of years.

Endowment mortgages have had such a bad press in recent years that, not surprisingly, hardly anyone chooses one these days and you might wonder why, if it were not for the persuasion of commission-hungry sales people, anyone ever did.

The idea of 'gearing'

In fact, there were – in the past – some good reasons for advocating an endowment mortgage or something similar. The idea was that a mortgage was a long-term loan, or form of gearing, at a very low interest rate. If you used some of that borrowed money to invest in the stock market, and if shares price rises were higher than the interest rate on your loan, at the end of the day, you would win. Not only would you be able to repay the loan at the set date, your savings would have produced a surplus. And that would be money for free, because the endowment package cost no more than an ordinary repayment loan.

It's worth pointing out that this method did, for many years, do exactly what it suggested, and many thousands of borrowers benefited by taking out mortgages on this basis. But there is a hugely important 'if' in the argument. It only works if investments in the stock market grow faster than the interest rate on the loan.

And in the last few years, it all went horribly wrong. Stock markets crashed and share values plummeted. What made matters worse was that the level of savings borrowers were told to make into their plans was set, with hindsight, much too low.

The life companies and lenders were so eager to persuade people to choose endowments that they made sure the route looked, on paper, cheaper than a repayment loan. And the only way they could do that was by cutting the level of savings required for a given loan. That, in turn, meant they were making more and more optimistic predictions about how fast the investments would grow. At the same time, they skated over the risk involved.

The end result is that millions of borrowers are stuck with endowments which are not going to produce anything like enough to pay off their mortgage. If you are in this position, read the trouble-shooting guide at the end of this chapter and act on it now.

Starting from here

If you're a new borrower, not lumbered by the mistakes of the past, should you automatically reject the idea of an endowment mortgage? If you want to play it safe, the answer is undoubtedly yes. But if you are prepared to take the risk, it may – but only may – provide bigger rewards. These days, using an endowment as your savings vehicle may not be the best choice, as they are not very tax efficient, as the underlying investments are taxable. Regular savings into an individual savings account (Isa) or a pension plan would be better.

Suppose, for example, you are self-employed and cannot join a company pension scheme. You have enough money to take out a repayment mortgage or to start saving into a pension plan but cannot do both. One option could be to take out an interest-only loan and start putting money into the pension.

Interest-only loans are, of course, cheaper than repayment ones, as you can see from the table on page 41. At 6%, for example, a 25-year repayment mortgage will cost around £652 a month for a £100,000 loan, an interest-only mortgage, just £500. You could use the surplus to start saving. Thanks to the initial tax relief on pension plans, the extra £152 per month is actually worth £194. If this sum is put into a pension fund which invests in equities (company shares) and if growth in the stock market outpaces the rate of interest you are paying on the mortgage, you will be quids in.

But it's not quite that simple. At the time of writing, the pension rules allow you to take only 25% of your fund as cash, which will then be available to pay off your mortgage, and you won't be able to take it until you reach 55. So it won't necessarily be a complete answer to repaying your mortgage.

In any case, you will need to be prepared to adapt as your life changes. You could, for example, switch over to a repayment arrangement after, say, ten years, when you have a bit more spare cash. Or if you receive an inheritance, you could use this to pay off some of the capital.

In this scenario, the responsibility for repaying the loan is all yours. You cannot simply sit back and expect everything to work out all right in the long run.

It is also possible to take out a 'part and part' loan. If you already have an endowment covering some of your loan which you want to keep, you can play safe by converting part of it to a repayment basis while keeping the rest interest-only.

The costs of buying and selling

If you have never bought a property before, stand by for a shock. One way or another, you are likely to have to find several thousand pounds. And if you are a second or third-timer, you may well still be shocked. The chief culprit in this is stamp duty but there are other costs as well. The main ones are:

◆ Legal fees;
◆ Land registry charges;
◆ Stamp duty;
◆ Valuation or survey fees;
◆ Removal costs;
◆ Mortgage fees such as an administration fee;
◆ Insurance costs – buildings and contents.

Legal fees

Typical solicitors' fees are likely to be £500 to £750, depending on the cost of the property and whether any complications emerge during the transaction.

Buying a leasehold flat may be more expensive than buying a freehold house, as the lease needs to be checked. Borrowers also have to pay the lender's legal costs, but these may be included in the total your solicitor charges. It may be worth shopping around among different firms to get the best quote.

Land registry charges

These are payable at the same time as solicitors' fees. Most property in England and Wales is already registered and the fees for transferring the title are on a sliding scale according to its value. For example, the charge is £100 for properties costing £80,001 to £100,000, £150 up to £200,000, £250 up to £500,000 and £450 for £500,001 to £1m. Scotland has a separate land registry system.

Stamp duty

Now that property prices have risen so far, stamp duty, payable by the buyer of a property, represents a big burden for just about everyone. Twenty years ago, most first-time buyers did not pay anything. Today is different: scarcely anyone escapes. There are two tiers of stamp duty. One relates to property in 'disadvantaged areas' which are strictly defined: by postcode in Scotland and by electoral ward in the rest of the UK.

Stamp duty

Disadvantaged areas		Other areas	
Property price	Stamp duty rate	Property price	Stamp duty rate
Up to £150,000	Nil	Up to £60,000	Nil
£150,001-£250,000	1%	£60,001-£250,000	1%
£250,001-£500,000	3%	£250,001-£500,000	3%
£500,001+	4%	£500,001+	4%

To find out about disadvantaged areas, call the stamp duty helpline on 0845 603 0135 or go to www.inlandrevenue.gov.uk.

Stamp duty is payable on the property itself, not any fixtures and fittings, so if the price you are being asked to pay is near one of the limits, it may be possible to do a bit of negotiation with the buyer to lower the price or perhaps agree a separate cash payment for fixtures. But don't push it. Any blatant manipulation of the rules could count as tax evasion and carry nasty penalties.

Valuation and survey

All lenders insist a valuation is carried out on your property before they decide how much to lend – and you pay for it. The valuation simply relates to the market value of the property and says nothing about its structural condition. Unless you are buying a brand new property, it would be wise to go for a more extensive report. Many lenders offer a report which is a combination of a valuation and basic structural survey. This is usually a cheaper alternative to a full survey and should be adequate for most properties. Both the report and the full survey will include a valuation, so you need not pay extra for this.

At some point in the future – but no one knows when – the government has decreed that property sellers in England and Wales must provide all potential buyers with a seller's information pack which will include a home condition report based on a survey. This will, in theory, shift the cost of this element from buyer to seller, although it remains to be seen whether buyers will be happy to rely on this. In any case, buyers will still have to pay for a valuation for their lender.

Typical valuation and survey fees

Property price Up to	Level one	Level two
£50,000	£185	£420
£100,000	£220	£420
£150,000	£250	£450
£200,000	£285	£500
£300,000	£355	£620
£400,000	£415	£750
£500,000	£475	£890
£600,000	£525	£1,030
£700,000	£575	£1,070
£800,000+	p.o.a.	p.o.a

Level one is a basic valuation only; level two is a combined valuation plus basic survey. Costs for a full structural survey are usually by negotiation.
Source: Halifax

Insurance and your home

Mortgage lenders insist you take out buildings insurance on your home, and it is only sensible to get contents cover at the same time. Insuring yourself is equally important – especially if you have dependants – to be sure the mortgage will be paid if you die or become too ill to work. See Section Four for more details.

Mortgage payment protection insurance

Mortgage lenders are keen to sell a specific type of insurance known as mortgage payment protection insurance (MPPI) – and the government is keen for people to buy it. The reason is that government help for borrowers has been cut back in recent years and it wants private insurers to fill the gap.

Government help

In most cases, if you become unemployed, you get no state benefits to pay the cost of your mortgage for the first nine months. Thereafter, some benefits may be payable but they are means-tested. If you have savings of more than £3,000, benefit is cut, and savings of £8,000 or more mean you get no benefit whatsoever. If you do qualify, payments are limited to the interest (no capital repayments) on the first £100,000 of a loan.

What MPPI offers

If you are unable to work through illness, accident or because you have been made unemployed, an MPPI policy will pay your monthly mortgage obligations for up to nine or 12 months, starting after 30, 60 or 90 days. There is usually a choice of deferred period and the longer you choose, the lower the premium.

Self-employed people may only be able to claim on the unemployment section if they cease trading altogether or go bust. They can choose a policy that provides cover only for accident and sickness. Employees with a decent sick pay scheme can buy cover just for unemployment.

These policies can be a sensible idea but they can also be pricey for what they actually provide. Mortgage lenders offer their own policies but you may get a better deal direct from an insurance company or by going to a broker. It's definitely worth shopping around and, as always, read the small print carefully. The cost is likely to be around £2.50 to £3 a month for each £100 of monthly mortgage payment if you are just buying unemployment cover, a similar sum for accident and sickness, and from about £5 a month to cover all three.

One tip: if you're young and in a low-risk occupation, you may do better by taking out a more extensive permanent health insurance policy (see Section Four). This is because premiums for PHI policies depend on the policyholder's age and occupation. If you're older and in a high-risk job, such as construction work, an MPPI policy could be a bargain, as they charge a flat rate for everyone.

Leasehold homes

Almost all houses in the UK are 'freehold', owned outright by their owners. Flats are a different matter. Traditionally, in England and Wales they have been sold on a long lease – typically either 99 or 999 years. The freeholder – perhaps the original developer – retains the freehold and charges leaseholders an annual ground rent. A very long lease is, in most aspects, very little different from a freehold and can have advantages in managing the property where there are communal parts used by a number of different flat dwellers. All leaseholders have obligations under their lease to contribute to the upkeep of the common parts such as the roof. Householders have had the right to buy their freehold since the Leasehold Reform Act of 1967. The rights of flat owners to do the same, however, only came in with acts passed in 1993 and 2002.

The rules on buying the freehold of a flat are quite complicated and require some co-operation with other owners in the block. There are two main options:

◆ You can club together with the other leaseholders to buy the freehold;
◆ Or if you cannot get enough of them to agree, you have an individual right to extend your lease by 90 years, as long as you have owned the flat for at least two years.

To be eligible for the right to buy the freehold, at least two-thirds of the flats in the block must be held on long leases, meaning an original term of 21 years or more. In addition, the participating group must hold at least half the total number of flats and if there are only two, both must participate. The body that actually buys the freehold is a company, owned by the flat owners, set up especially for this purpose.

If the freeholders and leaseholders cannot agree a price, either party can apply to a leasehold valuation tribunal, and if there is still disagreement, either can appeal to the Lands Tribunal, whose decision is binding.

The Leasehold Advisory Service, a private company funded by the government, provides free advice on all aspects of buying a freehold or extending the lease (see Appendix).

Equity release schemes

Thanks to the rise in property prices, many people have paper profits of thousands – maybe hundreds of thousands – of pounds locked up in their property. Equity release schemes let you liberate some of that cash to spend as you like, while staying in your own home. But this is not a matter of having your cake and eating it. There is, of course, a price to pay, and in some circumstances it can be a very heavy one.

One way to raise cash is to trade down to a smaller property. Equity release schemes are, financially, second best, but if you want to stay in your own home, there is much to be said for them. There are basically four ways you can get hold of the cash, and in all of them you must have reached a certain age to be eligible. Typically 55 to 60 is the minimum, though they are better value if you can afford to wait.

Interest-only mortgages

A number of lenders offer special, usually fixed-rate mortgages to retired people. You get your hands on a cash sum and may not even have to pay interest as the lender allows it to be rolled up, alongside the loan, repayable only after your death, or when the house is sold if you move to a residential home.

Once interest starts rolling up on a loan, the total owed can rise surprisingly fast, as it includes interest on the interest. Lenders protect themselves by restricting their maximum loan to a low proportion of the property value – typically, 20% of its current market value at age 60, rising to a maximum of 50% for a homeowner aged 80. And usually they protect you by offering a 'no negative equity guarantee'. This means they guarantee that, no matter how long you live in your home, the total of loan plus rolled-up interest will not exceed the value of your house on death, so you or your heirs will not face a hefty interest bill, although there may be nothing left when the house is eventually sold.

If your main need is extra income rather than a big capital sum, you should go for a drawdown mortgage, where you borrow small amounts regularly rather than one lump sum. That way, interest on the amount borrowed will rise more slowly.

Shared appreciation mortgages

These schemes charge a much lower interest rate – sometimes none at all – and on the surface seem attractive, but the deal is that when the house is sold, the lender is entitled to a proportion of the rise in the house price since the plan was taken out. In recent years, this has resulted in lenders getting huge sums on the sale of properties, leading to bitter complaints, usually from the offspring of the planholders. However, none have, so far, been upheld by the regulatory authorities because they believe the terms of the deal were clearly explained. The fact that it resulted in a big profit for the bank concerned is irrelevant. Many experts counsel against using such schemes for precisely this reason.

Home income plans

These combine a fixed-rate mortgage with an annuity. You borrow a capital sum from the lender and use the cash to buy an annuity, which pays you a fixed income for life. Part of the annuity payments are used to pay the mortgage interest, the surplus is extra income for yourself. With these, your debt does not grow over time, which means you will have more to leave to your heirs, but the income you receive will be lower.

Home reversion schemes

These do not involve mortgages at all. Instead you sell either the whole or a portion of your home to a reversion company in exchange for a cash sum. Because you have the right to remain living there, the amount you will be offered will seem disappointingly low compared to its current market value. The amount offered depends on your age at the outset – the older you are, the higher it will be. Typically, the range is between 35% and 60%. Suppose you have a home valued at £200,000 and decide to sell half to a reversion company. Depending on your age, you will be offered between £35,000 and £60,000 as a lump sum. Once you die, the reversion company picks up a full 50% of the proceeds, so if it has risen in value to £300,000, the company will get back £150,000.

Advice

If you're interested in any of these schemes, do get professional advice. There are pluses and minuses to each. One thing to watch out for is whether the extra income or capital is going to disqualify you from any state benefits you would otherwise get. And if you have children, it would be only fair to discuss the arrangement with them first.

Finding out more

The Financial Services Authority publishes a useful leaflet called *Raising Money From Your Home*. The charity Age Concern has a booklet and a good factsheet, while the trade association Ship (Safe Home Income Plans) also produces a guide. For contact details, see Appendix.

Buy-to-let mortgages

Buying residential property to rent out has become hugely popular in recent years and scores of lenders now offer specialist buy-to-let mortgages. They usually require a bigger deposit than loans for buying your own property – typically 20% to 25% – and interest rates tend to be 0.5% to 1% higher. When deciding how much to lend, lenders will usually take into account the expected income from rent, rather than relying solely on your earned income. Lenders can also dictate the type of tenancy agreement you have, with an assured shorthold tenancy the preferred option. The magazine *Moneyfacts* is a useful source of information on buy-to-let mortgages (see Appendix).

While there is, these days, a range of decent fixed and discounted products, it may be worth remortgaging your own home, assuming you have plenty of equity in it, as an alternative. You will need to let the Inland Revenue know the loan is to buy letting property, so you can claim tax relief on the interest paid against rent received.

The attractions of investing in buy-to-let property may seem obvious: you should get a good return on your money in rent, which should, moreover, increase over the long term. Meanwhile, you have a capital asset which should also rise in value.

Many investors see buy-to-let as better than a pension plan in providing an income for retirement, and it may well become even more popular as changes to the pension rules in 2005 will allow residential property to bc owned within a pension fund. But before you go ahead, do also consider the disadvantages:

◆ Tenants can cause trouble and won't always pay the rent;
◆ You may not always be able to find tenants;
◆ There will be ongoing expenses for council tax, insurance and general upkeep whether or not you have tenants;
◆ Managing agents' fees will take a bite out of the rent;
◆ Property prices and rental levels could go down but you will still have to meet the mortgage and other costs;
◆ Property is an 'illiquid' investment. It may take time to sell and you must, of course, sell the whole property at once. With more liquid investments such as shares, you can sell bit by bit, making use of your annual capital gains tax exemption over a number of years to cut down on tax. You don't have that option with property.

Managing agents expect to get between 10% and 15% of rental income for their services. As a rule of thumb, you need to achieve a rent of between 130% and, perhaps, 150% of the mortgage interest to cover your costs.

Finding out more

The Association of Residential Letting Agents (Arla) can provide advice and put buyers in touch with professional letting agents and buy-to-let lenders (see Appendix). It also publishes a 224-page *Buy to Let Guide*, in association with the Council of Mortgage Lenders. You can get it free from Arla member agents or by post for a nominal sum. The Consumers' Association also publishes *The Which? Guide to Letting and Renting*.

As the popularity of this form of investment has grown, a number of commercial companies have jumped on the bandwagon, offering courses at inflated prices on buying to let. Think twice before you spend money on any of these. You can probably get all the information you need elsewhere.

Trouble-shooting guide

Endowment mortgages

Millions of homebuyers have endowment policies which are predicted to produce a shortfall when they mature, meaning that – if they do nothing about it – they will have to find thousands of pounds extra to repay their loan on that date.

So what should you do?

◆ The first thing to consider is whether you have grounds for a successful complaint. If you think you do, don't delay – there are deadlines involved and if you carry on sticking your head in the sand, you may run out of time.

◆ The second thing to think about is how to deal with the situation from now onwards. Even if you succeed in getting compensation, this won't necessarily solve the problem entirely. You still have to decide how to repay the loan in the future.

Complaints

Nearly all borrowers with endowment mortgages have what is technically known as a low-cost endowment. This guarantees to pay off the loan only if you die within the term. Assuming you survive, there is no such guarantee: instead, you are relying on investment growth within the policy to pay off the capital sum.

Back in the 1980s and 1990s, when most of these endowments were sold, this fact was rarely pointed out. The sales people simply assumed investment growth would be more than sufficient to repay the loan and you would probably get a surplus as well. Costing no more – and sometimes less – than a repayment loan, they must have seemed like the investment equivalent of a free lunch. No wonder so many people took them out, and no wonder so many are now disappointed.

As it turned out, investment returns were much lower than anyone anticipated. Since 2000, life companies have had to write annually to their endowment holders, giving them an estimate of how much the policy is likely to pay on maturity. The estimate is given at three growth rates – typically, 4%, 6% and 8% a year. Estimates which show policies will meet their target even at the lowest growth rate are called 'green' letters; those which hit the target at the middle growth rate are 'amber', and those where the policy will only meet the target if the growth rate is 8% or more are called 'red'. Many borrowers have been receiving red letters in recent times. But note – these letters are not actually coloured green, amber or red – you'll have to check the figures quoted yourself.

Grounds for a complaint

The Financial Services Authority, which lays out the ground rules for making complaints to the Financial Ombudsman Service (FOS), has made it clear you cannot complain just because the performance of some investment has been worse than you expected. That would be tantamount to giving every investor a blank cheque and would speedily lead to the collapse of the financial services industry. It does, however, acknowledge people may have been 'mis-sold' an investment, through being misled over the degree of risk involved.

It is clear huge numbers of people were mis-sold endowments. They were never told there was any risk at all. If they had known, they would never have bought one and would have taken a repayment mortgage instead, where the capital is guaranteed to be repaid at the end of the term. And that, in effect, must be your argument – that you would never have bought the policy if you had known all the facts.

How to make your complaint

If you feel you are in this position, you should complain. To help you frame your complaint, get the free factsheet *Endowment Mortgage Complaints* from the Financial Services Authority (0845 608 2372). The Consumers' Association has also produced a sample letter, which you can find at www.endowmentaction.co.uk.

Who to contact

This depends on who sold you the policy. It may have been a salesperson employed by the life company, in which case you must complain to the company. Or it may have been an independent adviser, and you should complain to them. If you can't remember, or cannot now find the adviser concerned, the life company or the FOS may be able to help you track them down.

If you do not receive a satisfactory answer to this initial complaint, the company concerned will tell you that you now have a right to complain to the FOS and will provide details of how to do so.

Time limits

There are a number of time limits involved for making a complaint.

◆ **The date you took out the policy** If you bought the policy direct from a life company or one of its employees, it does not matter how long ago it was sold to you. But if you bought it from an independent adviser, complaints will only be accepted if this was on or after 29 April, 1988, when the rules on mis-selling came into force. One extra twist: if the adviser from whom you bought the policy has gone out of business, you will only get compensation if your policy was sold on or after 28 August, 1988, as this is when the compensation scheme came into existence.

◆ **The time you realised the policy was not guaranteed** This, of course, may be difficult to pin down, but the FOS has given a blanket ruling. It says you must complain within three years of getting your first red letter from the life company. If you don't, it is assumed you're happy and any later complaint will be turned down.

◆ **The time you started to take steps to deal with the problem** In law, investors have a duty to mitigate their losses once they realise matters are going awry. Some financial companies are beginning to argue that if an investor has shown he understands the drawbacks of his endowment policy by taking some additional action, this is the point at which any compensation should stop.

The moral of all this is that you should complain as soon as possible.

How compensation is calculated

If your complaint is upheld, you will probably be offered compensation. The idea is to put you back in the position you would have been in had you taken out a repayment mortgage at the outset.

The company concerned must calculate the amount of capital you would have repaid on the loan and compare that with the current surrender value of your endowment. It will also look at your monthly outgoings compared to what they would have been on a repayment loan and at the cost of life assurance, which is built-in with an endowment mortgage but must be paid for separately with a repayment loan. Mostly, it is assumed you would have taken out extra life assurance with the repayment loan, but you can argue this point if you were single and with no dependants at the time. The figure resulting from this sum is the amount of compensation you are due.

What to do once you get the compensation

The tempting thing may be to spend it; the sensible thing is to use it to pay off part of your loan, so making immediate savings on the interest. The only circumstance in which you should not is if you are tied into a special deal with penalties for early repayment. In that case, wait until you're out of the penalty period.

To escape the future risk of your endowment policy falling further behind its target amount, you should remortgage on to a repayment deal and – you might assume – surrender the life policy. But think first: endowments include life cover on the loan. If you have suffered a deterioration in health since you took out the policy replacement life cover would be much more expensive, so there are some grounds for keeping the policy running. Even so, you could convert part of your loan to repayment, building in an extra safety net.

Many people decide to convert their mortgage to a full repayment one, but cannot decide whether they should surrender the policy or keep it running until maturity. Would they, as many phrase it, be throwing good money after bad? Unfortunately, there is no simple answer as it depends not just on future investment conditions but also on the strength of the life company concerned. If the policy has been running for at least ten years, consider selling it on the second-hand market. The Association of Policy Market Makers (see Appendix) can put you in touch with firms that specialise in this. It is possible you would get a higher price than its surrender value.

3

Investment

In this section we will look at

Balancing risk and reward

Four types of investment

How the stock market works

Choosing an investing style

Managing your shares

Stockbroker services

Collective investments

Selecting funds

3

Investment

Investment is the core of most financial planning. Saving money on your insurances or your mortgage may make you a bit better off, but making good or bad investment decisions could mean the difference between a comfortable and a poor old age. Investing seems complicated. There are difficult issues to get to grips with, like risk. But if you have money in savings plans, pension funds, life assurance funds, unit trusts or other funds, you are an investor and the more you understand about it, the more able you will be to get a higher return for less risk. In this section we will look at:

◆ **Understanding risk** How to organise your investments to create a balance between risk and reward.

◆ **The four types of investment** Deposits, fixed-rate, property and equity investments and how they work.

◆ **Choosing an investment style** Are you more interested in value or growth?

◆ **Stockbroking services** Deciding whether it is best to pay for advice or to take the do-it-yourself route.

◆ **Collective investments** Unit trusts, Oeics, investment trusts and the rest and how they work.

Risk and reward

When faced with decisions about how to invest money, you will be pulled in different directions by two powerful motivations: greed and fear. If you want your money to grow, how much of it are you prepared to risk? If you are determined to avoid any loss, how low a return will you accept? Should you protect and preserve or venture and – hopefully – grow?

To answer these questions you will need to set aims for your capital over a reasonable period, say, at least five years. There is a simple trade-off: the higher the rate of return you aim for, the more the value of your investments will vary on a day-to-day basis. The longer the timescale of your investment and the more robust your character in the face of adversity, the better placed you will be to withstand such fluctuations.

Putting this in more concrete terms, if you want to make a return of 10% a year on top of inflation, you must put almost all your capital into equity investments. Stock markets nowadays tend to move together, so even after spreading your money around you will still find the value of your investments could fall by 15% to 20% in a month or 30% to 40% in a year. If you experience such a fall after your investments have already risen by 100% or more, you can shrug your shoulders and will probably suffer little anxiety while being patient. But if the value of your investments falls by 40% soon after you have invested, what then?

This is why even bold aims need to be tempered with caution and why even if your goals are ambitious, you will probably want to use the principle of diversification to reduce the risk of suffering a sudden 40% drop in the value of your capital.

Four types of investment

The world of savings and investment may appear very complicated but is in essence quite simple. There are only four major types of investment: deposits, fixed-rate, property and equities, though these can be packaged and combined in different ways. Each has different characteristics and uses, and the art of successful saving and investment is matching them to your needs.

Deposits

Deposits give you capital security. You can get your money back at whatever period of notice is agreed. Its security is effectively guaranteed by the institution you deposit money with, so the actual security depends on its financial status. We think of banks as secure, and indeed the large UK and European banks have huge amounts of capital and are well regulated. Smaller or newer banks even in the EU may comply with banking regulations while being considerably less secure, while banks located outside the EU may be subject to far less stringent regulation and have far lower capital resources.

Deposits earn a variable rate of interest. In each currency there is a going short-term rate of interest, which is usually determined by the central bank. Thus the interest rates payable on US dollar deposits are essentially determined by the Federal Reserve in New York, regardless of whether the account is in New York, London or Tokyo. Likewise, the interest rates payable on sterling deposits are determined by the Bank of England.

These central banks are the lenders of last resort to the financial system, and by setting the interest rates at which they lend to the banks, they also set the minimum rate at which any bank will generally lend money. This in turn determines how much they will pay to borrow money from you, which is what they do when you open a deposit account.

The rates offered on deposits will be in a range around this going rate. Central banks review interest rates monthly, and any change they make in their minimum lending rates will quickly be reflected in those payable on all types of deposit.

Fixed-rate investments

Fixed-rate investments offer a fixed return for a specified period, which may range from six months to 30 years. At the end of the period, you get your original capital back. In the meantime, you get a fixed rate of interest, which may be paid to you as income or accumulated with the original sum. With most fixed-rate investments, the only capital guarantee is at the end of the term. If you want to get your money back earlier, you may suffer a penalty or have to take your chances in the marketplace where prices could be below what you paid.

Though central banks can fix short-term interest rates, they cannot fix longer-term rates, which are essentially determined by supply and demand in the marketplace. Since governments usually borrow a lot of money, they have significant effects on longer-term rates but many other factors also come into play. The most important is inflationary expectations. Before you lend money to someone for ten years, you will want to have thought hard about what average inflation rate is likely and feel confident you will get a decent return on top.

Property

When you buy property you have no guarantees of its future capital value or the income it will produce. In this respect, property is like shares. But because it is a tangible asset most people regard it as 'safer' or less risky. Yet most people also increase the riskiness of their property investment by using borrowed money to buy. Any use of borrowed money increases the risk you incur.

When we buy our home, we put down as little as 10% of the purchase price and borrow the rest. If the price falls by 20% and we have put down 10%, we are in trouble – and this is exactly what happened to up to a million homeowners who bought using large mortgages in 1987-89 and saw the value plummet by 30% or more in the following five years. They had 'negative equity' – they owed more than their property was worth.

Using borrowed money to acquire an asset is called gearing (the American term is leverage). When it works in your favour, it dramatically increases the return on your money. If you buy a house for £100,000 using £80,000 you have borrowed from a bank, and the price rises to £120,000, then you have not actually made a profit of 20%. You only invested £20,000 of your own money and on this 'equity stake' you have made a return of 100%.

Gearing is the simplest way of increasing both the risk and the potential return from an investment – but also of increasing the potential loss, something you should never forget, especially when people start making pronouncements that the price of property 'can never go down'. It has, and it can again.

Many people talk about the huge gains they have made over a period of 20 or 30 years from owning houses, without ever appreciating that this was mainly the result of using mortgages to achieve a high level of gearing. The use of borrowed money meant an average increase in house prices of, say, 10% a year was translated into a return on their own equity of 30% or 40% a year. If they had invested in the stock market using borrowed money in the same way over the same period, they would have made even bigger profits – but most people would have regarded this as far too risky.

As this example shows, the perception of risk is highly subjective. Despite the experience of 1989-95, most of us still believe that owning a house with a large mortgage is less risky than investing in the stock market. Whatever you feel about this, the important thing in planning terms is to know what you are doing and understand the risk involved. If you feel the risk is too high, you can look for ways of reducing it.

For example, if you own a £100,000 house with a £50,000 mortgage and inherit £100,000, you may think about buying a second property. This may seem 'safer' than the stock market. But one essential principle of investment is that diversification – owning different types of asset – reduces risk. If you end up with all your capital in property, you are far more vulnerable than if you have some money in other types of investment as well.

Equity

Equity investments are those where both the income and the capital value can fall as well as rise. This broad definition includes property but the term 'equities' is usually used to refer to shares and funds that invest in shares. Equities may give you no security as regards capital value or income but they do offer prospects of growth in both. Over the long term, they have always produced higher returns than the other three types of investment, and there is no reason to expect the future to be any different.

The valuation of shares in general is largely determined by expectations of growth in companies' profits and dividends, and these depend on a wide range of economic factors including inflation and interest rates, as well as on specific factors affecting each industry. You can choose to invest in shares directly or through collective investment funds (CIFs) such as unit trusts and open-ended investment companies (Oeics).

Average returns

Given the quite different characteristics of the four types of investment, you would expect that the returns from each of them over a period of time would also be quite distinct. And so they are, as the table shows. The most important feature of all investment plans is the allocation of capital and savings to these different types of asset. The evidence shows this decision will play the largest part in determining the overall level of returns you achieve as well as the level of risk you incur, and that the choice of individual investments will play a relatively trivial part in the outcome.

Returns from three major types of investment

Average real annual returns

Period in years	10	20	50	104
Type of investment				
Cash deposits	3.1%	4.4%	1.8%	1.0%
Fixed-interest	4.6%	6.1%	1.6%	1.1%
Equity	3.2%	8.0%	6.9%	5.1%

Figures are the average annual return before tax but after adjusting for inflation up to December 2003.
Source: Barclays Capital Equity-Gilt Study 2004

Over periods of ten years and 23 years to end 2003, UK commercial property produced annual returns of 8.1% and 5.7% respectively after adjusting for inflation but before tax.
Source: Investment Property Databank

Managing risk and reward

Our wish to acquire more and earn high returns on our money is tempered by the fear of loss. A number of academic studies have shown the majority of people fear loss more than they value profit, and that we will seek to avoid the pain of loss more eagerly than we pursue the pleasure of profit.

But if we all have such an aversion to risk, how is it we have runaway stock market and property booms? The answer is that at times of excessive optimism we simply wave a magic wand and abolish the risk; we claim it does not exist and use all kinds of specious reasoning to justify a belief that investing is no longer as risky as it used to be.

So far, every such fairytale pretence that has led stock or property markets into periods of exceptionally rapid rises has been shattered by the realisation that the golden coach and horses were still, in fact, only pumpkins and mice. Time and again speculative exuberance has been transformed into panic and crash. Quite why we go on progressively more irrational binges of this kind, with their inevitably painful hangovers, is still unclear, but the character of speculative boom today remains much the same as for the past 300 years.

Managing and controlling risk is what the evolution of more complex financial instruments and personal financial planning is all about. But in order to manage and control it we need to understand its nature.

The dictionary definition of risk is 'the chance of loss or injury'. We insure against risks to our property and ourselves, but when it comes to investing our money, we have no choice but to incur some level of risk if we want our capital or investment income to grow.

Because there are different types of risk – the risk that inflation will erode your capital, that deflation will devastate companies' profits, that the high interest rates needed to cool an overheating economy will cause all financial asset prices to fall – there is no such thing as a risk-free investment. If you think you have found one, you simply have not done enough 'what if?' thinking about the possible outcomes. Because risk is unavoidable, your aim must be to manage and control it – which is why diversification among different asset types is so important.

The dictionary definition of risk does not correspond with how it is perceived by financial analysts or by the regulators who determine what may and may not be said to individual investors. To them risk means volatility. The greater an investment's variations in price, the riskier it is. Such volatility can be measured and analysed by sophisticated mathematical techniques, which can result in lists of more or less 'risky' (meaning more or less volatile) products, but these miss the central point about risk.

Risk is subjective

The essential point is that the common sense definition of risk, the chance of loss or injury, is subjective. My chance of losing money depends on me, my circumstances and how I behave; your chance of losing money depends on you, your circumstances and how you behave. If you invest in shares with the intention of keeping the money there for ten years, but then panic and sell when prices fall by 20%, where did the risk come from? It arose not just from the volatility of the shares you bought but also from your own behaviour.

Most important among the subjective factors or variables involved in risk are:

◆ **Timescale** The longer your money is invested, the less influence volatility has on the rate of return. After a long period even apparently large variations in price have little effect on this.

◆ **Resources** The pattern of behaviour of investments differs. If you hold a number of different investments each of which behaves differently, the ups and downs to some extent balance each other out. The more capital you have, the more you can diversify and damp down the effects of volatility. The less capital you have, the less able you are to do this.

◆ **Character** If you are the kind of person who gets a sick feeling in their stomach when they lose money or lies awake at night worrying about it, you had better avoid volatile investments. Even if you buy them for the long term, if they crash in price you may feel so bad that you sell, incurring a big loss. Someone with a calmer temperament may find it easier to sit out panics and slumps.

Because every investment embodies risk and you cannot avoid it, your policy should be framed to reduce risk to an acceptable level through diversification.

Four-way split

Most people will want to hold some capital in secure cash deposits, some in relatively secure fixed-rate investments and some in riskier equity investments – and most will also own their home and so already have an investment in property.

When considering where to invest extra capital, most advisers will ignore the value of your home in the allocation they propose; you should, though, consider your overall exposure to property as an 'asset class' if you are planning to make direct investments such as buy-to-let property. The higher the proportion of your capital in property and equities, the higher the returns you can expect over a period of ten years or more.

The table gives examples of the asset split you might use depending on the overall return you are aiming for and the variability in the value of your portfolio you are comfortable with. These assume you already have a significant investment in property in the form of your home and do not plan any more.

Allocating your capital to three types of investment

Your aim for annual real returns* from your capital

	2-4%	4-6%	6-10%
Percentage of capital in			
Deposits	40%	20%	10%
Fixed-rate	40%	30%	20%
Equity	20%	50%	70%
Total	100%	100%	100%
Expected volatility of			
portfolio's value	Low	Moderate	High

*Returns after allowing for the effects of inflation.

If you have only 10% of your capital in equities, even a 30% fall in their price will only lower the value of your whole portfolio by 3%. But if you have 80% of your money in equities, the day-to-day fluctuations in the portfolio's value will be far larger. This much, and the fact of higher long-term returns from equities, is certain. But there is no scientific formula for applying this. Investment is an art rather than a science and, at the end of the day, you have to be comfortable with your investments.

Fixed-rate investments

The fixed-rate investments discussed in Section One were short term, with maturity within five years. In relatively stable conditions – particularly when inflation is low and expected to remain low – longer-term fixed-rate investments may enable you to earn a return in excess of inflation with low risk. For example, with the UK inflation rate at under 2% in 2004, longer-term fixed-rate investments offered pre-tax returns of 5%.

Both governments and companies issue fixed-rate bonds with terms from ten to 30 years. Few investors buy these bonds directly, but you can invest in them through collective investment funds. As regards fixed-rate investments, it is important to understand the differences between buying bonds directly and through a CIF.

When you buy a fixed-rate bond, you are certain of the capital you will get at the bond's redemption and of the income you will get each year up to that date. When you invest in a CIF, you do not have these certainties. Because the manager may buy and sell bonds, the income may vary, and you do not lock in a specific capital redemption figure.

Managers argue that their skills in managing a portfolio of bonds more than compensate for this loss of certainty. This is probably valid as far as lower quality ('junk' or 'sub-investment grade') bonds are concerned, but it is less obviously true regarding the gilt-edged bonds issued by the UK government. If you intend to buy only high-quality longer-term bonds, you should certainly consider doing this directly via a stockbroker as an alternative to paying the relatively high charges involved in a CIF.

Most investors buy fixed-rate investments for their income, but if you reinvest the income tax-free, as you can when fixed-rate investments are held in an individual savings account (Isa), they can also form a stable, low-growth part of a diversified portfolio.

Property

Investing in residential property has become popular in recent years. There are three main reasons:
◆ It can produce a higher income yield than other investments.
◆ Between 2000 and 2003 the stock market was going steadily down.

◆ Rising property prices have produced capital gains for investors as well as rental income.

Buy-to-let purchases account for about a tenth of the UK housing stock, still a lower proportion than in most European countries.

If you invest in residential property on the same basis as you do in shares or other investments, the table shows how this might look.

Costs and rewards of buying to let

Purchase price of two-bedroom flat	£100,000
Gross annual rental income	£8,000
Less Insurance	£500
** Maintenance**	£1,000
Total deductions	£1,500
Pre-tax rental income	£6,500 (6.5% of capital)

If you are a basic rate taxpayer and pay tax on all this income, the net return will drop to 5.07%.

However, most buy-to-let investors finance their purchases through mortgages, in which case the sums look like this:

Purchase price of two-bedroom flat	£100,000
Gross annual rental income	£8,000
Less Interest on mortgage*	£4,125
** Insurance**	£500
** Maintenance**	£1,000
Total deductions	£5,625
Pre-tax rental income	£2,375 (9.5%** of capital)

* £75,000 at 5.5% interest-only **on capital invested of £25,000

When you borrow 75% of the purchase price, the margin between gross rental income and total outgoings is much smaller and can be eroded by 'voids' (times when you have no tenant). But the return of 9.5% on the equity investment of £25,000 is much higher than the return on an ungeared investment.

This higher yield should not blind you to the fact that the mortgage lender has first claim on the rental income. If you cannot find tenants, you still have to pay the interest and the loan must eventually be repaid. Hence the risk involved in geared buy-to-let investment is substantially greater than it is for outright purchase. Because economic conditions in the UK have been benign for the past decade, it is easy to forget the UK has seen unemployment rates as high as 10% and that similar rates have been seen recently in other European countries. Rising unemployment, which would certainly reduce the number of tenants able to pay the rent needed to cover outgoings, could result in a buy-to-let investment running at a deficit.

Another risk is interest rates. Most buy-to-let purchases are financed on fixed-rate loans, but many investors have gone for short-term fixes of three or four years. If interest rates are significantly higher when refinancing is required, this too could erode the net rental yield on the property.

As against this, investors who entered the market in 2000 have seen substantial capital gains on top of their rental yield. But you would be unwise to project similar gains into the future.

Even more important is the asset allocation issue discussed above. If you already own your own home, you probably have a substantial proportion of your net wealth invested in it. If you invest more in property, you may earn higher returns than on other investments – at the time of buying, this is an unknown – but you will certainly increase your level of risk. Diversification does not hold out the promise of instant gains, rather it reduces risk: when one investment sector disappears beneath the waves, you should still remain afloat.

If you do decide to pursue the buy-to-let option, do plenty of homework and research. Be very wary of 'off-plan' purchases of new property where you may be offered a guaranteed rental income for a few years. The vendors can easily afford this guarantee out of the profit they make on selling you the property and have every incentive to guarantee a high income to make the potential yield look attractive. You need to check what the market-level rental actually is, and this is what you should base your yield calculations on. Do not rely on any data from an agent who is acting for the developer.

You can invest in commercial property through collective investment funds, discussed below.

Equities

You can choose to buy shares on the stock market using a stockbroker, or you can invest in collective investment funds (CIFs) where professional managers make the buying and selling decisions. The advent of cheap online share dealing facilities has brought share investing within the reach of millions of investors, so it is a realistic option for at least some of your capital. But many people will also want to use CIFs to spread the risk. Below we consider ways of combining direct investment and CIFs.

Collective investments provide most of the benefits of the stock market without the pain of personal effort. So why invest in shares of individual companies? The principal answer is that you can achieve higher returns.

Successful companies, if you trace them back to their earliest beginnings on the stock market, have often shown returns on an original investment of several thousand percent, converting £1,000 into £100,000 or even more over a decade. You do not need to pick many shares that perform like this to become wealthy. So the challenge is to do this without incurring huge risks to your capital.

Academic studies over the past 30 years have produced convincing evidence that in developed markets such as the UK and US, the market in the shares of large companies is 'efficient', meaning almost all current information is reflected in share prices. The implication, which is borne out from studies of CIFs investing in large companies, is that it is very difficult to obtain a higher return by switching among the top 100 shares than by simply buying and holding all 100.

If you accept this, a logical approach is to use low-cost tracker funds to get your core investment in shares and concentrate your own share investing on smaller companies where the evidence of 'efficiency' is much weaker and where the prospects for rapid growth are better.

Today's stock market

The boundaries of the old national stock markets have been eroding for decades. Many British companies now have share listings in New York as well as in London. The major European exchanges are discussing merger plans. New all-electronic exchanges threaten the older established ones both in Europe and America.

As far as the small and mainly domestic focused UK companies are concerned, the choice is between a listing on the London Stock Exchange (www.londonstockexchange.com), a listing on the Alternative Investment Market (www.londonstockexchange.com/aim) or simply making arrangements for the shares to be traded privately, as they are through Ofex (www.ofex.com).

The LSE is more demanding than Aim in terms of its listing requirements and charges higher fees. Companies without track records cannot list on the LSE, for example. The level of 'due diligence' applied to checking the facts and figures is higher for an LSE than for an Aim listing.

In both cases the process affords some investor protection. You can be sure that no director of a company listing on either exchange will have a criminal record, for instance. If a company seeking a listing has entered any agreements or contracts with companies controlled by its directors, these will be fully disclosed. In these and many other areas, the structure of limited companies provides ample opportunity for founder-managers to cheat incoming investors, so the policing of listing requirements is an important feature of stock exchanges.

Naturally, promoters of new all-electronic exchanges focus more on the cheapness of dealing costs. It is in their interests to relax listing requirements to attract companies to them.

Ofex is not a market at all. It is simply a facility for trading shares in privately owned companies that have not been subject to any exchange's listing rules. Just because a business is a public limited company (Plc) this does not mean it is listed on a stock exchange. All it means is that it has more than five shareholders and pays slightly more in audit fees for its annual report than a limited company.

Individuals are not allowed to trade directly on stock exchanges. They must transact their deals through stockbrokers who are accredited members of the exchange. The brokers themselves are responsible for settling transactions, which means collecting and paying over the money. The security and dependability of settlement is another defining feature of developed stock markets, but this is notably absent from many emerging stock markets.

When you buy or sell shares, the broker deals with a market-maker. The market-maker buys and sells shares, like a wholesale greengrocer, aiming to make tiny profits on most trades. The market-maker risks its own capital in doing this, whereas the broker simply acts as your agent in fulfilling the orders you have given. Confusingly, big banks own both market-making and stockbroking companies, though they are kept separate by 'Chinese walls' designed by regulators to prevent companies exploiting information to profit at their customers' expense.

Shareholders are last in line

Shareholders in a business are the last in line when it comes to entitlements to take money out. A company has a legal responsibility to pay the following:
◆ Any taxes due to the government: income tax, capital gains tax, Vat or customs duties;
◆ Any taxes due to the local authority (business rates);
◆ Wages due to its employees;
◆ Money owed to its bankers;
◆ Payments due to its suppliers;
◆ Money owed to other lenders including bondholders.

All these rank ahead of shareholders. Only when they have been paid is a company entitled to make payments to its shareholders. Thus, shareholders bear the most risk. But since they are entitled to everything that is left after paying off these prior obligations, they also obtain very high returns when a company prospers.

Companies can make themselves more or less risky for shareholders. The principal factor is debt; the more debt a company has, the more profits it must make to pay the interest before shareholders get anything. The ratio of debt to equity is therefore one of the most important features of a company's financing.

The value of debt is simply all the debts of whatever kind added together. The value of equity is the amount shown in the balance sheet as attributable to shareholders. This is the total of all the amounts subscribed for shares plus the company's retained profits and the reserves created from them that it has set aside over the years, plus any excess over their cost of the assets owned by the business.

Analysing companies' accounts used to be a matter of combing through reports and calculating figures. But today a huge amount of this is done by providers of databases which can be accessed through the internet. This has removed a lot of the drudgery, but you should still read one of the basic books on valuing companies so that you understand the principles. Global investor's online financial bookshop (www.global-investor.com) has a wide range.

The valuation basics

◆ **Equity** A company's equity is owned by its shareholders. The equity is the value of the business net of all its liabilities. This is only partially reflected in its balance sheet, its statement of total assets and liabilities. The balance sheet will include all tangible assets, but may not include the market value of brand names, patents, intellectual property and key personnel.

◆ **Enterprise value** This is the value of the business including not only shareholders' capital but also the total of any outstanding debt.

◆ **Net asset value** The net asset value per share is the balance sheet figure for assets attributable to shareholders divided by the number of shares in issue. It may be close to the market value of the business in the case of, say, a property company that has recently revalued its assets. Most businesses have a market value far higher than their net asset value.

◆ **Market capitalisation** The capitalisation (or market value) of a business is the number of shares in issue multiplied by the share price. Several valuation measures relate this market value to other factors.

◆ **Price to sales** A company's market value may be less than the value of its annual sales if it consistently makes a low profit margin on those sales. But in the case of a fast-growing new high-tech company the market value can be as much as ten times its sales.

◆ **Price to book** A company's market value may be equal to its book value – as in the case of the property company referred to above. In most cases it will be far higher than the book value.

◆ **Earnings** The company's profits, after tax and permitted adjustments, are its earnings. Earnings divided by the number of shares in issue give earnings per share.

◆ **Price/earnings ratio** The price/earnings ratio (PER) is the share price divided by earnings per share. If the share price is 250p and the earnings per share are 15p, the PER is 16.7.

◆ **Dividend yield** Companies pay dividends on a per-share basis. The latest total annual dividends per share divided by the share price and multiplied by 100 gives the dividend yield. This tells you the return on your money you get in the form of income when you buy a share. If the share price is 250p and the dividend is 8.75p per share the dividend yield is 3.5%. UK companies' dividend yields are usually quoted net of 20% tax.

◆ **EBITDA** Earnings before interest, taxation, depreciation and amortisation. The rate at which companies depreciate their assets varies. Many analysts now use EBITDA to compare companies.

◆ **Profit margins** Profits before tax as a percentage of sales or turnover.

◆ **Interest cover** The extent to which annual interest payments on debt are covered by gross profits.

◆ **Return on capital employed** This is profits before tax, interest and dividends (but after deducting depreciation and amortisation) expressed as a percentage of capital employed, defined as equity plus long-term debt.

Fundamental and technical analysis

Fundamental analysis is the study of a company's business and prospects using tools like those described above. The basic tenet of fundamental analysts is that the more you know and understand about a business, the better placed you are to assess its value relative to its peers and you will, therefore, make better buying and selling decisions.

Technical analysis is the study of market-related data such as movements in share prices, the volume of shares traded and the ratio of rising to falling share prices each day or week. Technical analysis used to be mainly a matter of looking at price charts and trying to identify predictable trends. Computers have led to a huge array of extremely complex calculations all of which can be cross-related and monitored. A fashion for computer-driven share trading in the 1980s was temporarily halted by the 1987 crash, but today hedge funds – often speculative funds trading with borrowed money – are using similar methods on a large scale.

Many investors use fundamental and technical analysis to make decisions.

What is a good business?

Defining a successful company is difficult. Think of two of Britain's best-known brand names, both of which were, until the mid-1990s, long-term successes: J Sainsbury and Marks & Spencer. Both were regarded as blue-chip investments, both had huge financial strength and powerful brand names. Yet both lost the plot in terms of selling to their customers' needs. Sainsburys undercut its 'quality' image by embarking on a price-focused battle with Tesco – which it lost. Marks & Spencer's styling of its clothing range was perceived as so dull that its customers went elsewhere. Both companies' share prices crashed by over a third while their rivals bounded ahead.

These cases provide two important morals for investors:

◆ **Nothing is for ever** However good you think a company is, you must keep an eye on its performance. If its standards look as if they are starting to slip, investigate quickly and unless you find good reasons to expect a downturn to be only short term, sell.

◆ **You saw it first** Good or bad news on the high street is visible in the stores long before the City analysts can measure it in sales or profit figures. Busy Tesco car parks pointed to its success in winning customers from Sainsburys. Empty M&S clothing departments gave the clue to the story months before the shares crashed.

Trust your experience

There are many areas in which professional, full-time investors do enjoy advantages over individual investors. It is no good thinking that because you have access to lots of information on the internet you can compete with them. For a start, the professional fund managers mostly have first-class honours degrees, they spend all day thinking about investment and have access to far more information than you do.

The real advantage you have as an individual is your own experience. First, you have your own general experience of buying goods and services. Companies with clearly better deals for consumers are going to win business from rivals. Look for evidence of this around you, not just in the shops but also in services and utilities.

Second, you have your own particular skills and contacts. Perhaps you work in the packaging industry – in which case you should know something about the big packaging companies and which of them is doing well. Perhaps you work in the civil service – so which companies are winning contracts to install computers, develop software and subcontract services?

Use your network of friends and acquaintances to research and test ideas. If a store is busy in your town, is it doing as well elsewhere? If your cable company's service is terrible, is this just a local flaw? Is the new hotel going up on the edge of town part of a chain? And watch for local press reports on locally based listed companies – you will often get far more detail in these reports than in brief national press comments.

Warren Buffett, the world's most successful investor, defines a successful business as one with a franchise that is hard for someone to invade. A local newspaper is a good example. So long as you turn out a decent product, the advertising revenue rolls in – it is almost as good as a monopoly. Peter Lynch, a hugely successful US fund manager, saw quarries as having similar attractive qualities. No quarry owner tries to sell his gravel to people living on the edge of a competitor's quarry, but he is content to take a near-monopoly profit on all sales within a radius of his own hole in the ground.

Buffett sees global brands in the same light: he has been a long-term investor in Coca-Cola and American Express, for example, which must be two of his country's best-known brands. But with a brand, you still have to check that it is secure from competition or erosion of its profit margins by cheaper rivals.

Successful businesses are easy to identify with hindsight. But very few investors climb on board a company like Microsoft or Glaxo near the start of the journey. Still, the encouraging thing is that you do not need to. As Buffett remarks, it is far better to pay a fair price for a great company than a great price for a fair company. Buffett confessed in one of his shareholder reports that he only bought shares in Coca-Cola after 20 years of admiring it and consuming its products. He still made a fortune.

Big winners usually go on rolling ahead for many years so if you find one that you believe has the potential, do not be put off by the fact that the price has already risen a lot.

New issues

When a company makes its stock market debut it offers shares to investors. The American term for public issue is initial public offering or IPO and this term is gradually coming into use in the UK.

The company has to satisfy the listing requirements of the relevant stock exchange. This will require a report from its auditors as well as its directors. A prospectus will be issued giving the company's history, latest profit and loss account and balance sheet and usually an indication of likely profits for the current financial year. You apply for shares, which are usually on offer at a fixed price, by filling in an application and sending it in with your cheque.

When the stock market is especially buoyant, new issues usually get off to a flying start. Optimism is widespread, so people apply for more shares than they want, expecting to be able to sell them at a premium when dealings start. Over-subscription may mean that investors receive fewer shares than they applied for, possibly resulting in even greater demand when dealings begin. So when trading does start, new issues can soar away to a premium of 50% or, in the case of internet stocks in 1999, 200% on the first day.

If that all seems enticing, not to say intoxicating, sobriety is just around the corner. Detailed research into IPOs in the US has shown that investors on average get worse returns than they would by buying an index-tracker fund. This was not true for 1998 and 1999, years in which the internet and technology craze drove new issues to gigantic premiums, but the long-term evidence should make you wary of expecting instant riches from new issues.

Most of the truly brilliant long-term winners on the stock market could have been bought at any time in a period of two or three years and still have returned gigantic profits. Sponsors of IPOs like to create an air of excitement about new issues and pay heavily to public relations consultancies to achieve this. The reality is that an untried business needs a few years to prove itself. Even if the shares rise a lot, they will still offer huge upside in a couple of years' time and they will be a much less risky investment. For information on new issues, log onto Ample (www.iii.co.uk/newissues).

Penny shares

Many investors believe shares priced in pennies offer greater profit potential than those priced in pounds. This is simply not true. The upside potential of a share relates to the profitability of the business and not to how its shares are priced.

Many penny shares are in small companies that have fallen on hard times. Very few companies issue shares in pennies, and for a share to get from a typical issue price of 50p or £1 down to 5p, the business must have done something wrong. There may be recovery prospects. Or there may be hopes of a deal whereby entrepreneurs inject new assets into the company in exchange for shares. Developments like these can result in huge gains but they are rare.

Moreover, dealing spreads in penny shares can be enormous. Take a company whose total capitalisation is £5m with 50 million shares in issue. The 'middle' price quoted in the newspapers is 10p, but the actual prices are different. The dealing spread may be 11p to buy and 9p to sell. That is a 20% spread, which means the first 20% of any gains will go not to you but to the market-maker.

Dealing frequently in penny shares may or may not make you rich, but it will certainly help the stockbroker and market-maker to add a wing to their country mansions.

Choosing an investing style

There are many different styles of investing. The word style is used because this is not just about deciding on a method but about how you apply it. It also suggests that, as with fashion, what you adopt has to suit your character or you risk making yourself appear ridiculous – or, in the case of investing, poor.

The three styles described here are well defined and have been applied by many investors over long periods. But they are only applications of a set of rules within given boundaries. There is really no limit to the number of investment styles, each of which will be differently applied by every individual investor. So you do not have simply to adopt one. But the evidence does suggest that it is hard to be a contrarian part of the time and a growth investor some of the time.

You may succeed in applying two different styles if you do so to distinctly separate pots of money. But on the whole, you are probably better off deciding on one approach and then trying to refine it.

Value is biggest and best

Value investing is the approach that has been in use for longest and with the most consistent results. It was invented by Benjamin Graham, author of a tome on security valuation, and applied by him from the 1930s to the 1950s. Warren Buffett, whose company Berkshire Hathaway has produced annual returns far in excess of the average investment fund, is a Graham disciple, as have been many other successful investors.

The key features of Graham's approach are:

◆ **The business** Know and understand the business in depth: its history, its strengths and weaknesses, its opportunities, its finances, its management and its products.

◆ **The numbers** Value investing is very analytical. In particular, look at trends in terms of sales, profits and earnings; at the ratio of stock to turnover; at the ratio of short-term debtors to creditors; at the ratio of debt to equity; at the return on the capital employed in the business, adjusting for any accounting measures which may produce a falsely rosy picture.

◆ **The margin of safety** This was Graham's key contribution. He wanted to buy a dollar for sixty cents. In the 1930s, 1940s and the early 1950s it was easy to do so. If you analysed the numbers, many companies' shares were selling at sixty cents when the assets were clearly worth a dollar. Buying such a share gave the margin of safety Graham always wanted.

In more recent times, very few shares have been available on terms like that. This is partly because tangible assets such as land and buildings, important in Graham's day, now make up a small proportion of companies' assets. In a 'dematerialised' economy, the value of a company's brands, patents and key personnel is often more important than its tangible assets. Measuring these 'intangibles' is not as easy. The margin of safety may still be there but is harder to quantify.

Buffett has progressively moved from a strict interpretation of Graham's methods to one in which the value of a brand or 'franchise' provides the margin of safety.

Working with Mr Market

Value investors buy and hold. Buffett has held many shares for ten years or more and claims to pay no attention to market prices. He is fond of citing Graham's 'Mr Market' analogy. It goes like this. When you buy a share, think of yourself as becoming a partner in a business with Mr Market. Mr Market is very accommodating. Every day he turns up and states a price at which he will buy your share of the business, or sell his share to you.

But though the business may be stable, Mr Market's quotations will be anything but stable. 'For, sad to say, the poor fellow suffers from incurable emotional problems. At times he feels euphoric and can see only the favourable factors affecting the business. When in this mood, he names a very high buy-sell price because he fears that you will snap up his interest and rob him of imminent gains. At other times he is depressed and can see nothing but trouble ahead both for the business and the world. On these occasions he will name a very low price, since he is terrified you will unload your interest onto him.'

Buffett points out that under these conditions, the more manic depressive Mr Market's behaviour is, the better for you. But this is on one condition: Mr Market is there to serve you and not to guide you. It will be disastrous if you fall under his influence. Buffett sums up: 'Indeed, if you aren't certain that you understand and can value your business far better than Mr Market, you don't belong in the game.'

Value investing is austere, analytical and a touch arrogant. Yet the evidence is clear: its practitioners have included more of the most successful investors than any other style.

Growth investing

When the number of companies whose shares qualified as value investments shrank in the 1950s and 1960s, analysts cast about for other methods. One that was highly successful was the growth investing style of T Rowe Price, an American stockbroker. He argued that it was worth paying an apparently high price for shares in companies capable of rapid growth in profits and earnings, and the boom of the 1950s and 1960s proved him spectacularly right.

The market crash in 1969-70 then saw many growth company shares fall by 50% or more, and for a while growth investing was marginalised. But it returned in spectacular style in the late 1990s, as technology stocks soared to unprecedentedly high valuations on the basis of their supposed ability to produce very high rates of growth in earnings for many years.

◆ **The life cycle** Price believed that companies went through a life cycle. In their earliest and latest stages they were most risky. But the least risky time to own them was when they had established themselves and sales and profits were growing strongly. The aim was to own them until they entered the period of maturity and to sell them before they entered the period of decadence.

◆ **Cyclical and secular** The ideal growth stock is one capable of secular growth in earnings, which means it will continue to grow through several business cycles during which its sector and the whole economy expands and contracts. Shares in such a company will still fall along with those of its peers in a cyclical downturn but will recover much more strongly in the next upturn.

◆ **Moving on** When a company reaches a plateau, or when external conditions erode its ability to grow, its shares should be sold. Unlike value investing, growth investing is active in disposing of previously successful companies and replacing them with new hopefuls.

The high valuations sometimes attained by growth stocks lead to widespread scepticism. As so often happens in the stock market, rationality and emotion come into conflict.

Here is how another insightful American investor, Walter K Gutman, sees them reaching a resolution: 'Because no wealth you will ever have – even if you are the richest man in the world – will equal your dreams, stocks go to particularly high levels when a lot of people think they might equal their dreams. Those stocks that are called growth stocks might better be called dream stocks. But dreams are real – we have them every day. It's a big mistake to think that dreams are unreal and what is called real life is real. If dreams were unreal, it would be possible for you to feel richer than your dreams if you were the richest man in the world. When the dream of a new industry comes true, then the dream ends and the stocks sell more conservatively, relating to what is real rather than to what was dreamed.'

They're all wrong

Contrarianism is the investment style based on the view that if a great majority of investors are doing the same thing, it is usually wrong. Its application is more limited than the other styles and may best be thought of as a kind of medicine.

Edward C Johnson II, founder of the giant US mutual fund manager Fidelity, pointed out that contrary opinion was of little use in matters of fact. Where contrarianism comes into its own is as a defence against crowd psychology.

◆ **Evidence in favour** Study of transactions by small investors on the New York Stock Exchange over many years showed that when the vast majority were buying, you would be better off selling, and vice versa. In the second half of 1974, sellers consistently outnumbered buyers in the UK market and share prices doubled in the first few months of 1975. In summer 1987, buyers hugely outnumbered sellers and along came a 30% crash in October.

◆ **Greater fool** The greater fool theory of investment is that it does not matter if you buy at a foolish price so long as there is a bigger fool willing to pay an even more foolish price. But for this to work there must an adequate supply of bigger fools, and if this is to happen, crowd psychology must be in operation. As Johnson observed: 'Crowds, when they carry often sound ideas to foolish extremes, tend to commit suicide.' As successful old-time speculator in cotton Dickson Watts advised: 'Against the crowd, act boldly. With the crowd, act cautiously. It may at any time turn and rend you.' The contrarian looks for opportunities to act against the crowd.

◆ **You too** For contrarianism to work you have to apply it to your own pet ideas as well as to those of others. Why do you believe X? What would you do if you did not believe X? Used in this way, contrarianism is an attempt to undertake a very difficult task: to listen to what the market is saying, not what people (you included) are thinking and saying about the market.

Fads and fashions

Finding and holding on to a great investment for years while it makes you rich is one possible investment objective, and there is plenty of evidence to prove it is attainable. But this is not what the majority of professional investors do, and since the professionals own the bulk of listed shares, they are the ones who determine short-term and even medium-term market movements.

The problem with these professionals is that they are accountable to investors, advisers and trustees on a short-term basis. They are therefore motivated to attain short-term results. Generally, they will be accounted successful if they have done better than the average of their competitors over the last six to 12 months. So, in broad terms, they pile into sectors and shares they believe will go up in the short term and out of those they believe will go down in the short term. Their timescale is three to six months or at most a year and almost never more.

As long ago as 1935 JM Keynes, who was not only a great economist but also a great investor and speculator, spotted this. He wrote: 'It might have been supposed that competition between expert professionals, possessing judgment and knowledge beyond that of the individual investor, would correct the vagaries of the ignorant individual left to himself. It happens, however, that the energies and skills of the professional investor and speculator are mainly occupied otherwise. For most of these persons are, in fact, largely concerned, not with making superior long-term forecasts of the probable yield of an investment over its whole life, but with foreseeing changes in the conventional basis of valuation a short time ahead of the general public.'

Keynes equally acutely explained why professional investors would not, by and large, be long-term investors: 'It is the long-term investor, he who most promotes the public interest, who will in practice come in for most criticism, wherever funds are managed by committees or boards or banks. For it is in the essence of his behaviour that he should be eccentric, unconventional and rash in the eyes of average opinion. If he is successful, that will only confirm the general belief in his rashness; and if in the short run he is unsuccessful, which is very likely, he will not receive much mercy. Worldly wisdom teaches that it is better for reputation to fail conventionally than succeed unconventionally.'

Or, as Warren Buffett mischievously puts it: 'No individual lemming ever received a bad press.'

For a recent example of this truth, consider what happened to Phillips & Drew Fund Management, part of the Swiss banking giant UBS. PDFM is principally a value investor and disliked the high-tech stocks that started to perform so well from 1998 onwards, considering them to be overpriced and in many cases over-borrowed.

The result was that the portfolios it managed for clients contained none of these soaring tech stocks and therefore performed well below the average of their competitors for the following two years. PDFM was ridiculed by its rivals who had, as the saying goes, 'filled their boots' with high-tech stocks, and PDFM lost a significant number of clients as a result. Of course, PDFM did end up having the last laugh when the 2000-3 bear market saw prices of many of those same wonder stocks fall by 90% or more.

Sector rotation

The fads and fashions of the stock market are ever changing but 'sector rotation' is the old perennial. A few months of gloom from the high street, a couple of shop chains reporting profits not as good as expected, and suddenly all retailers' shares are heading down, the good along with the bad, only to rise again six months later when reports of 'equity withdrawal' from housing spark expectations of a spending boom.

In the meantime, the money goes into utilities because they are cheap on a yield valuation, so up go the utilities' shares. A slightly tougher-than-expected statement from a utility regulator, and down go water or electricity shares, only to rise again in six months when the companies announce exactly the same dividend increases as had previously been forecast.

Almost all the research and opinions you see cited in newspapers and magazines will reflect the current professional consensus. And you have a simple choice: try to find out what the consensus is as quickly as possible, so you can join in and keep up with it, or be aware of it but use it simply as another piece of information in your attempt to select long-term investments. If you do want to play alongside the professionals, you must recognise that you enter a race with a sizeable handicap.

Managing your shares

Cutting losses

Most professional investors agree that individual investors do worse than they could because they do not dump their losers but hold them all the way to the bottom. This is largely a matter of psychology. If you over-identify with your investments, the failure of one of them becomes a personal failure. It is a hard trap to avoid.

This is the test proposed by several professional investors. Regardless of what you paid for it and when you bought it, and knowing what you now know about the company, would you buy its shares at the present price? If not, sell.

Successful investors are divided on the issue of the use of automatic 'stop-losses'. Some investors when they buy a share set a stop-loss, a price at which they will sell if it falls. They argue that strict adherence to this policy may result in some disappointments, when a share bounces quickly back after falling through the stop-loss level, but it saves you from far worse losses on shares that keep going down. Many online brokers now allow you to set automatic stop-loss levels at which shares will be sold without you having to give further instructions.

It's all there

Doing your own research on companies is much easier in the internet age. An increasing number of Plcs have websites from which you can download annual reports and other investor information and these sites are easy to find using a search engine. Stockbrokers are starting to offer free research reports. Many offer access to charts of share prices. Independent sites tell you how many shares are rising and falling, which companies' directors are buying and selling, which shares are being most actively bought or sold by private investors, and many let you record your own portfolio and set alerts so that you are e-mailed when prices hit specified levels. All this and far more is available provided you are prepared to spend the time trawling through the ever increasing number of websites.

Some of the more useful include: Ample (www.iii.co.uk), Bigcharts (www.bigcharts.marketwatch.com), Citywire (www.citywire.co.uk/home), Digitallook (www.digitallook.com), Everyinvestor (www.everyinvestor.co.uk), Financial Times (http://news.ft.com/home/europe), Hemscott (www.hemscott.net), LSE (www.londonstockexchange.com), Reuters (www.reuters.com), Sharecast (www.sharecast.com), UK-Wire company announcements (www.uk-wire.com).

One way of learning about investing while having fun is to join an investment club. Members meet regularly, trade ideas, argue and choose shares in which their pooled money – quite small amounts, usually – is invested. An organisation called Proshare (www.proshare.org.uk) provides guidance on setting up or joining a club (see Appendix).

You need time

It is no accident that many of the most active individual investors are retired people. Finding and studying all that material, chatting on internet bulletin boards, even going to companies' annual meetings, simply takes up too much time for someone who has a full-time job and family responsibilities.

Share investing can be a part-time hobby if you stick to a few simple trading rules and do not over-commit yourself. But if you want to put a lot of your money into shares, be realistic about the amount of time you need to do this effectively. If you do not have the time, it may be better to use collectives for the bulk of your capital and to restrict your involvement with shares.

Stockbroker services

Stockbrokers offer two types of dealing service to individual investors:

◆ **Advisory** You may ask your broker for advice and the firm may also provide you with research material and newsletters. Dealing costs are typically 1.25% to 1.5% on the value of each trade. You will usually deal with the same individual or small group of individuals who will get to know you and your account.

◆ **Execution-only** The broker provides no advice and takes no responsibility for your investment choices. The firm simply provides a dealing and settlement service. The cost is usually under 1% on the value of a trade – and is often now provided on a flat-rate basis, with several services charging less than £10 per trade. Telephone dealing usually costs more than online dealing. When you phone you will normally talk to one of a group of order-takers who can call up details of your account on-screen there and then.

Until recently, when you bought shares you received a certificate. This was not legal title of ownership. It is the entry on the company's register that represents title to shares but it was traditional to issue certificates. Now most trading and settlement is handled electronically, registration of ownership has also gone electronic. Stockbrokers prefer you to hold your shares in a nominee account, which means that the broker operates one electronic account through which all clients' holdings are held. You can open your own account with the stock exchange clearing system (Crest) but the charges may be as much as £100 a year.

There are two problems with brokers' nominee accounts. One is that you do not receive communications from companies, because these go to the nominee and not to you. Some brokers allow you to have information redirected but they usually charge for this.

The second problem is security. Legally, you are the owner and if the nominee company went bust you should still be the owner. But in the past, people who were in the process of settling transactions found that if a nominee company did go bust it took many months to sort out their entitlement.

Brokers have two answers to this problem: insurance and use of third parties. If a broker runs its own nominee company, it should have a very large sum of insurance to cover any potential client losses and should be happy to tell you what cover it has. Or the broker may use an independent nominee company which is part of a financial group with much more capital.

Brokers who hold your shares in nominee accounts are obliged to send you periodic statements showing exactly what you hold.

You can compare broker costs at www.moneysupermarket.com/shares.

Self-select Isas

Many stockbrokers offer self-select individual savings accounts. This means you set up a plan with the broker, subscribe cash to the plan and then buy shares within the Isa.

Dealing costs are normally the same as for advisory or execution-only services, but there are extra charges to watch out for. Usually, they are in one of two forms. Brokers either charge on a per item basis for collecting dividends and paying money to you, or they levy an annual charge, typically 0.5% or 1% of the value of your investments, and make no extra charges for these services.

You will need to examine the small print carefully to work out the effect of these charges. But do think about the long term. A 1% charge on a £5,000 investment is only £50 a year, but suppose you treble your money in the next three years. Now the charge is £150 a year. Wherever possible, select plans with the lowest annual charges – and consider those with no or flat-rate annual charges so long as the per item charges are not going to cost you too much.

Isas allow you to buy shares in overseas as well as in UK companies. Watch out for higher costs here since commission rates of 2.5% or even more may be charged on purchases and sales of non-UK companies' shares.

If you want to take control of your own pension fund, you can do so with a self-select self-invested personal pension (Sipp). Several stockbrokers offer online Sipps with low costs.

Out-and-out speculation

If you are attracted by the idea of high-risk, short-term trading, or speculating, you can also consider spread betting through one of several specialist bookmakers. The costs of betting on the movement of a share price can be less than the in-and-out costs of buying and selling the shares, and, while the bookmaker may ask for a 'margin' deposit, this will usually be small by comparison with the capital you would need to invest to have the same profit potential. Since betting gains are tax-free, the package can look attractive. But the important point to remember with spread betting is that you can lose as well as make huge amounts of money.

Contracts for difference are another way of trading or speculating in shares. Unlike spread betting, the gains are taxable but the advantage is lower dealing costs and greater flexibility in placing stop-losses.

Collective investments

Collective investments, such as unit and investment trusts and others discussed below, undertake to manage money for you in stock market investments. Because they deal in large sums, their transaction costs are far lower than yours would be, saving you money as well as time and effort. But they also levy initial charges that balance this out.

Collective investments have annual charges too. The best way to view these is as a form of insurance premium. If you could not insure your home against fire or flood, would you rather own your own home or own a one-hundredth share in your own and in 99 other homes? Clearly this is less risky. Likewise, owning shares in 100 different companies is less risky than having them in one or two. So the annual charge on a collective investment includes the equivalent of an insurance premium you pay to reduce your risk of loss.

And just as the insurance premiums you pay over the years will reduce the overall return you make from owning a house, so the annual charges on collective investments will reduce the return. In the same way that you want the best cover for your home at the lowest possible cost, you will want the best type of collective at the lowest possible annual charge. And just as with insurance, there will be a trade-off between quality and cost.

The collective proposition

Collective investments in general – at least those in developed markets like the UK – offer a fivefold proposition to investors.

◆ **Risk** Spreading investment, as collective investments do, reduces risk as compared with holding a few individual securities.

◆ **Cost** The cost of buying and selling collectives is often similar to and can be lower than the cost of buying and selling individual securities.

◆ **Professional management** Collectives entrust your money to full-time professional investors.

◆ **Convenience** Owning collectives results in considerably less paperwork and decision making for the investor.

◆ **Regulation** Collectives are subject to well-defined legislation and prudential rules enforced by effective regulation, making fraud virtually impossible and providing adequate compensation in the event of a loss caused by any breach of the rules by the fund manager.

Unit trusts

Unit trusts are so called because they are constituted as trusts whose assets are held by a trustee. The trustee is part of a large financial group and must be separate and independent from the company that manages the investments, providing bomb-proof investor protection.

A unit trust holds a set of investments that are valued at least once a day. The price of a unit is the value of the investments divided by the number of units in issue. To this basic valuation are added the costs that would be incurred in buying the current investments. On top of this the manager adds an initial charge of up to 5%. This gives the offer price of units, which you pay when you buy. The bid price, what you get when you sell, is usually about 6.5% below the offer price.

Unit trusts may also be single-priced. In this case, the published price is simply the value of the investments per unit with a sales charge added separately for incoming investors. Unit trusts are 'open-ended' – they issue new units when investors want to buy and redeem them when investors want to sell.

They are 'forward priced': when you place an order to buy, you get units priced at the next valuation. After your purchase, you receive a contract note setting out the date and terms of the deal and either a certificate or a statement of your registered holding. As with shares, it is the entry on the register that provides legal title of ownership, not the certificate.

The unit trust manager handles purchases and sales of units and also the buying and selling of investments. But the investments and cash are all held by a custodian who is responsible to the trustee. The trustee is liable to investors for the safety of these assets.

Units may be bought from the managers or through independent advisers or stockbrokers. These advisers are entitled to commission of up to 3% on purchases and they may not only offer reductions in this commission but may also negotiate discounts with the managers. This means it is usually better to buy units through an adviser than direct from the manager.

Unit trusts may invest in shares and fixed-rate securities listed on stock markets. They may invest a small proportion of their assets in unquoted or private shares, but very few do because such assets are hard to value. Unit trusts may also invest in commercial and industrial, but not residential, property. Trusts are not permitted to borrow money to add to their pool of assets. They may use derivatives only if this results in no additional risk for investors. They may not hold more than 5% of their assets in any one security, so the minimum number of companies in which a trust will hold shares is 20 though most hold far more.

There are some 20 different types of unit trust, such as those investing in the UK for growth and for income, in America, Japan, and Europe, in technology or financial or health shares, in natural resources and in smaller companies.

Unit trusts pay dividends net of tax. The dividend is not subject to any more tax if you are a basic rate payer but higher rate payers will have an additional liability depending on whether the income comes from fixed-rate investments or shares. Unit trusts pay no capital gains tax on profits when they buy and sell shares. Individual investors will be liable to capital gains tax when they sell if their gains exceed their annual allowance.

Open-ended investment companies

In most of the rest of the world, collective investments take the form of companies rather than trusts. Recent UK legislation has permitted the creation of Oeics whose main difference from unit trusts is that they are companies, not trusts, and do not have two prices. Instead there is just one price. When you buy, the manager usually adds a sales charge to this.

Oeics have the power to redeem their own shares at their current net asset value, which is the value of the investments divided by the number of shares in issue. Like unit trusts, they have independent custodians who hold the assets. Each unit trust is a separate legal entity, but an Oeic may be a single company with 20 or more different funds within it. Oeics may also have different classes of share linked to the same investments. The class available to institutional investors, with a minimum investment of £100,000 or more, has lower charges than that available to individuals.

Oeics have similar investment powers and restrictions to unit trusts and a similar range of funds. The tax treatment is the same as with unit trusts. As from 2004, investment managers are permitted to offer new varieties of Oeic. These funds may borrow money and use derivatives. Such funds may offer 'risk limitation' by guaranteeing you can always sell at no less than 80% of the price you paid. In 2005 it is expected a new form of Oeic investing in commercial and/or residential property will also be available.

For more information on unit trusts and Oeics go to www.investmentuk.org.

Types of unit trust and Oeic

Most unit trusts and Oeics are 'plain vanilla' funds investing all their money in one type of asset, such as UK smaller companies, UK property, European fixed-interest, American smaller companies and so forth. Some are highly specialised such as funds investing in healthcare or in shares in Thailand. Other types of fund include:

◆ **Index-tracker funds** These enable you to link your investment to stock market indices such as the FTSE 100 or the Standard & Poor's 500.

◆ **Funds divided between shares and fixed-interest** These are designed to generate a higher income for investors and include 'distribution funds'.

◆ **Managed funds** These may include shares abroad and in the UK as well as fixed-interest.

◆ **Limited risk funds** These use derivatives to limit losses – see below.

The Investment Management Association (see Appendix) places funds in categories so their performance can be compared with that of their peer group.

Charges and costs with unit trusts and Oeics

The key cost figure for unit trusts and Oeics is the total expense ratio (TER). At present this is not disclosed as a single figure in sales documents, though it probably will be within a year or two. For the time being, the only figure managers disclose is the annual charge, which for unit trusts is typically between 1% and 1.5%. Additional charges (such as custodian fees) mean funds with management charges of 1.5% usually have TERs between 1.75% and 2%.

While it may be reasonable to pay charges at this level for actively managed funds, the evidence is that if you are investing only in large UK companies, it is not worth paying these costs for active management and, over time, an index-tracking trust with annual charges of less than 0.75% is likely to produce better returns.

While some index-tracking trusts make no initial charge and have annual charges of less than 0.75%, there are still several levying initial charges and higher annual charges, so even with trackers it is worth shopping around, or you can use exchange traded funds and get an even better deal.

Exchange traded funds

Exchange traded funds (ETFs) are a recent innovation. They are index-tracker funds that are listed on the London Stock Exchange. A merchant bank creates a portfolio of, say, the top 100 companies' shares in which the value of shares in each company corresponds to their place in the FTSE 100. Shares in this pool are then listed on the LSE and can be bought and sold like any other share. The value of the ETF changes in line with the relevant index. ETFs have two advantages:

◆ Unlike unit trusts and Oeics, they are constantly revalued and you do not have to wait for a daily valuation point – you can buy or sell at any time during LSE trading hours.
◆ There is no initial charge and annual charges are under 0.5%, making them cheaper than any unit trust or Oeic tracker fund. You can buy and sell ETFs through an online stockbroker at less than £10 per deal, which on a purchase of £5,000 would represent 0.2%. You can hold them in an Isa if you wish.

Fund supermarkets

Several major financial services companies offer fund supermarkets. The concept is still evolving, but the basic idea is you set up an account and buy whatever funds you want, managed by different investment firms, within it. Fund supermarkets usually offer a self-select Isa, so you can do the same within an Isa account.

The promoter of the fund supermarket may not own the technology. Fidelity Funds Network is one of the two biggest fund supermarkets, and you can either transact directly with Fidelity, or you can use the same system but through an independent financial adviser. Some of the IFAs using the system offer larger discounts on some of the available funds than you can get if you transact with Fidelity.

When deciding which fund supermarket to use, and whether to go direct or through an IFA, the most important issues are:
◆ How many different funds and managers can you get access to through the service?
◆ What are the minimum investments per fund for lump sums and regular savings?
◆ What level of discounts from initial charges are offered?
◆ What resources, in terms of factsheets, fund manager interviews, newsletters and so on does the operator offer?

Fund supermarkets are rapidly capturing a large slice of the investment market. Do not underestimate the convenience factor. With some supermarkets you can access an online valuation of your holdings. But at a minimum you will receive at least a half-yearly consolidated statement showing all your investments – a big improvement over getting half-a-dozen valuations on different dates from different fund managers.

Switching from one fund to another within a supermarket is virtually instant, whereas it can take weeks if you are dealing direct with two different fund management companies.

Investment trusts

These are the oldest form of collective investment, dating back to 1868. They are simply companies whose shares are listed on the London Stock Exchange. They hold a portfolio of shares in other companies, so their assets consist entirely of investments. The value of the investments divided by the number of shares in issue gives the net asset value per share (Nav). However, the share price in the marketplace may diverge substantially from the net asset value. When a share price is below the Nav, it is said to be at a discount, and if it is above Nav, it is at a premium.

The most important factor giving rise to discounts or premiums is supply and demand, which itself has several contributory causes. Investment trusts are 'closed-end' funds: they do not create and redeem shares on demand. They issue a fixed number of shares that are then traded on the stock market between investors. Depending on the type of investments a trust holds, investors may be more or less enthusiastic about their prospects. The more enthusiastic they are, the higher in relation to Nav the share price will be.

Investment trusts are permitted to borrow money to add to their investments. The Nav of a highly geared trust will rise and fall more in relation to the prices of the underlying investments it holds than the Nav of a trust with no borrowings. So when the price of its investments is rising, the shares of a highly geared trust are likely to trade at or above Nav, while when its investment are falling, they are likely to fall to a large discount to Nav.

Investment trust managers prefer not to have their shares trading at large discounts and use several techniques to avoid this. One is to provide subsidised low-cost savings plans to bring in new investors. Another is to buy back some of their shares from investors.

Investment trusts are taxed on the same basis as unit trusts and Oeics. To qualify for these concessions, they pay out almost all their income as dividends and meet certain investment criteria. Some managers run investment companies which are very similar to investment trusts but do not meet these requirements. To avoid adverse taxation of capital gains, they are usually registered in an offshore tax haven, though they are listed on the London Stock Exchange.

Investment trusts are allowed to invest in companies whose shares are not listed on any stock market. Some trusts specialise in venture capital and place most of their money in such investments, which are naturally far riskier than companies that have attained a stock market listing. The majority of investment trusts hold only a small portion of their assets in unlisted companies.

The more recent split-capital investment trusts have a more complex structure and the different categories of share offered may incorporate much higher risks, as has emerged in a scandal surrounding the creation of highly geared split-capital funds by a group of managers each of which supported the launch of new funds by other managers in a so-called 'magic circle'.

Confusingly, some classes of share in some split-capital trusts are very low risk and secure investments while other classes in newer split-capital trusts are very risky indeed. This is a sector where you need to tread with extreme care.

Find out more from the Association of Investment Trust Companies (www.aitc.co.uk).

Selecting funds

Most collective investment funds, besides stating that they will invest in a particular geographical area or type of share, have an objective which is not written into the prospectus. It is to produce investment returns that put it among the top 25% of all funds of a similar type. Only funds that achieve this with some consistency will attract the support of investment advisers, and investment advisers account for over three-quarters of all the new subscriptions to collective investment funds.

Only a small minority of collective investment funds succeed in achieving this kind of 'top quartile' performance consistently year after year. The majority produce performance that is more erratic: a year of better-than-average results is followed by a worse-than-average one and so on. Academic studies have fairly convincingly shown that past performance on its own is not at all a reliable indicator of future performance.

How then do you choose a good collective? The consensus among investment advisers is to undertake detailed research into the investment process, to try to understand how and why investment managers make their decisions. The theory is that successful managers will have common characteristics.

Unfortunately, reality does not support this theory any more than it did the previous one that past performance proved superior talent. The few collective investments that have demonstrated consistent long-term success have been run by individuals with widely different methods: by 'mavericks'.

This is not a pejorative term: Warren Buffett, the world's most successful investor, is a maverick. He does not conform to the norms almost all other investment managers accept. Nor do the long-term successes among UK collective fund managers. Each is a one-off, so it is hard to identify them by conventional yardsticks.

The absence of a convincing theory about how you pick winners among collective funds has fuelled a trend towards index tracking. But just because you cannot be sure a fund is going to produce the best performance does not mean you should only buy index-tracking funds.

For a start, in the UK, European and Japanese markets, there is a cycle during which shares in small and large companies respectively produce higher returns. In the UK the cycle used to last about four years and though, like most cycles, this is less dependable than it used to be, the mid-1990s saw UK small companies performing very poorly indeed compared with larger ones, a trend that appeared to reverse during 1999. Index-tracking funds miss out on the high returns produced by smaller companies during such upturns.

They also produce relatively little income. This is because many of the largest companies in terms of their market value pay low dividends. So if you need an income from your investments, you will have to look at actively managed funds, where the managers seek out shares that pay high dividends. The Investment Management Association classifies these funds as UK equity income.

Finally, stock market indices work well for the American and UK markets but far less well for Japan and Europe. In Japan, there have been many periods in which the majority of UK unit trusts have produced higher returns than the most representative Japanese stock market index. In these areas, index-tracking funds have less to offer.

When it comes to collective fund management, quantification – of performance or processes – is part of the problem, not the solution. Investment advisers produce ever more sophisticated ways of permuting, combining and interpreting the historic performance numbers, but you should not be overly impressed.

Investment is an art, not a science and it is better to think of the talented fund manager as an artist rather than as a scientist. Just as one artist prefers landscapes and another portraits, managers thrive best in particular market conditions. Well-informed professional advisers who stay in close touch with the leading fund managers often have a 'feel' for this and know which managers are 'on song' at any time. You may also get a sense of this from the reports and interviews with fund managers in newspapers and magazines.

You may hanker after hard evidence, but hard-nosed analysis has shown most of this is useless. The fact that a more touchy-feely approach to selection conflicts with our ideas about money actually says more about our ideas than anything else.

Managing investments is a process that involves both reasoning and emotion, and all the evidence is that it is the emotional aspect, in terms of the fund manager's character, that is the more important. If you ask why this should be so, here is a clue. How would you feel if the price of an investment you had just bought suddenly fell by 30%? Do you buy more, sell or just hold on? Turbulent emotions make it more difficult to reach the right decision.

Perhaps we should eliminate feeling and let the computer choose? So far, the results of doing so have been disastrous: judgment is not a purely rational faculty and computers do not have it. There is no alternative to accepting that investment is a tough game and that its winners will display emotional strength rational analysis will find hard to identify.

For performance information on unit trusts, Oeics and investment trusts, see Morningstar (www.morningstar.co.uk), Standard & Poor's (www.funds-sp.com/registration_features.cfm) and Trustnet (www.trustnet.com).

Stock market swings

Economic growth, interest rates, politics, oil, elections, war… there is no end to the factors that affect the world's stock markets. So it is not surprising that over different periods their performance varies. However, the online databases that allow you to look at fund performance are limited by the fact that the data is up to today's date. What would it have looked like up to a different end date? The table over the page gives you figures for several different sectors.

If nothing else, these should show that today's doghouse investment can be tomorrow's superstar and that today's superstar can easily be in the doghouse tomorrow. Buying last year's best performers has rarely been a successful investment strategy, but fund managers continue to promote most actively funds that have shown the greatest recent success.

How investment returns from collective funds vary year by year

Total return from an initial investment of £1,000

	Return in calendar year				Five-year return to end of	
	1996 £	1998 £	2000 £	2003 £	1996 £	2003 £
Unit trusts						
UK income & growth	1,073	1,063	970	1,162	1,775	1,087
UK smaller companies	1,108	903	957	1,312	1,867	1,509
Europe	1,080	1,225	974	1,216	1,974	928
Japan	828	1,032	672	1,191	1,099	1,424
North America	1,073	1,126	967	1,078	2,282	835
Emerging markets	951	737	780	1,331	1,639	1,416
UK fixed-interest	1,034	1,098	985	1,078	1,466	1,195
Building society account	1,036	1,046	1,038	1,020	1,261	1,157
UK Retail Price Index	1,027	1,028	1,029	1,024	1,134	1,111

Unit trusts: average performance of the sector. In 1999, UK income & growth was replaced by UK equity income. The UK fixed-interest sector has also been redefined. Offer to bid prices with net income reinvested.

The figure for the Retail Price Index shows how much you would have needed at the end of the period to buy what £1,000 would have bought at the start.

Life insurance funds

Life insurance companies run many funds and offer lump sum investments linked to them. Unlike unit trusts, Oeics or investment trusts, when you buy an investment from a life insurance company you do not become legally entitled to any of the assets. You buy a policy whose claim value against the company may be defined in terms of units or in other ways.

Unlike these other investments, too, life insurance companies pay tax on their income and their capital gains. Individual policyholders do not pay capital gains tax on any gains, nor do they pay basic rate income tax on any gains or income. But higher rate taxpayers may become liable to tax on their profits or withdrawals from the policy at a rate equal to the difference between the basic rate and the higher rate of income tax.

The funds offered by life insurers fall into four categories: with-profits, unit-linked, guaranteed and high income.

◆ **With-profits** Lump sum investments in a with-profits fund earn bonuses. Usually one rate of bonus is paid annually and an extra 'terminal' bonus may be paid on encashment or death. Added together these bonuses usually give a rate of return somewhat greater than the best rates available on deposits.

◆ **Unit-linked** Like unit trusts, life insurance funds invest in shares or fixed-interest securities in the UK or overseas. Insurers also offer managed funds which divide their investments between shares, fixed-rate investments and property, as well as property funds which invest in commercial, industrial and retail property.

◆ **Guaranteed income and growth** Some insurers offer fixed returns with capital guarantees over periods from two to ten years. The rates are usually somewhat better than the net rates available from deposits.

◆ **High income** See structured capital at risk products (Scarps) below.

In general, the average performance of unit-linked insurance funds has been significantly worse than that of the comparable unit trust average over most periods, a difference that is only partly explained by life funds' less advantageous tax position. For most investors, unit trusts or Oeics are a better way to invest in shares, fixed-interest or property than life assurance funds.

With-profits bonds

From the late 1980s onwards, life insurers offered lump sum investments in their with-profits funds, which split investment between shares, property and fixed-interest investments. Up to 2001 these offered returns averaging up to 9% a year. The returns were good because most insurers held a high proportion of their funds in shares, which performed extremely well, and distributed a high proportion of these gains as bonuses.

The 2000-3 bear market coincided with a more rigorous approach to life insurance regulation (see Section One). The result was that insurers had to reduce the proportion of the fund invested in shares and cut the bonuses paid. Many insurers also applied a 'market value adjustment' to their funds, reducing the cash-in value by up to 20%.

The consequence is that there are now hundreds of thousands of investors who hold with-profits bonds where minimal or no bonuses are being paid and where high market value adjustments are being applied. These conditions seem likely to persist for the following reasons:

◆ A lower proportion of the fund is now held in shares which means future gains and hence bonuses will be lower.

◆ Companies need to rebuild the 'free capital' they hold to support tougher regulatory requirements, again reducing the likely level of future bonuses for several years.

In addition, many insurers have launched or are in the process of launching new with-profits funds conforming to the new standards proposed in the Sandler Report (see page 20). This means they will not be promoting their old with-profit funds to new investors and have little incentive to remain competitive in terms of bonus payments. The result is a class of 'with-profit prisoners' in the form of investors in old funds with heavy exit penalties. If you are in this category, you should certainly obtain independent advice on your situation.

Since the conditions that have given rise to this position were almost entirely unforeseeable, it is unlikely many people will be able to claim compensation. If an adviser recommended a with-profits bond on the basis of it being a lower-risk investment suitable for your circumstances prior to 2001, this was probably a fair assessment at the time. So you will need to consider whether to accept the penalty and cash in to seek a better investment elsewhere.

Alternatives to with-profits

The financial services industry is adept at inventing new products and the reduction in attractiveness of with-profits bonds has left a big gap in the market. New forms of open-ended funds are being created, some of which may fulfil investors' desires for an investment that provides higher returns than cash deposits but with less volatility than an investment in shares. An important requirement for many investors is also a higher income than can be obtained from an equity investment.

Distribution funds

Typically these hold 40% to 60% of their assets in fixed-rate investments and the balance in shares, usually higher yielding shares. This combination means they can offer an initial yield significantly higher than pure equity funds. Also, their prices should be less volatile than those of pure equity funds, though a sudden slump in price is still possible.

Lifestyle funds

Here the manager asks you to decide your term of investment and commit to this at the outset. If you choose, say, a 15-year term, at the start almost all the fund will be invested in shares, but by year 12 more than half will have been switched to fixed-rate investments and by year 15 it will all be in cash. Funds like these with pre-determined asset allocations linked to time will certainly reduce the level of risk, but until they have been running for many years, we will not know how they compare with pure equity funds.

Structured capital at risk products

Scarps is the regulator's term for funds that create guarantees over the level of capital or income using financial derivatives. One set of these – 'precipice bonds' – has proved disastrous for investors. Many investors with precipice bonds issued before the 2000-3 bear market lost more than 50% of their capital. You should never confuse a small probability of an event occurring with a low risk. New and tougher Financial Services Authority rules on promotions mean the promises in future will be less exuberant.

Scarps generally do one of two things: guarantee that you cannot lose any money over a five-year term but will get some proportion of the gain made by the FTSE 100 index, or guarantee you a set rate of income each year, but promise to return all your original capital only if a certain index has remained above a critical level. These can be highly complex products requiring careful thought. But the major point to note is that with most of them, while you may get a gain of 100% of the FTSE 100 index, this will only be the capital change in the index.

Over a five-year period, if you owned all the shares in the FTSE 100 (or a tracker fund), you would get dividends equalling a return of more than 15% on your money. Effectively, with most structured products, you give up this 15% to secure the guarantee – and history shows that this is usually a poor bargain.

Another point to watch for is 'averaging', where the opening or closing level of the index is taken as an average over a period of up to six months or even longer. While this can reduce the chance of loss, it also reduces potential gains, and since in the long term the trend of the stock market is upwards, averaging will usually cost you more in lost gains than it delivers in protection from loss.

Successful fund manager Peter Lynch said one of his guidelines was: 'Never invest in anything you can't illustrate with a crayon.' Most Scarps fail this test.

Limited risk funds

Here the fund manager uses 'dynamic asset allocation' or financial derivatives or both to underwrite a guarantee that you will never suffer a loss of more than, say, 20% of your initial investment. Dynamic asset allocation means adjusting the proportion of the fund in shares, fixed-interest and cash in response to changing financial conditions. Since this involves reducing investment in shares when share prices are falling, they will necessarily give up a significant part of the gains on any recovery after a period of falling prices. Again, it is likely to be many years before it will be possible to judge the success of these funds.

Your choice

What all these funds do is take all or part of the asset allocation decision out of your hands, and if you lack the confidence to set your own investment policy such investments may have their uses. But if you are prepared to think through your own appropriate asset allocation, you will be able to implement it for yourself at far lower cost. Not only do the specialised funds described above have annual expense ratios of 1.5% to 2% (which means the first 1.5% to 2% of returns earned go to them and not to you), but the techniques they use to reduce volatility also have a cost, which in the case of funds using derivatives is likely to be at least another 1% to 2% a year.

Using the Isa

The individual savings account is a tax-exempt 'wrapper' that can be put around unit trusts, Oeics and investment trusts as well as shares. It comes in two forms, mini and maxi. A mini-Isa permits you to invest up to £1,000 each year (£3,000 in 2004-5) in shares, unit trusts, Oeics or investment trusts. A maxi-Isa raises the maximum to £5,000 each year (£7,000 in 2004-5).

Most unit trust, Oeic and investment trust managers offer Isas that can be wrapped around their own funds. With unit trusts and Oeics, there is usually no extra charge for this: you simply pay the same charges as you would in the relevant unit trust or Oeic. With investment trusts, there is often an additional cost. Within an Isa offered by a manager of unit trusts or Oeics, you may invest in one or more funds and switch between them without losing the tax-exempt status. Almost all unit trusts and Oeics qualify for inclusion in Isas.

Both income and gains within an Isa are tax-free. As far as share dividends are concerned, the basic rate taxpayer receives the same net income within an Isa as if the shares are held directly, while a higher rate taxpayer holding shares in an Isa avoids the extra income tax on dividends.

The fact that Isas are exempt from capital gains tax may not be of much benefit to you today if you have only small sums to invest, because you are unlikely to exceed the annual threshold below which you pay no capital gains tax. But if you put £5,000 into an Isa each year, by the end of ten years you are likely to have an investment that could generate taxable gains, so the scheme may still save you tax eventually.

If you invest in an Isa run by one fund manager then want to switch your money to a fund run by a different one, you will have to switch your Isa. Though you are allowed to do this, there may be extra costs. The alternative is to set up a self-select Isa. You can do this with a fund supermarket (see pages 93-94) or a stockbroker and can alter your funds whenever you want and may also secure discounts on purchases.

Given the tax breaks, it is clearly worth using the Isa for your first £5,000 of savings and/or investments each year. Each year you can, if you want, set up an Isa with a different manager. But after a while you will have a mass of paper to deal with, which is why having one self-select plan is a better method.

Investing for growth or income

Most advisers quickly categorise people into 'investing for growth' or 'investing for income'. But what you are in fact investing for is always the same: a set of future flows of cash. The more precise you can be about what cash you need when, the better you can design your investments to maximise return and minimise risk.

Advisers who do not have sufficient training or experience in investment will often fail to ask you in enough detail about this. If you are vague – and given the uncertainties of the future this is understandable – try to be less so. Think about all the events that would require you to cash in investments, and what events among your family would lead you to want to change them. If it is likely you will want to help your daughter by contributing towards her first home purchase in about five years, for example, match this by placing more money into fixed-interest investments rather than shares.

One mistake many retired investors make is to become too concerned with capital values rather than income. Throughout the 2000-3 bear market, in which share prices fell by 40%, dividends continued to grow – admittedly only by 1% a year, as compared with the 5% or more by which they tend to grow in 'normal' times. But the point is that if you invested in shares for income, it did not decline precipitately in the 2000-3 bear market, nor did it do so in previous bear markets. It would require a 1930s-style depression, in which GDP shrinks for several years, for a significant decline in UK dividend payments to be likely. If your principal aim is a steadily rising income, the right attitude to UK shares is to buy and hold.

Some advisers recommend retired investors progressively switch their investments from shares into fixed-interest. But someone aged 65 is likely to live to 80, and on a 15-year timescale it does not make a great deal of sense to switch into fixed-interest purely to avoid fluctuations in capital which – so long as your main requirement is income – need not actually affect you. A more realistic strategy – though requiring attention and care to manage – is to maintain a high percentage of your capital in equities but to sell some and take profits whenever share prices reach what seem to be high levels.

Precipice bonds offered apparently higher rates of income. So does buying property to let. But what about the security of the income? That is where the risk lies. 'The higher the income, the higher the risk' is as true today as it was 100 years ago.

For income investors, the right strategy over the past 50 years has been to settle for the lowest income you could get by on – because by investing more in shares you got both a rising income (which other investments did not provide) and capital growth.

Investing for children

Banks and building societies offer a variety of accounts for children's savings, but if you are investing for children, the stock market is the natural choice.

From 2005, each child born after September 2002 will have £250 invested in the Child Trust Fund (CTF) by the government (£500 if household income is below a certain level). A further sum will be placed in the account by the Treasury when the child is aged seven. All the funds must remain there until the child is aged 18, at which point they will be paid direct to them. The CTF will be tax-free. The maximum level of charges will be 1.5% a year.

Parents and others will be allowed to contribute a further £1,200 a year to each child's CTF. Each child can have only one so the choice is important. The 'default' fund which all providers must offer will combine shares and fixed-interest and will progressively switch to fixed-interest and cash as the 18th birthday approaches. Some CTF providers will offer other options including pure equity funds.

For well-off parents, grandparents or others, another way to give a child a head start in life is to set up a stakeholder pension. There is no minimum age for stakeholder pension schemes, and up to £2,808 may be contributed each year, which will be topped up by the tax relief to £3,600. When the child 'comes of age' he or she can start adding his or her own contributions to the plan. For more on stakeholders, see Section Five.

The advent of tuition fees has meant that many students graduate with debts of more than £15,000 – and for medical students, for instance, the figure can be far higher. Many parents will want to assist their children through college years and particularly if more than one child is involved, some advance provision through savings will be required – see Section One.

The savings calculator at www.e-gismos.com/savings.asp may be helpful.

Investing for retirement

One of the main aims many people have for their capital is to make it grow so it can be used to top up their pension income in retirement. The key issues here are how much capital you need and how much risk you are prepared to take to get it.

For the free capital you accumulate outside your pension schemes, you can, as a basic rate taxpayer, take a 4% net annual return as a reasonable benchmark. On that basis, and assuming you want the capital to remain intact, you need £25,000 to generate annual income of £1,000. When you draw income from a pension scheme, all the capital is converted into a lifetime income. Assuming you convert some of the capital into income each year, around £16,000 would be needed to provide a net income of £1,000. For more on saving through pension schemes see Section Five.

For many people, the amount of capital required to provide a comfortable standard of living in retirement will represent a challenging target. You will probably need to do two things to improve your chances of achieving this:

◆ Add to your regular savings as much and as often as you can, using equity funds (see Section One).

◆ Hold as high a proportion of your capital as you feel comfortable with in shares or share collective investment funds.

Investment advice

The biggest problem with investment is finding good advisers and avoiding bad advice. Advisers' qualifications are improving, and regulators are getting tougher on companies that give poor advice, but your best protection against poor advice is simply to be better informed (see Section Seven).

There are honourable exceptions, but generally you will do well to avoid advisers employed by big high street banks. With investment advice it is all down to the quality of the firm and individual giving you the service, and continuity of advice from a qualified, experienced adviser is likely to serve you best.

Trouble-shooting guide

Most investments in the UK are regulated by the Financial Services Authority, which has extensive powers to punish wrongdoers. Its Financial Ombudsman Scheme also provides a relatively speedy (compared with the courts) means of resolving complaints.

If you are dissatisfied with advice you have been given, your first step is to complain to the firm in question, which should follow a complaints procedure set out by the FSA. If you are dissatisfied with its response, you can take your case to the Financial Ombudsman Service (see page 213).

However, the following areas are not regulated in the UK:

◆ Direct property investment whether in the UK or abroad;

◆ Tangibles such as wine, whisky, art, antiques and gemstones;

◆ Overseas investments that are not covered by local regulations and compensation schemes.

In these areas, *caveat emptor* applies with special force. There have been numerous frauds and scams.

A growing area of concern is 'boiler room' operations. These are 'stockbrokers' operating from outside the UK and using telephone sales to persuade UK investors to buy shares in what seem to be real businesses but are often no more than cleverly constructed facades including company websites, press announcements and financial statements, all of which give the impression of a substantial and promising business.

Ask yourself why the promoters would need to seek investors as far afield as the UK if their propositions were so good, and why they are doing so in a way that is illegal.

Some of these brokers may have authorisation in another EU country, and if so, under EU rules they may legally promote in the UK. But any reputable and sizeable firm wanting to do business in the UK will set up an operation here. The Financial Services Authority website (www.fsa.gov.uk/consumer) lists known operators of boiler room and other scams.

4

Insurance

In this section we will look at

Life insurance

Critical illness cover

Income replacement insurance

Accident, sickness and unemployment cover

Private medical insurance

Buildings and contents cover

Insuring cars and other vehicles

Protection for pets, holidays and special events

4

Insurance

Everyone needs insurance. If you have a car or a house, you'll certainly need to protect them against damage, theft and other causes of financial loss. And it is the same with other possessions – there are policies that provide financial protection for virtually everything you own, from your furniture to your pets and from your coin collection to your caravan.

And what about you and your family? If you have any dependants, you need to insure your life. There are also persuasive arguments for private medical cover and insurance that provides an income if illness or injury forces you off work for an extended period, or provides a lump sum that can be used to clear debts and fund any necessary lifestyle changes.

It doesn't end there. Travel insurance is essential for those heading abroad. Those organising events need insurance in case unforeseen problems cause cancellation and to cover their legal liabilities. In short, there are few things on earth that do not have an associated insurance plan of one kind or another.

Whatever you're buying, however, it is essential to get the right combination of cover and cost. There is no reason to celebrate a low premium if you aren't getting adequate protection. And there's certainly no point paying good money for a policy that is inappropriate or inadequate.

This section looks at the full range of policies. Here you will find information covering:

◆ **Protecting yourself, your family and your financial well-being** Life insurance, medical plans and so on.

◆ **Protecting your possessions** Household and motor insurance, policies for bikes, caravans etc.

◆ **Special occasion insurance** Travel insurance, weddings, fetes and the like. Remember: the only thing that's less fun than insurance is not having a policy when you need to make a claim. So bite the bullet, decide what cover you need and get the best policy at the best price.

That's Life...

Even if you've only ever had the most fleeting of dealings with the world of insurance, you'll know one thing for sure: it's wrapped up in mumbo-jumbo that seems designed to put you, the customer, at a disadvantage. Insurance companies have developed their own language. They talk of indemnities and deductibles, exclusions and moratoriums. They sprinkle their communications with bewildering calculations and offer options and alternatives that simply add to the confusion. No wonder nobody likes them.

To their credit, some insurers are wrestling with this problem. They are trying to jettison the jargon and streamline their offerings. They still have a long way to go, but at least they've acknowledged the problem. Take life insurance. Shouldn't we stop being so squeamish and call it death insurance instead? After all, that is why you buy it – to pay a lump sum or an income to your dependants if you die.

And why do we sometimes read the word 'insurance' and other times 'assurance'? What's the difference? Strictly speaking, insurance is a policy which will pay out if a certain event occurs, while assurance pays out when something that is definitely going to happen actually happens. So, you insure your car against accident or theft, and you insure your life against the risk of death within a certain period – known as the term of the policy. But you can also assure your life, so that the policy will pay out when you eventually shuffle off this mortal coil, whenever that time comes.

As we work our way through the myriad policies on offer, we'll translate any industry-speak and explain the workings of the contracts so you know what you are buying and where you stand.

Term insurance

If you thought you'd left the word term behind at school, think again. In this case it refers to the length of time the policy operates – or, as the insurers say, is in force. If you die during the term, the policy pays out what is known as the sum insured. If you survive, the policy comes to an end and that's that. You don't get any money back.

A lot of term insurance is sold to match a specific debt, usually a mortgage. Thus, if you die, the debt will be cleared and will not be a burden to those you leave behind. Some lenders even insist such cover is in place or at least recommend you take out a policy.

If you have no dependants, you do not really need life insurance, even if you have a large mortgage. If you died, the lender could simply repossess your property. If you do have family, however, it makes sense to have life cover over and above what is needed to pay off debts. You need to provide funds for everyday expenses and general living costs stretching into the future.

This is true even if you are not the main breadwinner or even if you don't bring any money into the house. If you were to die, your partner would need funds to pay for such things as housekeeping and childcare while he or she carried on working.

Grim, this, isn't it? But these uncomfortable facts are better dealt with than brushed under the carpet. Too many bereaved people have to cope with money worries on top of their grief.

Types of term

◆ **Level term** You pay a fixed premium for the duration of the policy and a fixed lump sum is paid out if you die within the term.
◆ **Decreasing term** The premium stays the same throughout, but the amount of cover falls over the term of the policy in line with a decreasing debt, such as with a repayment mortgage. This reduces the total cost.
◆ **Family income benefit** Instead of paying out a lump sum, these policies pay an income for a specified length of time.
◆ **Single and joint policies** It is possible for one person to take out a policy for themselves, or for a couple to take out a joint policy – ideal if they are using the insurance to cover their mortgage.

How much cover?

First, get enough cover to clear your mortgage and other debts (credit and store cards, personal and car loans and so on). Next, work out how much money your dependants would need each year and how much would have to be invested to generate that amount. Say you want to provide an income of £15,000. At today's rates, that would mean investing around £300,000 – enough to generate adequate funds for day-to-day living and to create a base for the family's future financial well-being.

What determines the cost of cover?

Insurers calculate their prices according to your:
◆ **Age** You pay more as you get older.
◆ **Gender** Men pay more than women.
◆ **Term** The longer the policy lasts, the more it costs.
◆ **Sum insured** The bigger it is, the bigger the premium.
◆ **Smoking** Smokers pay up to half as much again.
◆ **Health** Ill-health bumps up the premiums.
When you take out insurance, you are asked if you have any major medical complaints or if you have a family history of heart disease or other instances of early death. If the answer is yes, the premium will increase. In some cases the insurer will ask your doctor for a medical report or you may be asked to attend a private clinic for a check-up. This is particularly likely if you are seeking a sum insured of £250,000 or more.

Cover through your pension

Those in personal or company pension schemes can get tax relief on term insurance premiums at their highest marginal rate, which means a basic rate taxpayer saves 22% of the cost, a higher rate taxpayer 40%. You can only spend up to 10% of your pension contributions on term cover though, and you can't buy insurance through a stakeholder pension. Ask your company or pension provider for details.

The good news about premiums

The price of term insurance has fallen in recent years because, in general, we're living longer. More of us survive serious illnesses and road accidents, and the fear that Aids would kill tens of thousands of people has proved unfounded. These factors have allowed insurers to trim their premiums. Competition from new entrants to the market, such as Virgin, Direct Line and Marks & Spencer, has also helped.

In the mid-1990s, a 30-year-old man could expect to pay around £37 a month for a £300,000 sum insured over 15 years. Today someone of that age would pay around £16 – less than half.

Policies in trust

Make sure any policy you buy is written in trust. If it is, the proceeds of a claim will go straight to the beneficiary of your choice. If it isn't, the money will be added to your estate, which will delay payment and potentially create inheritance tax problems, as you pay 40% tax on everything in your estate over £263,000. The company selling you your policy should automatically arrange for it to be written in trust. If in doubt, ask.

Where to buy

As with most kinds of insurance, you can buy direct from the company or from an independent financial adviser (IFA). With term cover, there are no variable factors such as investment performance to worry about, so all that should concern you is the price. This is one of the few instances where the lowest premium is invariably the one to choose.

IFA Promotion (0800 085 3250, www.unbiased.co.uk) will give you details of IFAs in your area. You can buy over the telephone from the likes of Direct Line (0845 3000 233), Marks & Spencer (0800 363422) and Virgin (0845 6102 040) or shop around over the internet. Good starting places include www.find.co.uk, www.moneyextra.com and www.financial-discounts.co.uk. Internet sites will let you obtain comparative quotes and buy online.

The cost of decreasing term insurance

Competitive monthly premiums for a 25-year policy with an initial sum insured of £100,000

Male, non-smokers

Age 35	Scottish Widows	£7.60
	Tesco	£7.98
	Legal & General	£8.02
Age 40	Tesco	£10.52
	Scottish Widows	£10.73
	Legal & General	£10.79
Age 45	Legal & General	£26.17
	Liverpool Victoria	£27.50
	Scottish Widows	£27.98

Male, smokers

Age 35	Tesco	£12.43
	Norwich Union	£12.78
	Legal & General	£13.27
Age 40	Tesco	£18.78
	Norwich Union	£19.18
	Legal & General	£20.34
Age 45	Legal & General	£57.49
	Friends Provident	£60.44
	Liverpool Victoria	£66.30

Female, non-smokers

Age 35	Tesco	£6.99
	Lutine Assurance	£7.25
	Scottish Widows	£7.30
Age 40	Lutine Assurance	£8.97
	Tesco	£9.16
	Legal & General	£9.26
Age 45	Legal & General	£19.48
	Liverpool Victoria	£20.50
	Friends Provident	£21.46

Female, smokers

Age 35	Tesco	£10.61
	Friends Provident	£10.76
	Norwich Union	£10.93
Age 40	Tesco	£15.70
	Norwich Union	£16.08
	Friends Provident	£16.19
Age 45	Legal & General	£42.69
	Friends Provident	£44.98
	Scottish Equitable	£45.64

Joint (male age shown; female three years younger), non-smokers

Age 35	Tesco	£9.97
	Norwich Union	£10.28
	Lutine Assurance	£10.56
Age 40	Tesco	£13.89
	Norwich Union	£14.17
	Legal & General	£15.26
Age 45	Legal & General	£38.26
	Liverpool Victoria	£40.10
	Friends Provident	£41.33

Joint (male age shown, female three years younger), smokers

Age 35	Tesco	£16.50
	Norwich Union	£16.86
	Legal & General	£18.69
Age 40	Tesco	£26.40
	Norwich Union	£26.86
	Legal & General	£28.93
Age 45	Legal & General	£83.73
	Friends Provident	£90.25
	Scottish Provident	£99.82

Source: Term Direct

Other types of life insurance

The best way to provide funds for your dependants in the event of your death is through term cover. But there are other forms of life insurance with heavy investment links.

Endowments

These are policies with a core of life insurance but their main aim is to provide a lump sum on maturity, often to clear a mortgage debt. As you may have read in the press, many endowments have failed to meet expectations, leaving policyholders with substantial shortfalls on their mortgage obligations. If you have an endowment and are concerned about how it is performing, you should check with your financial adviser or with the Financial Services Authority. See pages 58-61 for further information and guidance.

Whole-of-life policies

As the name suggests, these last for your life and pay out when you die. Remember: a term policy is only in force for a specified period and if you live to the end of it, you get no return. The whole-of-life approach is investment oriented and intended for those seeking to build a legacy rather than to provide cash in a crisis. And as the policy is guaranteed to pay out, the premiums are higher.

A section of the whole-of-life market is devoted to those aged over 50 or 60. Here policies guarantee to pay a certain amount in return for a given premium, which is either paid for life or for, say, 20 years. These policies, which can be arranged as individual or joint contracts, are often used to provide money for funerals or tax planning purposes.

A word of warning: some insurers sell policies known as flexible whole-of-life investment plans, where the premiums are set at a certain rate for ten years on the assumption that the underlying investment will grow at a certain rate. But making assumptions about investment growth is a dangerous pursuit. If the investments do not match the expectation, premiums can double or the sum insured can be halved. And this can happen again at subsequent 'review' anniversaries. If you need a whole-of-life plan, make sure the premiums and the sum insured are fixed and guaranteed. Flexibility will not always work in your favour.

Funeral plans

If you thought contemplating the need for life insurance was bad enough, how about working out the cost of your funeral and taking out a policy accordingly? Many elderly people are anxious not to leave their heirs with a financial burden so make arrangements to cover the cost of their send-off. With even a relatively modest funeral costing around £1,500, this can be valuable foresight.

The plans on offer either accept a lump sum payment or a regular premium and guarantee to pay the cost of the sort of funeral service and arrangements you stipulate. Make sure:

◆ The policy promises to pay all the costs;
◆ Cover remains valid if you move to another area;
◆ You have the flexibility to alter your requirements if you choose.

You need to know whether the policy commits you to a certain firm of undertakers. Ensure also that your family, solicitor and executors are fully aware of any arrangements you make.

Critical illness cover

◆ Over 250,000 people a year in the UK develop cancer. A third of all people contract cancer at some point, but more than a third of men and nearly half of women who get cancer live at least five years.
◆ Over 120,000 people a year in the UK suffer a stroke, but more than 80,000 of them survive for a year or more.
◆ There are more than 100,000 people alive in the UK who have suffered from kidney failure.
◆ Over 5,000 people a year in the UK require major organ transplants.
◆ A quarter of men and a fifth of women suffer a serious illness before they reach 65.

As the facts and figures suggest, serious illness is commonplace. But what is easy to forget is that many people recover and have to adjust to a new set of circumstances. Along with reduced physical capacity and vulnerability to further medical setbacks, one of the major factors they have to confront is financial difficulty. The illness may force them off work for a lengthy period, or even permanently, and any money they receive from their employer or from the state will rarely be sufficient to meet their needs.

This is where critical illness cover can play a part. Just as term insurance pays out if you die within the specified period, so critical illness insurance pays out if you are diagnosed with a serious illness. As with term cover, you select a sum insured based on what you think you would need if disaster struck. You choose whether you want the policy to last for a given term or for life (the former option is cheaper).

Again, the cost will be determined by your age, sex, occupation, health and whether or not you smoke. A basic policy providing £100,000 of cover over 30 years for a 35-year-old man would cost around £40 a month. A woman would pay slightly more because, statistically, women are more likely to fall ill. If the policy was set up to run until death, the cost would be around £60 for the man and slightly more for the woman. This is because women generally live longer and so have more time in which to contract an illness. The cash payout is tax-free.

Policies cover the major illnesses such as heart attack, cancer and multiple sclerosis and total permanent disability. That said, insurers have different ways of defining this condition. Some require that you are unable to carry out your job or any other form of work, or they may apply a test linked to 'activities of daily living' such as washing yourself and moving around the house. If you cannot manage these by yourself, the policy will pay out.

Some conditions are excluded, such as Aids, addictions, depressive illness and self-inflicted injuries. Insurers also differ in their attitude to diseases such as Alzheimer's and Parkinson's. You may, for example, have to reach a given age before a claim will be paid.

In all cases, read the product literature before buying. You can also visit the website of the Association of British Insurers (www.abi.org.uk) for further information. Note that, with a critical illness policy, any claim brings the policy to an end. You cannot claim for more than one illness.

Variations on a theme

Critical illness can either be bought as a stand-alone policy or combined with another contract:

◆ **Critical illness and term**   The policy pays out either when you contract an illness or die, but not on both occasions.
◆ **Critical illness and whole of life**   The policy guarantees to pay out when you die, unless you contract the illness first.
◆ **Critical illness and endowment**   You can link this policy to your mortgage so the debt is paid off if you fall ill or die.

Income replacement insurance

◆ At this moment, around 7% of the working population is claiming state sickness benefits.
◆ More than two million people have been ill and off work for more than 26 weeks.
◆ Over one million have been claiming state invalidity support for more than 12 months. Of these, more than 600,000 have been sick or disabled for longer than three years.
◆ A quarter of men and a fifth of women will suffer a serious illness before reaching 65.
◆ You are 20 times more likely to have a breakdown in health lasting more than six months than you are to die before reaching 65.

While critical illness cover provides a lump sum in an emergency, income replacement insurance provides an income – and it keeps on doing so until you are fit to return to work or you reach retirement age.

With these policies, it is not a case of having one or the other. The chunk of cash provided by a critical illness policy may be swallowed by the cost of adapting the house to accommodate a wheelchair, buying a new car and paying for a convalescent holiday. Or, of course, it may be used to clear debts. It won't meet living expenses well into the foreseeable future.

Income replacement insurance does pretty much what it says on the tin. It delivers a tax-free income that boosts statutory sick pay and other benefits and prevents you from having to dip into your savings.

Note: remember how we mentioned the insurance industry's love of obscure phrases and odd words? Income replacement insurance used to be widely known as permanent health insurance. Understandably, many people confused it with straightforward health insurance, which pays medical fees, so the industry has largely adopted the new phraseology.

How it works

◆ It replaces income while you are off work through sickness or injury.
◆ You choose the level of income to be paid.
◆ The amount of income, when added to your benefit entitlements, will never exceed around two-thirds of your normal pay, so claimants are not better-off staying at home.

Cost is determined by:

◆ The chosen level of income;
◆ Age;
◆ Gender;
◆ Occupation;
◆ Health;
◆ Whether or not you are a smoker;
◆ The deferred period.

Deferred periods

Most periods of sickness last a relatively short time, and income replacement policies don't pay out as soon as you are off work, because the cost would be astronomical. Insurers ask you to choose a deferred period, which is the number of weeks before your policy kicks in. The longer the deferred period, the lower the premium because there is a greater chance you will recover before a payout is required. It is, then, a question of balancing the pain of paying the premium with the relief of claiming your cash. The choice of deferred periods is usually four, 13, 26 or 52 weeks.

Own job, any job?

As if this type of insurance were not complicated enough, insurers have different approaches to when a claim will be paid. This is the 'own job, any job' distinction. Make sure you find out which cover you are buying to avoid any nasty surprises.

◆ **Own job** This pays out when you are unable to follow your own occupation.

◆ **Any job** This pays out when you are unable to follow any occupation, regardless of what you did before.

The own job cover is better and is, therefore, more expensive. With this, you simply have to demonstrate that you cannot do your job. With any job cover, you will not be able to claim if you can switch from your current occupation to a different sort of work, which might oblige you to seek another form of employment. There have been instances where people in high-pressure management jobs have been forced to take work as, say, car park attendants.

This own job, any job distinction also applies to state benefits. After 28 weeks, Incapacity Benefit is only paid to those judged unfit to do any job. Decisions about entitlement are made by government inspectors.

To make a claim, you will need to be signed off by your doctor. Expect an occasional visit from one of the insurance company's representatives. There will be lots of smiling and well-wishing, but they are really checking you are not staying off work for longer than is justified.

Index linking

Policies offer a choice of level and index-linked payouts. The latter option bumps up the premium but means your payments keep track of rising prices.

Give us a waiver

Income replacement policies pay out as many times as is justified, so long as you keep paying the premiums. It is, therefore, worth paying the premiums even while you are making a claim. Obviously, funds will be tight in such a circumstance, but insurers have anticipated the situation with a waiver of premium option.

This is a form of insurance within insurance and means that, if you make a claim, the premiums will continue to be paid on your behalf. This sub-cover costs more but can be well worth the investment.

What about sick pay?

Before you buy, check what your employer offers in terms of sick pay. Your firm is obliged to pay statutory sick pay at a rate of £64.35 a week for 28 weeks unless you have paid insufficient National Insurance contributions, in which case you can claim state Incapacity Benefit. After 28 weeks, you move from statutory sick pay to state benefits – which are hardly generous, as the table opposite shows.

Some companies pay more than the statutory minimum, and for longer, especially for senior staff. You may even be able to select income replacement from a menu of employee benefits. Others may stick to the legal minimums. If you are self-employed, you will need to make your own arrangements.

What about state benefits?

There are three types of Incapacity Benefit:

◆ **Short-term lower rate benefit** This is paid if you don't qualify for sick pay.
◆ **Short-term higher rate benefit** This is paid if you have been sick for more than 28 weeks and fewer than 52.
◆ **Long-term benefit** This is paid if you have been sick for more than 52 weeks. Additional payments may be made if you have dependants. Leaflet GL23 from post offices has full details.

Incapacity benefits

Short-term lower rate (first 28 weeks)

Basic rate	£54.40
Adult dependency increase	£33.65*

Short-term higher rate (weeks 29-52)

Basic rate	£64.35
Adult dependency increase	£35.65*
Child dependency increase	£11.35*

Long-term rate (week 53 onwards)

Basic rate	£72.15
Adult dependency increase	£43.15*
Child dependency increase	£11.35*

Age addition to long-term rate

Incapacity before 35	£15.15
Incapacity between 35 and 44	£7.60

* Payment made only if there are dependent children or there is a dependant over age 60. Payments may be made via Child Tax Credit.

The cost of income replacement cover

Monthly premiums for a healthy 35-year-old, non-smoking accountant on an own job basis. Benefit: £1,250 a month (50% of salary) with policy terminating at the age of 60

Male premium

Deferred period	4 weeks	13 weeks	26 weeks	52 weeks
Level benefit	£43.64	£19.76	£15.29	£12.90
Index-linked benefit	£47.69	£23.90	£19.45	£17.73

Female premium

Deferred period	4 weeks	13 weeks	26 weeks	52 weeks
Level benefit	£74.12	£32.32	£24.51	£20.33
Index-linked benefit	£81.20	£39.58	£31.79	£28.78

Source: Swiss Life

Accident, sickness and unemployment cover

Accident, sickness and unemployment (ASU) cover also goes under the name mortgage payment protection insurance (MPPI), and it has come in for some stick of late. Its basic purpose is to pay your mortgage while you are unable to earn a living. But there have been instances where policyholders have had what seemed to be perfectly reasonable claims turned down, usually on the basis of the policy small print. Clearly, before buying you need to acquaint yourself as closely as possible with the minutia of the contract.

How it works when you don't

You buy a policy, either from your lender or direct from a firm such as Royal & SunAlliance or Norwich Union and pay a premium each month. To qualify for a policy, you must have been in continuous employment for a given length of time (six months or a year, depending on the insurer). You must also work a minimum number of hours each week (usually 16), must not know of any impending cause of unemployment and must be in good health.

Policies must be in force for a qualifying period before a claim will be paid. This varies from 30 days to six months. Some insurers only impose a qualifying period for claims related to unemployment, as opposed to sickness or disability. After claiming, benefits will not be paid until another waiting period has elapsed. This varies from 30 to 90 days. You can only secure potential benefits up to a certain amount, with a maximum of around 125% of your monthly mortgage payment.

If you become unemployed or unable to work through accident or sickness, the policy pays a designated amount, sufficient to cover your mortgage and associated costs, such as household insurance premiums. Payments are made for a limited period, usually 12 months or two years, or until you return to work. Most insurers will not offer unemployment cover to the self-employed.

The cost of ASU

There is no individual cost calculation with this type of insurance. If you meet the insurer's criteria, you pay a standard rate. Expect to pay about £5 a month for every £100 of potential monthly benefit.

What about state aid?

Previously, a person on Income Support would have half of their mortgage interest paid for the first 16 weeks of their claim. Thereafter, the full amount of interest was paid. But we live in more straightened circumstances today.

Those who have had a mortgage since before October 1995 and who make a claim for benefit receive no payment for two months and then get 50% of the interest for the following four months. Full interest payments are made after six months. Those who have taken out their mortgage since October 1995 and who subsequently become eligible for Income Support receive nothing towards the cost of their mortgage for the first nine months of the claim.

Any such state benefits are means-tested, which means those with savings and investments of more than £3,000 will receive a reduced benefit, while those with more than £8,000 or a spouse or partner who works more than 24 hours a week, or who has another source of income, will not qualify. It is estimated 80% of borrowers would not qualify for state benefit for one reason or another.

Note also that Income Support only pays the interest on the first £100,000 of a mortgage – a modest amount in today's housing market. And the contribution is only towards the interest. There is nothing to help repay the capital debt. ASU cover, therefore, has its attractions, and is a lower cost option than income replacement cover. But remember that many restrictions apply.

Private medical insurance

Interest in private medical insurance (PMI) has grown in recent years as the woes of the National Health Service have multiplied. Why wait in a queue if you can secure rapid, high quality treatment through an insurance contract?

It is beyond the scope of these pages to explore the political and moral arguments aroused by such a question. Suffice to say that around eight million people in the UK enjoy PMI, either through a company scheme or a private policy.

There is not much enjoyment to be had, however, from paying the premiums, which have increased sharply of late, sometimes by as much as 20% in a year. This is because medical equipment, procedures and the salaries and fees paid to the private medical profession are expensive and growing more so. Medical science is developing apace, but such progress must be paid for by those who use it. To help those of more modest resources access the PMI market, insurers have introduced budget policies, which exclude many conditions.

Cost factors

Your premium will be determined by your age, occupation, sex, whether or not you smoke and your medical history. Also relevant is the quality of hospital you choose. If you want luxury hotel-standard care, be prepared to pay for it. The more conditions and treatments excluded from the policy, the cheaper it will be. You can buy an individual policy or extend it to your family. If you choose a large excess – the amount you pay towards the cost of any claim – the premium will reduce. If you get cover through work, it counts as a taxable benefit.

What is covered?

◆ **Professional fees** These include bills for consultations and specialist physicians, anaesthetists and surgeons.
◆ **Hospital charges** These are for accommodation and nursing, either in a private hospital or in a private bed within an NHS hospital.
◆ **Specialist treatments** These include physiotherapy, chemotherapy and radiology.
◆ **Also covered** Drugs, tests, X-rays, dressings and treatments, out-patient treatments and home nursing should be included.
◆ **Cash benefit** This sum (say, £50) is paid for each night you are in hospital. Policies known as hospital cash plans provide this benefit alone for a cost of around £3 a week.

What is not covered?

Different policies offer different levels of cover, with some offering a lower premium in return for a longer list of exclusions. However, there are a number of exclusions which are common across all contracts, including:
◆ Fees payable to a GP;
◆ Treatments not recommended by a GP;
◆ Dental treatments (except those requiring an operation);
◆ Cosmetic surgery (except when made necessary by an accident);
◆ Routine tests and examinations (such as for sight and hearing);
◆ Vaccinations;
◆ Pregnancy and childbirth (although complications arising in pregnancy may be covered);

◆ Abortion;
◆ Infertility treatment;
◆ Self-inflicted injury;
◆ Alcohol and drug dependence;
◆ Aids;
◆ Injury sustained in war.

Remember, you need to disclose as fully as you can all details of your medical history. If you have what is termed a pre-existing condition when you buy cover, that condition will either be excluded from the scope of the policy or a moratorium will apply. This means you will not be able to claim for that condition for a specified period of, say, two years.

Dental health schemes

As with PMI, private dental arrangements have soared in popularity as state provision has declined, if not in quality, then certainly in quantity. Images of hundreds of people queuing to register at an NHS dentist are enough to set anyone to sucking a pensive tooth.

Dental health schemes enable you to have routine and emergency work carried out at no extra cost. Your monthly subscription is worked out in advance by your dentist to reflect your dental history and the state of your teeth. If you can't chew blancmange, expect a hefty bill. As part of the arrangement, you are required to visit the dentist on a regular basis. You may also have to undertake a course of treatment before you are allowed to join.

The cost varies between £10 and £25 a month, although your starting price may rise or fall if your teeth get worse or better. You will also have to pay a registration fee. For example, Denplan (0800 401402), the main company in this market, makes a charge equivalent to your monthly payment.

Such schemes pay for routine treatment, preventative care, accident and emergency treatment, oral cancer treatments and wisdom teeth extraction. They can also cover major restorative work such as crowns, bridges and dentures. But they do not pay for everything. For example, you may have to pay for the materials used in crowns, bridges and dentures. There may also be a bill if your dentist has to sub-contract work to a laboratory or refer you to a specialist. And purely cosmetic work will not be included.

If you belong to such a scheme, you should be able to reclaim the cost of emergency dental treatment you have anywhere in the world. If you go into hospital under the care of a consultant dental surgeon, you will receive a nightly cash benefit. Denplan pays £50 a night.

Remember, these plans are run by the dentist and it is through the dentist that you join. You will therefore need to find a dentist who organises such a scheme.

The NHS 'option'

Of the 31,000 dentists in the UK, almost half have either gone private or have stopped accepting new NHS patients – hence the clamouring hordes whenever a new NHS dentist opens his or her doors. Even if you find an NHS dentist willing to take you on, you will probably have to pay 80% of the cost of treatment, up to a maximum of £378.

Who gets free treatment?

◆ Children under 18;

◆ Those under 19 in full-time education;

◆ Women who are pregnant or who have a child under 18 months old;

◆ Anyone receiving Income Support or Job Seekers' Allowance;

◆ Families with a certificate for full help with the cost of NHS services.

Pensioners, the unemployed, students and others get free treatment only if they fall into one of these categories or have low income. Check with the dentist (ask for form AG1) or get form AB11 from your post office.

The cost of NHS treatment

Basic examination	£5.48
Extensive clinical examination	£8.20
Simple scale and polish	£8.64
Two small x-rays and one small filling (from)	£8.64
One large filling (from)	£9.60
A precious metal crown (from)	£15.08
An upper or lower metal denture (from)	£104.72
A full set of plastic dentures (from)	£118.88

An NHS dentist may also charge for a broken appointment if reasonable notice is not given.
Source: NHS

General insurance

Few cheques are as dispiriting to write as the ones to pay insurance premiums. Little wonder: you're paying good money – probably a lot of good money – for something you hope never to use. And if you do use it, it will only be because something has gone wrong.

It's not surprising that marketing professionals refer to insurance as a 'distress purchase'. And as if to add insult to injury, you pay 5% on top in tax. In some cases, such as travel insurance, insurance premium tax is a whopping 17.5%.

But as we've noted already, the one thing more distressing than having to buy insurance is not having a policy when you need to make a claim. So if you have to buy cover – and in the case of motor insurance, you legally must – it makes sense to get the right policy at the best price.

Over the next few pages we'll be looking at all the main types of insurance for things you own, such as your house and belongings, your car, bikes and other vehicles and your pets. We'll also explain how you can protect events such as fetes and weddings against unforeseen problems or inclement weather.

There are few things for which you can't buy insurance. You can even take out a policy against the risk of having twins.

Home from home

There are two types of home insurance: one to protect the bricks and mortar – buildings insurance – and one to protect your possessions – contents insurance.

If you own your property, you need both. If you're renting, your landlord should have a policy to take care of the property itself, but you will need to insure your belongings.

Insurers tend to offer both types of cover and you can often earn a discount (perhaps of 20% off the total premium) if you buy them from the same firm. This also means you'll have only one renewal date to remember each year.

There are, however, significant differences in premium levels from firm to firm, so it is always worth shopping around to check you've got the best deal.

This is certainly the case if you bought your buildings insurance through your bank or building society when you arranged your mortgage. For years, insurers have paid huge commissions to lenders to encourage them to sell home insurance as part of the mortgage deal, because they know borrowers are a sort of captive audience. And the lenders have been happy to go along with the arrangement. Some charge a so-called 'administration fee' of £25 or £50 to anyone who chooses to go elsewhere.

But with commissions sometimes reaching 40% of the premium, and with lots of companies competing for your business, it is easy to pay the fee and still save money. Some companies will even pay it on your behalf and handle the paperwork involved in transferring the business. And remember: you only pay the penalty once, but if you get a better deal, you will enjoy the savings every year.

Buildings cover

Three main factors determine the cost of buildings insurance:

◆ **Rebuilding cost** This is not the market value of the property. When you put a figure in the 'buildings sum insured' box on the proposal form, you are saying how much it would cost to reinstate the building if it were destroyed. In many parts of the UK, this will be far less than the price for which it would sell.

You can consult a surveyor for an accurate sum. Your broker or insurance company should also be able to give you an idea, since they will know the figures applying to similar properties in your area.

◆ **Type of property** Insurance premiums are based on the property being of standard construction. If there is anything unusual about it, such as being listed or having a thatched roof, expect to pay more.

◆ **Location** Just as the 'L' word is the most important in an estate agent's vocabulary, it has a mighty impact on the cost of buildings cover. Insurers know from experience which areas are prone to the major perils afflicting buildings: subsidence and flooding. If you live in one, you will pay much more for your insurance than if you lived on top of a granite mountain.

Subsidence

Houses built on clay soils are at risk of subsidence. The problem is that the ground expands and shrinks according to how wet it is. That plays havoc with foundations and results in worrying cracks in brickwork and, in extreme instances, major structural problems and collapses.

Insurer Churchill has reported subsidence related claims rose by 300% in 2003. If you are buying a house, you are strongly recommended to have a full structural survey before completing. The £500 or so it will cost could prove a wise investment.

If your house is in a subsidence zone, not only will your premium be higher but you may face a hefty 'excess' (the amount you must pay towards the cost of any subsidence related claim). It is not uncommon for this excess to be £1,000 or even £5,000.

If the subsidence is particularly bad and your property has already been affected, you may be required to carry out remedial or preventative work before an insurer will provide cover.

Flooding

It is estimated more than 1.3 million properties in the UK are at risk of flooding. And with pressure mounting to build new properties, there are concerns that more developments will occur on flood plains and in other vulnerable areas. There is also the issue of climate change, which may, according to some forecasts, result in the twin perils of heavier rainfall and rising sea levels.

As we've seen from heart-rending news reports, very little can be done to hold back a torrent from a river that has burst its banks. But if you know a flood is on its way, you can at least move your valuables upstairs or out of the property completely.

The Environment Agency's Floodline (0845 988 1188) carries information on flood threats for specific areas. Locations deemed most at risk include those around the rivers Severn, Thames, Humber and Tees, major estuaries such as the Wash and the East Coast of England, from Lincolnshire to Essex. Parts of Kent, Lancashire, East Wales and Central Scotland have also suffered in recent years.

If your house is rendered uninhabitable by a flood, your insurance should pay for alternative accommodation while repairs and restoration are carried out.

Contents cover

The premium for your contents cover is determined by the value of your possessions and where you live. In crude terms, the more crime ridden your area, the bigger your premium will be.

Your first task is to calculate your sum insured. Most people choose a figure far lower than would actually be required to replace all their belongings if, say, they were destroyed by fire. It is best to go room by room and list everything, from the carpets to the lampshades, from the curtains to the mirrors and from the furniture to books, CDs and DVDs.

Some insurers provide a guide to finding out the accurate contents sum insured. There is no benefit in deliberately picking a low amount to secure a lower premium – if you do that, you may find any claim you make is reduced so that you don't receive the full value of the lost items.

It is always a good idea to keep receipts for any major purchase – three-piece suite, new TV, freezer – so you can demonstrate to the insurer exactly how much it needs to pay.

Most policies provide 'new for old' cover, which means any replacement you receive following a loss is the current model, rather than a replica of one you may have bought some years ago. Some insurers will arrange to source, obtain and deliver goods themselves; others will simply send you out a cheque for the appropriate amount.

Precious items

Policies stipulate a maximum value that can be attached to any one item – perhaps £1,500. If you have jewellery or art or equipment worth more than this, tell the insurer. It will either adapt the contract to accommodate the item in question or recommend a separate policy. Either way, you may have to keep the piece in a safe or in a certain part of the house.

Other features of home insurance

◆ **All risks** One of the most baffling of all the baffling phrases beloved of insurers is 'all risks'. This simply means you are covered if you take your belongings outside the home and either lose or damage them.

◆ **Bicycles** You can include bicycles on your contents insurance, but there will be a limit on the value – say, £250. You may also have to keep them locked and out of sight of the road.

◆ **Helplines** If you suffer a broken window, burst pipe or other domestic emergency, you may be able to get rapid assistance via a dedicated helpline on your contents insurance policy. If such a service is provided, keep the number to hand.

◆ **Legal expenses** Some policies provide legal expenses insurance. This will pay your costs if you are obliged to defend yourself in a civil action.

◆ **Home-working** As more people work from home, insurance policies are adapting to meet their needs. You may be able to extend your contents insurance to cover the equipment you use in the course of your work, and this may apply whether you are self-employed or an employee working from home on an occasional basis.

Care is needed here. If you are bringing work (and equipment) home, check with your employer to see what cover is provided by its commercial insurance. If you are self-employed, is the cover provided by your contents policy adequate? If not, you could probably get a stand-alone homeworker's contract for around £100 a year, and your accountant will confirm it is a legitimate business expense.

If you work at home but choose not to extend your contents cover, tell the insurer anyway. A burglary claim was once rejected by the insurer on the grounds that it did not know the person was working at home. It argued that, if someone else was aware expensive computer equipment was present, a burglary could be planned specifically to obtain it. The non-disclosure was sufficient to invalidate the policy.

Safe and secure

Burglary is distressing and potentially dangerous, and victims inevitably agree no amount of financial redress can right the wrong suffered. It is much better to prevent rather than to attempt to cure. There are more than a million burglaries every year in the UK. Try not to become part of the depressing statistic. Measures you can take to protect yourself include:

◆ **Locks** Fit them and use them. All doors and windows should have them. Make sure garages and conservatories are secure, since these can provide access to the house proper. Don't leave windows open while you are out and think very carefully about leaving them open while you are asleep.

◆ **Alarms** These can serve as a useful deterrent. Your policy may specify the type of alarm and monitoring service required. You might also consider triggered lighting. If you live in a large house, the insurer may send a consultant around to provide advice.

◆ **Neighbourhood Watch** These community groups can be effective as long as everyone participates fully. The police will provide enthusiastic support to those establishing such schemes.

◆ **Dogs** Never underestimate the power of a fierce bark.

◆ **Safes** It is sensible to keep precious items in a safe. Some wealthy people even have a decoy safe to deflect attention from the principal objects. It is also worth considering keeping items of particular monetary or sentimental value in a bank vault. Banks charge upwards of £15 a year for such a service, depending on the value of the items or documents.

Get your motor running...

Motor insurance is a legal necessity. That fact doesn't stop an estimated one million people driving without cover, but most of us understand why it is essential to have protection in place.

That knowledge can appear scant consolation when writing out a cheque for many hundreds or even thousands of pounds (the average cost of cover is around £700 a year). That said, some solace may be derived from the fact that, this year at least, motor insurance premiums are relatively stable. After several years of steep increases, this will be welcome news to drivers.

The overall movement of premium rates is determined by levels of competition between insurers and various other industry factors. But down at street level, there are a number of things you can do to control the cost of cover.

Shop around

Whether it's Michael Winner offering more ham than a pig farm, a nodding dog, a musical telephone or a camp admiral with a stuffed parrot perched on his shoulder, there are dozens of motor insurance firms vying for your attention. You can normally get a quote in a minute or so over the telephone, so it is easy to compare prices.

You can also use the internet. A site such as www.find.co.uk has many useful links, but simply tapping 'UK motor insurance' into your search engine will throw up lots of results. And you can get a quote and buy online as well.

High street insurance brokers are declining in number but they are being replaced by internet and telebrokers who will trawl the market on your behalf in search of a good deal. But you may still have to go direct to a couple of firms (such as Direct Line or esure) which do not sell through brokers, just to ensure you have covered the market.

No claim, no pain

A no-claims discount – they don't seem to call it a no-claims 'bonus' anymore – can slice a huge amount off your premium. The discount increases year on year until it's worth around two-thirds of the total premium. You can then take out insurance to protect your discount so you are able to make a given number of claims in a specified period without being shunted back to zero.

Easy street

Where you live has a big impact on your premium for two reasons. One is theft, while the other is the typical number of vehicles per mile of road. In short, if you live in a busy urban area you will pay more than someone who lives in the sticks.

Age and gender

You can't control how old you are, and changing your sex is not exactly an easy option, but it is the case that older people and women tend to pay less for their motor insurance.

This is entirely logical. Forget what Les Dawson told you: women are better drivers. At least, they are involved in far fewer serious accidents. And if men are the main culprits, then young men are by far the worst offenders. Something about the cocktail of hormones and horsepower is dangerous – insurers have the facts to prove it and they charge accordingly.

Type of car

In essence, the bigger, flashier, faster and more expensive your car, the bigger the premium will be. Many car adverts even specify which insurance group the vehicle falls into, so that you have an idea how much it will cost you. Insurers rank all main car types into groups to make their calculations easier and a tad more transparent.

New cars often come with a year's free insurance – which is well worth having. But be prepared for a hefty premium when you emerge into the cold reality of the market.

Additional drivers

You can extend your policy so a named person or persons can drive your car or so anyone can do so. But be aware that the latter option costs more. Also, if your list of named drivers includes your 17-year-old son, you'll pay heavily for the privilege.

Off-road parking

Insurance will cost less if you park the car off-road at night. A driveway is good, a carport better and a locked garage best of all.

Classic cars

Special cars deserve special policies. If you have one that is more than 20 years old, you can elect to insure it under a classic car contract.

The essential difference is the cover can be limited and tailored to the precise requirements – and this can both provide better protection and save money compared to a conventional policy.

In addition to the usual factors such as where you live and the type of vehicle, the premium will be affected by the annual mileage. Do you rarely venture onto the Queen's highways in your prized machine? Or do you proudly show it at rallies at every opportunity? Policies come with limited mileage bands of, say, 1,500, 3,000 or 6,000 a year. The lower the distance, the lower the premium.

Security is important with older vehicles, which present little challenge to a modern car thief. You may not want, or may not be able, to fit alarms or tracker devices, but try to keep the car off-road, especially at night.

Excesses and discounts

With both motor and household insurance, the size of the premium will be affected by excesses and discounts. The excess is the amount you pay towards a claim. Most policies have a standard excess of £50 or £100 – the idea being to put people off making claims that are more costly to administer than they are to pay. Remember that a buildings policy on a house prone to subsidence will have a high excess applicable solely to subsidence claims. You can volunteer to increase the excess by as much as you want – and the higher the amount, the lower your premium will be.

You obtain discounts in various ways. Both motor and household policies reward you for not making a claim, although the discounts on motor policies tend to be higher (60% or even 65%) than on household contracts (up to 40%).

You can also get discounts for combining buildings and contents cover and for fitting security devices. Household policies may even specify which sort of locks you have to fit. If you then fail to use them or to set the alarm or tracker device on your car, you may invalidate the cover.

Many motor and household insurers offer a discount if you buy online – you can save up to 10% this way.

Paying by instalments

Most insurance policies can be paid for in instalments. But watch out: while some companies simply divide the premium by 12 to arrive at the monthly amount due, others add an interest charge of up to 6% to make up for the fact that they are not getting the whole amount up front. Paying by instalments is convenient and useful but that doesn't mean you should have to pay for the privilege.

Other covers

Caravans

Caravanning is increasingly popular, except when you're stuck behind one in a traffic jam. If you are one of the happy millions who like to have a home away from home, make sure you have appropriate insurance. More than £12m-worth of theft claims are made every year by caravanners, and these vehicles are often seen as a soft touch by thieves.

◆ **Security** You have two worries: losing what's inside the van and losing the van itself. You need to take care where you park at night – always opt for a site that has security of its own. An unguarded, unfenced farmer's field is risky and you may get back from your evening stroll to find you've had uninvited guests.

  Many losses are reported from caravans parked in the driveway of the owner's home, either for casual theft of the contents or theft of the vehicle itself. You need sturdy locks on the doors and windows and a wheel-clamp and/or hitchlock.

◆ **Touring** If you tour with your caravan, make sure your car's insurance policy provides full protection. It is essential to have at least third-party cover in case other people are injured in an accident and you are found liable. Check any geographical limitations on cover if you plan to venture overseas.

◆ **Sub-letting** If you allow others to use your caravan, either towing it with their own car or using it when sited for a holiday, your cover may be affected. Read your policy details and make your tenants aware of the situation, since they may need cover of their own.

Motorbikes

Motorcycling is dangerous. Statistics suggest you are up to six times more likely to be killed or injured while riding than while driving a car. What's more, thieves love motorbikes. They're relatively easy to steal and there is a ready market for big, powerful machines from the leading marques.

  Little wonder insurers are wary. And when insurers are wary, the premiums can soon become scary. Younger male drivers can find themselves paying more for their insurance than they did for the bike itself.

  Indeed, things got so bad in the 1990s that the leading insurer in the market, Norwich Union, stopped offering cover to anyone under 28. It eventually changed its mind, not least thanks to the improvements in security devices such as deadlocks, immobilisers, alarms and industrial-strength chains. But premiums are still high.

  Ironically, one of the main sources of claims at the moment is not tearaway youths but 'born again' bikers – men in their 30s and 40s – who can afford motorbikes with plenty of oomph, perhaps more than their modest biking skills can handle. And this is no laughing matter: it is thought that one of the main reasons why the annual death toll on British roads has stuck stubbornly at the 3,400 mark since 1996, despite considerable improvements in car design and other safety measures, is the number of casualties among middle-aged male motorcyclists.

When you buy motorbike insurance, you have the same basic issues as with car cover: security, location, age of vehicle and size of engine. You can also get a no-claims discount and pay by instalments if you choose.

One of the leading brokers in this market is Bennetts (www.bennetts.co.uk).

Pleasure craft

Anyone taking a craft onto a river, canal or in-shore waters must by law have liability insurance to meet any potential damages claims that arise out of an accident. If you sail into international waters or the national waters of another state, different rules may apply, so check before weighing anchor.

If you hire a boat for the day or for a cruising holiday, the insurance should be included in the price – but check just the same. Likewise, if you borrow a craft or if you lend yours to someone else, make sure everyone knows their responsibilities and reads the fine print of the relevant policies.

If you have a pleasure craft, chances are you'll want some insurance beyond the legal minimum. This will pay for repairs if it is damaged and cover you for theft of any gear you may have on board. And with sat-nav systems increasingly common, it certainly makes sense to have adequate insurance. That said, you should also fit security devices to deter and prevent any acts of casual piracy. Some policies may insist on security being in place, with discounted premiums as an incentive.

Reckon on paying around 1% of the price of the boat in insurance premiums – unless you have a powerful speed boat, where the increased liabilities are likely to push the figure closer to 5%.

Animal magic

Pet insurance – and the equine equivalent if you keep horses – is a good idea if only because vets' fees can make the flushest of us whinny and whimper. The reason is similar to that applying to medical treatment for humans: the range and complexity of procedures has advanced, meaning we can do lots more to help the injured and sick recover whereas in the past they might have died. But such progress costs money.

Pet insurance starts at around £70 to £90 a year for a cat and £100 to £130 for a dog, depending on the breed and the age of the animal. In any case, the animal will need to be over ten weeks old and under ten years and not already suffering from an ailment. Certain breeds may be excluded from policies at earlier

The Sunday Times Money Guide
The Sunday Times Money Guide

ages – Alsatians, for example, are increasingly prone to back and hind leg problems at six or seven years.

The cost of equine cover is determined largely by the value of the beast. You should be able to extend the policy to cover tack and other equipment. Check your motor policy before you tow a horse-box – additional premiums may be required. Pet insurance provides:

◆ **Cover for vet's fees** This is only for illness or injury. Policies do not cover the cost of vaccinations or of neutering and spaying.

◆ **Third-party liability** This covers you in case your pet causes an accident that results in injury or damage and you are found liable.

◆ **Death** A death benefit will be payable up to the purchase price of the animal if it dies prematurely from an illness or accident (not old age).

◆ **Boarding fees** If you have to go into hospital, the policy will pay for the animal's accommodation while you are away. If you prefer to leave it with a friend, you will qualify for a cash amount per night instead.

◆ **Advertising and reward** This covers the costs associated with trying to secure the return of your pet if it is lost. An equine policy will also cover the cost of bringing the animal home.

◆ **Loss by theft or straying** The policy will refund the purchase price after a given length of time has elapsed, but you may have to pay the money back if the animal is subsequently found.

◆ **Holiday cancellation** If you are obliged to cancel your holiday because of a pet's illness, the policy would reimburse the cost of the holiday. This cover is not available via standard travel insurance.

◆ **Accidental damage** This covers damage caused by your pet, either to your property or someone else's and plugs a gap in many household policies.

Travel insurance

Most travel insurance used to be sold alongside a holiday by the travel agent: 'Going to Tenerife for two weeks? Here's your two-week travel policy. We'll talk again if you decide to go skiing in the winter.'

But just as the competitive market exposed the rip-off deals on home insurance concocted by insurers and mortgage lenders, so the high cost of travel agents' insurance has been brought to light by companies selling annual policies.

These annual contracts sometimes cost less than two-week deals, yet they offer year-round protection, regardless of the number of trips made. For example, a family of four might pay £130 for an annual contract but closer to £200 for a single-trip plan.

Travel agents still sell single-trip policies and special holiday prices may be linked to taking the cover. But many insurers and brokers advertise annual plans in the press and other media which are much more reasonable.

The only real restrictions on an annual policy are that there may be a time limit of, say, 31 or 60 days for each trip and hazardous sports may be excluded altogether or only covered with payment of an additional premium. Business trips will normally be included. Special policies exist for backpackers.

Protecting events

Fetes

If there isn't a film version of an Edwardian comedy set in an impossibly perfect Home Counties village, starring Hattie Jacques and Wilfred Hyde-White and entitled *Tempting Fete*, there should be. Anyone who has been involved in organising an outdoor event knows that the best laid plans are as nothing before the caprice of the British climate. The sodden flight to the church hall may have moments of hilarity but such an outcome can devastate the chance of raising funds for a worthy cause. The insurance available for organisers covers a range of contingencies:

◆ Cancellation or reduction in takings because of weather;
◆ Third-party liability cover;
◆ Non-appearance of a celebrity;
◆ Damage to equipment or the venue;
◆ Theft of takings.

Weddings

Weddings cost a fortune, so the modest cost of an insurance policy can be well worthwhile. The protection extends to:

◆ Weather damage to a marquee;
◆ Double-booking of a venue;
◆ Loss or theft of presents;
◆ Loss of or damage to photographs or videos taken at the event.

Liability covers will also be provided.

Twins

From weddings, in one short bound, to twins… A policy here covers the extra costs associated with having two babies when only one was, as it were, expected.

Trouble-shooting guide

Having paid a hefty wedge of cash for your insurance, you will want the comfort of knowing the policy will pay out when you need it. But every year thousands of claims are turned down because policyholders think they have cover they don't or because they invalidate the cover they have.

In a recent high-profile case, entertainer Cilla Black's claim for the loss of possessions when her home was burgled was rejected. The reason? The policy stipulated the doors and windows must be locked and they were not.

The same reasoning applies to items inside cars. If you leave a bag or wallet in full view in an empty parked vehicle, your policy is unlikely to pay up. If you put them in the boot, however, you should be okay.

Critical illness insurance has thrown up problems in the past, with genuinely sick individuals not receiving any payout because their specific ailment was not covered. Life insurance claims have also been rejected because the policyholder did not give full details of their medical condition when they applied for the policy.

The trick with insurance is to understand what you have bought and to meet the terms and conditions laid down. Reading the policy literature will take a lot of time and provide little entertainment but at least you'll know where you stand. Pay particular attention to any section headed 'Exclusions' or 'Restrictions of Cover'.

If you get into dispute over your policy, there are certain rules and procedures to follow.

Where did you buy the policy?

Did you buy direct from the insurer or through a broker? Did the policy come as an adjunct to another contract, such as insurance for a new car? Did you buy through another service provider, such as your mobile phone company or a utility firm?

In the event of a problem, your first port of call should be whoever sold you the policy. Only head straight to the insurance company if you bought direct from it. If you used a broker, it should help clarify the situation and give you support if you have a valid argument. That is one of the ways they earn their commission.

All firms will have a complaints procedure if you feel you have been unfairly treated. This will probably be explained in the product literature, where you should also find information on who to contact in the first instance.

Make sure you follow this procedure to the letter. Not only will this show the company you are serious, it will also stand you in good stead if you are ultimately disappointed with its response and decide to take your complaint to the next stage.

The Financial Ombudsman Service

Only consult the Financial Ombudsman Service when you have fully exhausted the company's own complaints mechanisms. If you haven't, the ombudsman will simply refer you back to these.

The ombudsman deals with complaints regarding all sorts of insurance policies and the vast majority of companies and brokers belong to the scheme. There is no guarantee the ombudsman will find in your favour, but you are guaranteed a fair hearing by people who know the business. There is no cost for using the service. See Appendix for contact details.

Hints and suggestions

To help get the most from your insurance policy and to help ensure your claim is successful:

◆ Keep receipts for your purchases, especially expensive home entertainment equipment and jewellery.

◆ Take photographs of your most precious belongings.

◆ Mark items with your postcode, either in a hidden area or with an ultra-violet pen. This will identify your belongings if they are recovered.

◆ Make sure you have adequate cover.

◆ Discuss your requirements in full with the insurer or broker before you buy.

◆ Tell the insurer of any significant changes to what is being insured – for example, if you modify your car with, say, additional headlights.

◆ Provide full information whenever it is required, both when applying for cover and making a claim.

◆ With medical cover, inform your insurer of any pre-existing conditions. If in doubt, spell it out.

◆ Prevention is better than cure so use locks and alarms wherever possible – always use them if they are a condition of the policy.

5

Pensions and Retirement

In this section we will look at

What the state provides

Changes to the pension rules

Company pension schemes

Topping up your company provision

Stakeholder and personal pension plans

Preparing for retirement

Annuities and the alternatives

Investing after retirement

5

Pensions and Retirement

Retirement can be one of the best periods of your life, when you are finally able to do all the things you always wanted to but couldn't because of work commitments. You can travel the world and enjoy your leisure time and your family to the full. But it could be a different experience altogether if you are struggling to make ends meet.

Having an adequate retirement income is likely to make all the difference. This is why in this section we will be looking at how you can make sure you build up a sufficient pension and how you can get the best out of your finances when you get to retirement. We will act as your guide through the pensions maze and beyond. Read on for:

◆ **How the state pension scheme works and the extra benefits available** Knowing how little you are likely to get from the state when you retire will help to concentrate you mind on making those extra savings for retirement.

◆ **How pensions are changing** The government wants us to save more and is bringing in various improvements it hopes will encourage us to do so.

◆ **What to expect if you are a member of an occupational or company pension scheme** Why being in a company scheme is generally good news but not without its snags.

◆ **How stakeholder and personal pensions work** Here's the lowdown on the next best thing to company pensions.

◆ **How to get the most out of your pension at retirement** We take you through your options.

◆ **Your tax position in retirement** How to avoid paying more tax than you need to.

◆ **A strategy for investment after retirement** Adapting your investments to fit your changing requirements.

◆ **Paying for long-term care** Longer life expectancies mean a growing number of us will need professional care when we become elderly.

Pensions

Many people are likely to receive a combination of state and private pensions. The state scheme still provides the bulk of most people's retirement income through a combination of contributory and means-tested benefits, but the government has been trying to encourage people to save more themselves. The problem is that as people move jobs, they can acquire a patchwork of pensions, causing considerable confusion. In the first part of this section, we will be going through the essential elements of the schemes that may provide your income in retirement.

What the state provides

The first step in any pension planning exercise is to find out how much you can expect from the state. It may not be much but at least it will be secure and index-linked. Once you know what you will be getting, you can start working out how much you need to save in your own pension plan.

Apart from the basic state retirement pension, you may be in line to receive an additional state pension. In the following sections there is an explanation of how these schemes work. But the easiest way of finding out what you can expect is to ask for a pension forecast from the Department for Work and Pensions (DWP). The Retirement Pension Forecasting Team (0845 300 0168) will fill in your application over the phone. Alternatively, get form BR19 from your local DWP office or the internet and send in a written request.

This forecast will show how much pension you have already built up and how much you will receive at state pension age assuming you continue paying contributions. It will also show whether you can improve your state pension by paying voluntary contributions.

The basic state retirement pension

You will receive your pension at the state retirement age which is currently 65 for men and 60 for women. But the retirement age for women will soon start rising to bring them into line with men. The change is being phased in between 2010 and 2020. It means women born between April 1950 and April 1955 will have a retirement age of somewhere between 60 and 65, while all women born after that will have to wait to age 65. For a full listing of women's retirement ages see *A Guide to State Pensions*, booklet NP46, available from DWP offices or its pensions website (www.thepensionservice.gov.uk).

However, you do not have to start collecting your pensions at these ages if you would prefer to work longer. Until now, if you wanted you could delay your retirement by up to five years and your pension would be increased by 7.5% for each year you deferred in addition to the usual index-linking. But the government is planning to offer the alternative of having the pension you have foregone paid as a lump sum when you retire, with interest added at 2% above base rate. The lump sum will be liable to tax. This option is expected to be available from April 2005. After that it will also be possible to defer your pension for as long as you want. If you opt for extra pension instead of a lump sum, it will go up by 10.4% for each year deferred instead of 7.5% as now.

How much will you get?

Everybody who has paid an adequate number of National Insurance contributions when employed, self-employed or on a voluntary basis will receive the full basic state pension, currently £79.60 per week (for 2004-5). A married couple will receive an additional pension of £47.65, giving a total of £127.25, where a wife has not paid sufficient NI contributions for a full pension herself. These pensions will increase each year in line with the Retail Price Index.

Your National Insurance contributions

To get a full basic state pension, you must have been paid or been credited with full-rate NI contributions for 90% of your working life. Your working life is considered to start at age 16. This means men must have contributed for at least 44 years and women 39 years. After 2020 women will also need 44 years of contributions. Only full tax years of contributions qualify. If your contribution record is incomplete, you will get a reduced pension, but you must have contributed for at least 11 years (ten for women) to get anything. With 11 years' contributions, you will get the minimum amount of 25% of the basic pension.

Gaps in your contribution record

Gaps can be created in your record by periods spent in higher education, when you worked incomplete years or worked abroad. Some countries have reciprocal arrangements with the UK though, so contributions made to their social security systems count towards your UK pension. Contact the DWP's Pension Service for details if you live in the UK (see Appendix) or the International Pension Centre if you live elsewhere (0191 218 7777).

You may be able to fill these gaps by paying voluntary NI contributions. The current rate is £7.15 a week. Normally you have up to six years to make up for missing contributions. However, anyone wanting to fill gaps between April 1996 and April 2002 is being given longer as the Inland Revenue failed to notify people in time. Although it is generally worth considering making voluntary contributions, it will not be worthwhile if they don't help you achieve at least ten qualifying years. And if you are a married or divorced woman, you may get a better pension by claiming on your husband's NI contributions.

Moreover, not all periods when you are not working will affect your pension because you may qualify for NI credits. Those who qualify include:

◆ Children who stay on at school until age 18;
◆ Those receiving Jobseekers' Allowance and/or registered as unemployed;

◆ Those who are incapacitated and receiving Invalidity Benefit;

◆ Men of 60 and over who have stopped work, providing they do not live outside the UK. From 2010 credits will also be given to women in this age group.

Home responsibilities protection

Fewer years of NI contributions will be required if you qualify for home responsibilities protection (HRP) because you have stayed at home to look after a child or someone who is sick or disabled. HRP has been available since April 1978 and is given automatically to anyone receiving child benefit for a child under 16 or Income Support to look after a sick or disabled person. You can also apply for it on form CF411, available from DWP offices, if you are looking after someone for at least 35 hours a week who is receiving Attendance Allowance or a similar benefit. However, even if you receive HRP, you will require at least 20 years of ordinary NI contributions to qualify for a full pension.

Additional state pensions

Who gets them

A variety of schemes to provide additional state pensions have existed since 1961. First there was the graduated pension scheme which went on until 1975 and was open to people who earned more than around £9 a week. Then came the state earnings-related pension scheme (Serps). If you were an employee between 1978 and 1988 you had to contribute unless you were a member of an occupational scheme which provided you with a similar pension. After 1988, it became possible for individual employees to opt out of this part of the state scheme and have a personal pension instead. In April 2002 Serps was renamed the state second pension (S2P).

How much will you get?

Serps pensions are related to your earnings between the upper and lower earnings limit during the time you were contributing. When it was introduced, the Serps pension was designed to provide a pension equivalent to 25% of these earnings for the 20 best years of your working life, but it was later reduced to 20% of earnings averaged over your whole working life.

S2P, introduced in 2002, provides more generous benefits than Serps for lower earners. It is also earnings linked at present but the government is planning to change it to a flat rate benefit, possibly from 2006. Once in payment all additional pensions are inflation linked.

Contribution conditions

You only have to contribute to Serps or S2P for one year to receive some benefit when you retire. If you are a carer or someone with a long-term disability which prevents you working, you may receive credits towards S2P, unlike with Serps where no credits were given. However, carers looking after children will receive S2P credits only if their children are five or under. S2P credits will not be provided for the unemployed.

Opting out of S2P

You are free to opt out of S2P and have part of your NI contributions paid into a personal or stakeholder pension instead, as was also possible with Serps. When this option was introduced in 1988, the government offered incentive bonuses to those who opted out, but the current level of NI rebates are regarded by pension experts as neutral. This means, all things being equal, they will produce a similar pension to that which you can expect from S2P when invested in a personal or stakeholder scheme.

So there is no clear financial advantage to opting out of S2P. Choosing whether you do so will depend on whether you prefer the certainty of a state pension or having control of your own pension pot. If you opt for your own pension, you will be taking a risk on the investment markets, although there is no guarantee S2P will not be changed by future governments. If you are currently opted out of S2P you can opt back in. Your pension provider can explain how to do this.

The pension credit

Pensioners on low incomes have always been able to claim extra means-tested state benefits to supplement their pensions. In October 2003 this system of benefits became known as the pension credit. As well as providing extra income for those who need it, it introduced an additional benefit for people with modest pensions or savings, so those who have made an effort to save do not feel as though they are being penalised for their prudence.

The pension credit therefore consists of two elements. Some people may qualify for one or the other, some for a bit of both:

◆ **The guarantee credit** This provides extra income for people aged 60 or over on low incomes. It makes up the difference between whatever income they do have and the level set for the guarantee credit which is £105.45 per week for single people and £160.95 per week for couples for 2004-5.

◆ **The savings credit** This is available to those aged 65 or over. People whose total income is more than the basic state pension but below the guarantee credit limit will first of all have their income made up to the guarantee limit.

They will then receive an extra savings credit equivalent to 60p for every £1 of income they have in excess of the basic state pension but less than the guarantee credit limit. The maximum savings credit for a single person in 2004-5 is £15.51 and for couples it is £20.22. Pensioners whose total incomes are over the weekly guarantee credit limits of £105.45 if they are single or £160.95 if they are married may still get some savings credits but they will be reduced by 40p for every £1 by which their income exceeds these limits. No credit is currently payable for single pensioners with incomes over £144 or couples with more than £211.

When assessing entitlement to pension credit, the first £6,000 of savings will be ignored. Further savings will be assumed to produce income of £1 a week for every additional £500. As every £1 of pension will be counted in the assessment, people may be better off building up their first £6,000 of savings outside a pension.

Pensioners who think they may be eligible for pension credit and have not already been assessed should contact the Pension Service (0800 991 234, www.thepensionservice.gov.uk). Anyone who applies before October 2004 and is found to be eligible will have their credits backdated to October 2003. Future pensioners will have their income and entitlement to pension credit assessed when their state pension is being calculated.

Making your own pension provision

As the previous pages have demonstrated, a state retirement pension will provide you with little more than a safety net. By providing the guaranteed pension credit, even the government admits the basic pension is not enough to live on. This means the only way you can be sure of having enough income is to make your own provision. At present most people fail to save enough. Not long ago the Association of British Insurers identified a £27bn gap between what people are actually saving and what they will need for their later years.

One of the problems is that many people have been put off pensions by various scandals such as Equitable Life and company pension fund shortfalls, not to mention poor stock market performance. But it is important to remember the vast majority of retired people who have been members of pension schemes are reaping a steady and reliable income as a result. Moreover, pension schemes remain one of the most tax-efficient ways of saving for retirement. Your contributions are topped up by income tax relief from the taxman, invested in virtually tax-free funds and, at retirement, there is the opportunity to take part of your pension as a tax-free lump sum.

Future developments

To help restore confidence and encourage people to make better use of pension schemes, there are a number of government proposals in the pipeline. Here are some of the main changes due to be introduced over the next year or two.

Sandler products

To help the government work out how to encourage people to save more both generally and for their retirement, it commissioned the Sandler Report. This suggested a range of easy to understand, low cost products. These will include the stakeholder pension (see pages 153-156).

Better protection

The Pension Protection Fund is scheduled to be introduced in 2005. This will pay for the pensions of employees of companies that collapse leaving insolvent final salary schemes. The fund will be financed by a levy on other companies with final salary schemes.

Simplification of the contribution rules

At present the amount you can invest in a pension varies from one scheme to another and is influenced by your employment status, how much you earn and even how old you are. From April 2006 the situation will become a lot simpler. The old rules will be replaced by a total contribution limit starting at £215,000 per person per year, subject to a ceiling of 100% of earnings (or £3,600 a year if greater). As long as individuals keep to those limits they will be allowed to contribute to any scheme they want.

There will also be a maximum lifetime pension fund limit starting at £1.5m, increasing to £1.8m by 2010 and reviewed at five-year intervals thereafter. If funds exceed this amount they will be subject to a recovery tax of 55%. Most people will not be affected by these fund limits. However, some high earners will find their pension funds already exceed the lifetime limit when the rules change. They can protect their funds from the extra tax charge by registering them beforehand. This amount will then be treated as their personal lifetime allowance but no further contributions will be permitted. Those likely to be affected should seek professional advice.

Simplification of the benefit rules

The way you can take your benefits from a pension also varies from scheme to scheme. From April 2006 there will be uniformity across money purchase schemes. After that, it will be possible to take up to 25% of your fund as a tax-free lump sum, while the remainder provides your regular pension, normally through the purchase of an annuity. Final salary schemes may still retain their own rules.

Early retirement deferred

After April 2010 the minimum age at which it will be possible to take benefits from a pension will rise from 50 to 55.

Planning your pension

For many people, pension choices are dictated by employment status. For employees it generally makes sense to opt for the scheme offered by your employer. Nowadays, all employees, unless they work for businesses with less than five employees, have to be offered access to some form of pension scheme by their employer. For other people, a stakeholder or personal pension are the main choices.

Company pensions

Company, or occupational, schemes come in various forms. The main distinction is between final salary, which provide pensions linked to earnings, and money purchase, where the pension depends on the amount of money in your pension pot at retirement. The huge advantage of both is that your employer will be contributing to your pension, so you are likely to get more at retirement than if you had to pay for it entirely yourself. Therefore, not joining a company scheme would mean you were effectively turning down part of your salary.

The ground rules for each type of scheme are the same. You can contribute up to 15% of your income. The maximum pension you can take is two-thirds of your final earnings. You can swap part of your regular pension for a tax-free lump sum of up to one-and-a-half times your final salary. A spouse's pension and life cover of up to four times your annual salary may also be provided.

After April 2006 when pension simplification is introduced (see previous page), these limits will no longer apply to future contributions and benefits. But final salary schemes may still apply their own benefit rules.

Final salary schemes

Final salary, or defined benefit, schemes are traditionally regarded as the Rolls-Royce of pension schemes. They promise your pension will be a fixed proportion of your pay when you reach retirement depending on how long you have worked for your employer. So, in theory, they offer security and no need to worry about investment returns or interest rates as you would in a money purchase scheme.

Both employers and employees have to make regular contributions towards a final salary pension. These are normally invested in funds which include shares, fixed-interest and property. Employers are expected to make up any difference between the value of the funds and the amount needed to pay members' pensions. However, in recent years, poor stock market performance and increasing life expectancies have resulted in growing shortfalls in many funds. This has pushed up the costs for employers and led an increasing number to modify their schemes or even close them to new and sometimes existing members to cut costs.

Moreover, because the promises on final salary schemes are only as sound as the firms making them, some employees have found their pensions are worth little or nothing if their employers go bust and are unable to top up their funds.

Public sector employees have not had to worry about the health of their pensions as these are normally financed on a pay-as-you-go basis directly out of current members' contributions and out of taxation. However, the increasing cost of paying pensions to members who are living ever longer is also leading to changes here too, such as crackdowns on early retirement.

Despite these difficulties, final salary schemes are still generally a good option. In comparison to other schemes, employers contribute more and employees usually get higher pensions. The proposed introduction of the Pension Protection Fund in 2005 should also give greater security to members.

How final salary schemes work

Typically members are asked to contribute around 5% of their pay towards their pension, while the employer pays the remainder of the cost. The amount of pension you get when you retire depends on several factors:

◆ **The accrual rate** This is normally 1/60th or 1/80th of your final salary for each year of pension scheme membership.

◆ **Number of years in the scheme** If you have been a member for, say, 20 years you would get a pension of 20/80ths or 20/60ths, that is a quarter or a third of your final earnings. The maximum you can get is two-thirds of your final earnings.

◆ **How your final salary is defined** This may be defined as your average earnings over the last three to five years of your employment. Alternatively, to reduce their costs, some employers have introduced career average schemes, where your pension is linked to your salary averaged over the whole time you were a member of the scheme.

◆ **How much of your salary is pensionable** Not all of your income may count towards your final salary pension. Part of it may be considered to be covered by your state pension and any overtime or bonuses you earn may also be disregarded. A recent trend is for employers to introduce hybrid schemes where only part of your salary is covered by a final salary pension, with the remainder linked to a money purchase pension.

◆ **Whether you take a cash sum** Most pension schemes give you a choice of giving up, or commuting, part of your pension and taking a tax-free lump sum instead. In the public sector you are usually given a lump sum automatically.

Money purchase schemes

The other type of company scheme is money purchase, also called defined contribution, where a pot of money is built up to provide your pension at retirement, normally through the purchase of an annuity.

The disadvantages of these schemes over the final salary variety are that employers usually contribute less and it is more difficult to predict how much pension you will get. The advantage is your pension savings are ringfenced so they will not be affected by anything which happens to your employer.

How money purchase schemes work

The main factors which will influence the size of the pension you get from a money purchase scheme include:

◆ **How much is contributed** The more that is contributed, the larger the pension pot will be. Employees on average are asked to contribute around 4% of their income, while the average contribution by employers is about 7% of pay. Some employers will match or make larger contributions if employees agree to pay more.

◆ **Investment growth** Investment returns will have a decisive effect on the size of your pension pot. These will depend on general economic and stock market conditions as well as on the type of assets your contributions are invested in and the skills of the investment managers.

In some money purchase schemes, contributions are pooled and the investment managers and their strategy decided by the fund's trustees. In others, the trustees decide on the investment manager but members are given a choice of funds. If you are given a choice, read Section Three on investing to help you decide on the most appropriate funds.

◆ **Annuity rates** To convert your pension pot into a regular income, an annuity will have to be purchased. Annuity returns fluctuate in line with long-term interest rates but the amount you get will also depend on the type purchased – for example, whether it pays a fixed or increasing income and whether it provides a spouse's pension.

At present, occupational schemes are obliged to use any pension benefits earned since April 1997 to purchase an annuity which provides limited price indexation, which means it must increase by 5% a year or the rate of inflation if less. But the government is planning to relax that provision to give pensioners more choice.

Topping up your company scheme

Very few employees clock up the maximum benefits in their pension scheme since most either move jobs, take career breaks or have gaps in their contribution records for other reasons. So if you have cash to spare it is a good idea to consider topping up your pension. There are several ways of doing this. The advantage of using a pension scheme as opposed to, say, individual savings plans (Isas) is that your contributions will be boosted by income tax relief.

AVCs and FSAVCs

All occupational schemes must offer members a facility to make additional voluntary contributions (AVCs), although this provision will be relaxed in 2006. There is usually a choice of investments ranging from deposit accounts to equity funds. The alternative is to save through a free-standing AVC (FSAVC) with an outside provider. As both types of scheme work on a money purchase basis, investment performance and charges are key considerations. AVC schemes usually have significantly lower charges than FSAVCs. So unless their investment performance is exceptionally poor, you will normally be better off choosing AVCs.

The amount you can pay in AVCs/FSAVCs will depend on how much you are already contributing to your pension. The overall limit on employee contributions is 15% of earnings. So if you are paying, say, 4% to the main scheme you could pay another 11% voluntarily. There may be added scope for making AVCs/FSAVCs if you receive extra income from such things as bonuses, overtime and perks and your main scheme contributions are related to your basic pay only.

One of the disadvantages of making AVCs/FSAVCs in recent years has been the rule that the accumulated fund could only be used to buy an annuity. Under the simplified pension rules to be introduced in April 2006, these schemes will be treated like all other money purchase schemes, so it will be possible to take 25% of the money as a tax-free lump sum. If you have an AVC/FSAVC coming to maturity, you may therefore prefer to wait until April 2006 before you take the benefits.

Added years

Some final salary schemes, usually those in the public sector, offer employees the option of buying added years as an alternative to money purchase AVCs. Added years are not cheap but they are worth considering as they will provide a guaranteed amount of additional pension, which will increase in line with your main scheme benefits. But if you are considering early retirement, check how any added years will be treated.

Stakeholder pensions

At present anyone who is a member of a company pension scheme and earns less than £30,000 a year can also take out a stakeholder pension (see pages 153-156) if they want to make extra savings. Until now these schemes have been an attractive alternative to AVCs as part of the benefit could be taken as a tax-free lump sum at retirement. However, the planned changes to the pension rules in April 2006 mean this difference will disappear.

Salary sacrifice

Another way of topping up your pension is by giving up some of your annual salary and having your employer redirect it into your pension. The advantage is that no National Insurance needs to be paid on this money, so your employer can use the saved NI component to enhance your pension contribution.

When you change jobs

When you leave a company, you will need to consider your pension options carefully. If you have a lot of money tied up in the scheme, it is advisable to take professional advice. If you have been a member of a final salary scheme and decide you want to take the value of your benefits elsewhere, it is particularly important to get expert help to make sure you are getting fair value.

If you have been a member of a company pension scheme for less than two years, you may be offered a refund of contributions, less tax, but if you are given other choices, such as a pension transfer value (see below), it will be more tax efficient and will ensure you don't have a gap in your pension provision. If you are given the cash back, make sure you don't spend it as you will regret it later.

If you have been a longer serving member, you will usually have up to three alternative ways in which you can deal with your pension from your old scheme. But there is no rush to make a decision. Transfers from old schemes can be requested up to a year before your original retirement date. However, if your old scheme is under-funded, your ex-employer may be able to refuse a transfer or reduce its value. Bear in mind that once you have made a transfer, you cannot reverse the decision.

Leave your pension where it is

If you take no action your pension will stay in your old scheme until you reach your old company's retirement age. You may also retain some other benefits such as provision for a dependant's pension on your death.

If it is a final salary scheme, the value of your pension will be calculated when you leave on the basis of your earnings at that time and then increased annually at least in line with the Retail Price Index, up to a maximum of 5% a year at present. The main snag with this approach is that earnings typically rise faster than prices, so the value of your pension may gradually start to lag behind your current earnings. If your ex-employer runs into financial problems and your old scheme becomes under-funded, your pension may also be hit.

If it is a money purchase company scheme, your cash will remain invested in the pension fund and its value will move in line with the investments in it. It will not be affected by any change in your old employer's fortunes.

Transfer to a new employer's scheme

If your new employer offers you membership of a pension scheme, it may be possible to transfer the benefits, although your new employer is not obliged to offer this facility.

If you are moving from one final salary scheme to another, unless you are switching between public sector schemes, you will probably be offered fewer years of pensionable service in the new scheme than you had before. If you are on a higher salary, a switch may still be worthwhile as your pension at retirement will be related to your improved earnings. But check that your new scheme is not under-funded before you make any decision.

Transferring between money purchase schemes is easier. Your pension pot from your old scheme will simply be moved across and invested in your new one. But there may be cost implications which you will need to take into consideration.

Transfer to an individual pension scheme

If you would prefer to have the pension under your own control, you can transfer it to a stakeholder or personal pension plan. This will enable you to decide the investments yourself, particularly if you use a self-invested personal pension (Sipp) (see pages 157-158) and may give you greater flexibility over how you take the benefits at retirement.

However, you should consider the risks very carefully if you are contemplating a transfer from a final salary scheme, as you will be swapping a defined benefit for the uncertainty of a money purchase arrangement. Even if you were a member of a money purchase scheme, it may not be advantageous to transfer to an individual pension scheme. The costs, for example, may be higher.

Other pension schemes

Around 35% of the UK workforce are covered by company pension schemes. For the remainder there are a wide variety of other schemes available including stakeholder, personal and executive pensions, small self-administered pension schemes and funded unapproved retirement benefit schemes.

This range is likely to shrink considerably after pensions simplification takes place in April 2006. With the exception of stakeholder and personal pensions, most of the others are expected to disappear and existing holders of these schemes should consult a professional adviser in the meantime to establish how they can get the best out of their plans in future.

Stakeholder pensions

Introduced in April 2001, stakeholder pensions have become the first step in pension planning for most people who do not belong to a company pension scheme, as well as a top-up option for some people who do belong to company schemes (see page 151). If you are in one of the following groups, a stakeholder pension may be right for you:

◆ **An employee** If your employer does not have a company scheme and employs five or more people, you must be offered access to a stakeholder pension instead. Your employer does not have to pay anything into this on your behalf, although some do. If yours does, you should definitely join. Even if there is no employer contribution, it may be a good idea to join the scheme your employer has nominated. It may be cheaper than an individual policy and, if you are not very good at saving, having your employer deduct your contributions from your pay at source will avoid the temptation to spend the money on other things. You can either have a flat rate contribution, say £50 a month, or a percentage of your pay, say 5%, deducted and paid into your pension. You can vary the amount at six monthly intervals.

◆ **Self-employed** As a self-employed person, you will only qualify for the basic state pension, so having your own plan is vital. In the past, if you were self-employed with irregular earnings, committing yourself to saving regularly in a pension could be a problem, but one of the advantages of stakeholder pensions is their flexibility. Minimum contributions can be as little as £20 and they can be stopped and restarted at any time without penalty.

◆ **A non-earner** You don't have to be working to take out a stakeholder pension, so if you take a career break you can still contribute up to £3,600 a year to a pension, or someone else can contribute on your behalf, and receive basic rate income tax relief. There is no minimum age for stakeholder pensions either, so they can be taken out for children, although it means they won't be able to access the money until they reach 55. Because tax relief is given at source, the maximum that actually comes out of your pocket is £2,808 a year.

How stakeholder pensions work

Stakeholder pensions are sold by a variety of pension companies but the basic outline of how they work is the same. Here are some of the main points:

◆ Most people aged up to 75 are eligible. The main exceptions at present are members of company schemes earning more than £30,000 a year and controlling directors, but this rule will be relaxed after April 2006.

◆ Contributors must be UK residents although if someone moves abroad they can continue contributing for up to five years.

◆ Minimum contributions are £20 either as one off or regular payments. Pension companies cannot force you to make regular contributions.

◆ Contributions of up to £3,600 per tax year can be made. Higher contributions are allowed providing they fall within the permitted limits for personal pension plans, which currently vary according to age and earnings (see page 157). Higher contributions can continue for up to five years after the relevant earnings have ceased. After April 2006, new simplified contribution rules will apply (see page 147).

◆ Contributions are paid net of basic rate tax by everyone including the self-employed and non-earners. The tax is reclaimed from the Inland Revenue by the pension company. Higher rate taxpayers have to claim their extra relief through their self-assessment returns.

◆ Charges on stakeholder pensions are restricted to a maximum of 1% a year. Any additional charges for extra services must be optional.

◆ No additional charges can be imposed if a saver wants to transfer their pension to another company.

◆ A choice of investment options may be offered, but schemes must stipulate a suitable default option for savers who prefer not to make their own choice. In future, under the Sandler proposals, the default option must be a lifestyle fund. These are funds where savers' contributions are normally invested in equities initially and switched into safer fixed-interest investments as retirement draws near.

◆ When a stakeholder pension is taken out, savers have a 14-day cooling off period in which they can change their mind and get their money back.

◆ At present a pension can be taken from a stakeholder plan any time from age 50 but after 2010 the minimum age will be 55. The proceeds must be used to buy an annuity by age 75, although 25% can be taken as a tax-free lump sum.

How much will you get from your stakeholder pension?

As stakeholder pensions are money purchase schemes, where you build up a fund to buy your pension, the main factors that will determine the amount of retirement income you get are as follows:

◆ **The amount contributed** The more you put in, the more you are likely to get out at retirement. Starting earlier rather than later also gives more time for your savings to accumulate. As the table over the page shows, a woman of 40 would have to save more than double the amount a woman of 30 would to achieve the same pension (assuming the same level of growth).

The best way to ensure you build up sufficient retirement income is to save a percentage of your earnings. A rule of thumb suggested by a pension expert for those who are just starting to save is to take your age and divide it in half. In other words, if you are 30, you should save 15% of your income, if you are 40 you should save 20% and so on. There is also a useful internet calculator set up by the Financial Services Authority and the Association of British Insurers at www.pensioncalculator.org.uk to help work out what you should be saving.

◆ **Investment growth** The returns on your contributions will have a major impact on the value of your pension at retirement. They will depend on the type of assets you invest in, general economic and investment conditions and the skill of your investment managers. No manager is good at everything, so it's usually wise to choose a stakeholder pension which offers links to external fund managers. For more on making the right choices when you are saving for retirement see Section Three on investing.

◆ **Charges** No matter how good your investment returns, high charges can erode them. On stakeholder pensions, charges are restricted to a maximum of 1% a year but there are still variations. Some providers charge less or they may operate a tiered system so the more you invest the lower your charges become.

The easiest way to compare charges on stakeholder pensions is to look at the comparative tables on the FSA's website at www.fsa.gov.uk/tables.

◆ **Annuity rates** At retirement you can take 25% of the money in your stakeholder fund as a tax-free lump sum, but the remainder will have to be used to buy an annuity. You will need to shop around for the best rate (see page 163).

Monthly premium required to achieve pension at age 65

Pension per year	Male age		Female age	
	30	40	30	40
£10,000	£97	£195	£104	£209
£15,000	£143	£289	£153	£310
£20,000	£189	£382	£203	£413
£25,000	£235	£478	£252	£513

Figures based on 7% return in a stakeholder scheme.
Source: Legal & General

Personal pensions

Personal pensions, like stakeholder pensions, are individual money purchase arrangements, so the amount you get at retirement will depend on how big a pot you manage to accumulate and on annuity rates at retirement.

Personal pensions have been largely replaced by stakeholder pensions in recent years but there are still circumstances where a personal pension may be a good choice. However, bear in mind this type of pension may be more expensive, so it is important to make sure it is right for you. Unlike stakeholder plans where annual charges are limited to 1%, with no penalties for transfers or stopping contributions, there are no restrictions on charges made on personal pensions.

The impact of charges can be compared by visiting www.fsa.gov.uk/tables. These show, for example, that a 35-year-old saving £100 per month would pay over a third more in charges for the most expensive personal plan than for the most expensive stakeholder plan.

The same amounts can be contributed to both personal pensions and stakeholder pension. Any contributions which exceed £3,600 per tax year gross must currently fall within the personal pension limits shown in the table opposite.

For the highly paid, there is a further limit on contributions as a result of the 'earnings cap' – the maximum amount of earnings against which contributions can be made. For the 2004-5 tax year the cap is £102,000. After pensions simplification is introduced in 2006, this limit will no longer apply.

Personal pension contribution limits

Maximum contribution for 2004-5 is the lower of:

Age at 6 April	% of earnings	Cash amount*
Up to 35	17.5%	£17,850
36 to 45	20%	£20,400
46 to 50	25%	£25,500
51 to 55	30%	£30,600
56 to 60	35%	£35,700
61 or over	40%	£40,800

*For those affected by the earnings cap

There are circumstances in which personal pensions are well worth considering, for instance if your employer invites you to join a group personal pension scheme. Some employers offer employees membership of a group personal pension scheme instead of a company or stakeholder arrangement. Since there is a rule with group personal pensions that employers have to contribute the equivalent of 3% of your pay, you would be unwise to turn down the offer of joining it and hence lose out on that contribution.

In other respects being a member of group personal pension scheme is no different to having your own personal plan, except you and your fellow employees all have policies with the same company which has been chosen by your employer. You will be able to choose the fund in which you want your savings invested, although the choice will depend on the company your employer has selected.

If you change employers you will be able to take your plan with you but your new employer will not have to contribute. You may be able to continue contributing yourself, particularly after 2006 when the pension contribution rules are being simplified. Or you could stop your contributions and make your plan 'paid up', leaving your money invested until retirement. Or you could transfer your accumulated fund to another pension plan but you need to check there are no extra charges for doing this.

You might also consider a personal pension if you want the wider investment choice of a self-invested personal pension (Sipp). It is worth remembering that pensions are essentially tax-efficient wrappers for investments. Traditionally these investments have been the pension companies' in-house funds. But savers have become increasingly aware in recent years that one company's investment skills may not be good enough. This has led to a growing number of pension plans which offer access to external investment managers.

But you may feel this is not enough either. You may prefer the idea of being able to control your investments via a Sipp. With these policies an insurer or professional company will provide the pension wrapper but you or your adviser can decide on the investment policy. Investments permitted within a Sipp include shares, gilts, investment trusts, unit trusts and commercial property. From April 2006 it will also be possible to hold residential buy-to-let property which can be financed by borrowing up to 50% of the value of fund in the form of a mortgage. Do consult Section Three when you are considering your investment strategy for your pension.

The drawback of Sipps is they are often more expensive than ordinary personal or stakeholder pensions. There are setting up costs and the costs of buying and selling investments to consider. Unless you have the time and the expertise, you will also have to pay an investment adviser. All this probably adds another 1% to 1.5% a year to the cost, so you will need to be confident the investment performance you can achieve will be better than with an ordinary scheme.

Many people transfer existing pension funds into a self-invested scheme. The minimum recommended amount is £100,000 but even then, unless you are going to make full use of the investment powers, an ordinary pension offering a choice of external fund managers may be more cost efficient.

Reviewing your existing provision

One of the easiest mistakes to make with your retirement planning is to assume once you have contributed to a pension you can more or less forget about it. It's understandable though, since many people tend to end up with bits and pieces of pensions from periods with different employers and different pension plans, so they lose track of what their overall pension is actually worth.

Giving your pensions a regular healthcheck is vital. If you have not received statements from your current and past pension providers recently, contact them and ask for up-to-date projections of your likely benefits. This will help you to work out how much more you need to save.

If you have individual policies or AVCs/FSAVCs or have been a member of a company money purchase scheme where you could choose the investment funds, check their performance. Pension fund performance figures can be found in publications such as *Money Management* and *Investment, Life & Pensions Moneyfacts* (see Appendix). Transferring to another fund or provider could help to improve the returns on your pension.

If your previous pension company has closed its doors to new business and switched to a very conservative investment policy, this could be another reason to consider a switch to a provider with better investment prospects.

If you have a personal pension taken out before the introduction of stakeholder plans in April 2001, it is also important to check the charges. When charges on stakeholders were set at 1% a year, some companies brought the deductions on their old personal policies into line. But others did not. If you have an old-style higher charging contract, a switch to a different provider could save you money and boost your future returns.

However, no transfer should be carried out until you have evaluated any benefits you may be giving up, such as a guaranteed annuity rate or loyalty bonuses. There may also be exit penalties. If you feel out of your depth when it comes to reviewing your pension provision, seek professional advice. You may have to pay a fee but it could bring considerable rewards in the long run.

Trouble-shooting guide

Lost track of your past pensions?

When you near retirement, you should be contacted by any pension schemes to which you have belonged in the past and informed about your entitlements. But if you have moved house your old scheme may have lost contact with you, so you will need to get in touch with them.

However, tracking down old employers may not be easy if they have been taken over or gone out of business. If you find yourself in this position, contact the Pension Schemes Registry (0191 225 6316, www.opra.gov.uk). It should be able to provide up-to-date information about how you can contact your old scheme. In theory, the registry only covers scheme details available from April 1975, but it does cover some before then, so it is always worth a try.

Your employer wants to close the company scheme

In recent years, an increasing number of companies have faced problems meeting the costs of their final salary schemes. Widespread under-funding has come to light due to poor performing stock markets and increasing government regulation.

As a result, many companies have closed their schemes to new members and some have also decided existing members will not be able to build up further benefits. Alternatively, some have reached agreements whereby both employers and employees pay higher contributions to maintain benefits. But a few have decided to wind up altogether. Unfortunately, there is nothing employees can do to stop their employers doing these things.

Your company pension benefits are not what you expected

Your first step should be to use your scheme's internal disputes procedure. Write a letter to your pension manager setting out your complaint. Ask your human resources department for help if you are not sure who to contact. Keep a copy of the letter. You should receive an answer within two months. If you are not satisfied, take your complaint to the trustees of the scheme or, with public sector schemes, the appropriate government department. If they do not deal with it adequately, you can turn to the Office for the Pensions Advisory Service (0845 601 2923, www.opas.org.uk).

If Opas cannot deal with the matter and thinks you have a good case, it will pass your complaint to the Pensions Ombudsman. If the ombudsman decides in your favour, he can award compensation if appropriate. His decision is binding, though you or the pension scheme can appeal to the High Court on a point of law.

You have problems with your personal or stakeholder pension

Your first complaint must be to your pension company. For more details on making an effective complaint to a financial services organisation, see page 212. If you are not satisfied you can take the matter to the Financial Ombudsman Service.

Retirement

Planning for the big day

As you approach retirement, the first thing you need to do, money-wise, is to find out what your likely income will be once you stop working. Much of this ground has been covered earlier in the section, but here is a quick check list of what you will need to find out, and how to go about it. The first step towards this is to get a forecast of your state pension.

State pension

From April 2004, the full basic pension was £79.60 a week for a single person and £127.25 for a couple. But you won't necessarily qualify for the full sum. The amount of basic state pension you will receive is based, broadly, on the number of qualifying National Insurance contributions you have made, as an earlier part of this section outlined.

But to translate theory into practice, you need to get a personal forecast based on your contribution record. You need form BR19, available from local offices of the Department for Work and Pensions or from 0845 300 0168. You can also fill in the form on line at www.dwp.gov.uk. You can ask for the forecast at any time up to four months before your state retirement age. The forecast will include figures for your entitlement to all the various (past and present) state schemes as well as the basic scheme, including graduated retirement benefit (in force from 1961 to 1975) and the state earnings-related pension scheme (Serps) which was around from 1975 to 2002, as well as its successor, the state second pension (S2P).

Patchy record?

If the forecast shows your national insurance contribution record is patchy, meaning your basic state pension will be less than the maximum, it may not be too late to do something about it. In theory, you can pay extra sums now to fill up your record, but there is a time limit – you can only pay missed contributions for the previous six years.

Retiring early?

If you retire before state pension age, it may be sensible to pay voluntary contributions to protect your full entitlement to a pension. But men who retire after 60 (but before their state pension age of 65) will usually have their contributions automatically credited for this period. From April 2010, when the state pension age for women starts to exceed 60, this will apply to them as well.

Retiring late?

Currently if you retire after state pension age, you can defer your pension and in return it will be increased by roughly 7.5% for each year you wait, with pro rata increases for shorter periods (the minimum deferment is seven weeks).

From April 2005, under the new Pensions Bill proposals, people who retire late will be able to get a lump sum instead, with an interest rate of at least 2% above the Bank of England base rate. Typically, this will result in a lump sum of £30,000 for a man deferring an entitlement of £100 a week for five years. The government has said this sum will not affect eligibility for means-tested benefits such as the pension credit, but full details are not known as yet. The lump sum will be taxed at your marginal tax rate for the year you receive it and won't push you into a higher band. Alternatively, you can choose to take a higher pension: once the bill becomes law it will increase by 10.4% for each year of retirement.

Is it worth deferring the pension, either under the current rules or after April 2005? It's impossible to be categoric. If taking the pension means you are pushed into the 40% tax band, the answer may well be yes. If not, perhaps not, but it really depends on your circumstances.

Company and personal pensions

To find out how much pension you will get from a company scheme, speak to your pensions department. It should, in any case, have been keeping you informed on a regular basis.

All personal pensions are money purchase schemes, as are many company schemes. If you have this type of plan, which is also known as a defined contribution scheme, bear in mind any figures you get in advance of retirement will be estimates. The actual amount of pension depends on the value of your fund and annuity rates when you retire. If you want to make an educated guess, take the current value of your fund and look at current annuity rates (see the table on page 166). Hopefully, your fund will grow between now and the time you retire, but to be on the safe side, don't build in too high an assumption of future growth.

Choices on retirement

If you are a member of a final salary scheme, you don't have much of a choice. If you are in the private sector, you must decide whether or not to take the lump sum available on retirement or to go for an increased pension. If you are in the public sector, you don't usually have this option: you get a tax-free lump sum automatically alongside a pension.

For everyone else, there are a number of choices to be made which can be highly confusing. They are also extremely important because making the wrong decision can mess up your finances for the rest of your life. So take time to understand and consider your options, and be prepared to take financial advice to ensure you are getting the best possible deal.

People in company schemes have their hands tied to some extent, unless they transfer before retirement to a personal pension plan. Company schemes which are contracted-out of the state second pension (as most are) require part of the pension fund to be converted into an index-linked annuity, but there is a free choice with the rest. People with personal, self-employed or stakeholder schemes have a free hand over what to choose.

The new Pensions Bill and an associated Finance Bill propose important changes to these rules which are expected to come into force in either April 2005 or April 2006 and will apply to everyone retiring after that date.

Annuities

As the pension rules stand, anyone with a pension plan must, at some stage, convert this to income by buying an annuity. It does not have to be when you retire but must happen by the time you reach 75. In essence, this rule won't change after April 2006. There is also a minimum age: at present, you must be 50 or over before you can start taking an income from your pension fund. From 2010, this will increase to 55.

How annuities work

An annuity is an income guaranteed for life – however long that might be. You hand over a lump sum to an insurance company and it pays you the income. Die tomorrow, and you have lost all your capital. On the other hand, live to 110, and the insurance company is obliged to keep paying, even though 'your' money has long ago run out.

Insurance companies work out what rates to offer on annuities by making an educated guess as to how long their annuitants will, on average, live. There will be some who die early, some who live long, and what the insurers gain on the early deaths goes to subsidise the longer lived. Rates also depend on the interest the insurer can earn on your capital in the meantime. This means looking at long-term interest rates. Because annuity income is usually fixed at the outset, insurers must buy long-term gilts or bonds to be sure of getting the same income over the years. So if long-term interest rates fall, so will the level of annuity rates. At the same time, if it becomes evident people in general are living longer, annuity rates will also fall, as insurers face the prospect of paying out for longer.

Pension annuities are always taxed as earned income.

Buy now or later?

Unless you are already 75, you don't have to buy an annuity immediately on retirement. You can opt for an income drawdown scheme or phased retirement, both of which are described in detail below. But these options all entail some investment risk. If your pension is going to form the main part of your income in retirement and your funds are relatively limited, say £250,000 or less, most experts would encourage you to buy an annuity as soon as you retire.

The annuity choice: getting advice

If you have decided to buy an annuity, it is essential to get independent advice. You don't have to but you would be foolish not to. The pension company with whom you have built up your fund will always offer you its own annuity, but you are under no obligation to accept and you could well do better elsewhere.

Some people are put off the idea of getting advice because they know they will have to pay the adviser commission. But it's really a no-lose situation. If it turns out your original pension company does, in fact, provide the best rate, you can accept it and pay no commission. But if the rate is better elsewhere, you will benefit even once commission is taken into account. The difference between the best and worst rates on the market can be up to 10%, so that could mean 10% more income every year for the rest of your life, in exchange for a certain amount of legwork now.

Some advisers, incidentally, offer the choice of paying fees or commission. If your pension fund is large, say £300,000 or more, you may do better by paying a fee and enjoying an enhanced annuity rate.

One thing to check – which an adviser should do for you – is that any annuity quotations are on the same basis as the one offered by your original provider. If, for example, its rate is based on a joint life annuity payable until the second death, and your partner is five years younger than you, this should not be compared to a single life annuity from another company, based only on your own life.

Types of annuity

Annuity rates are based not just on your age at the time you buy but a number of other factors as well, and there are several decisions you will have to take.

Fixed or escalating

Annuities can be fixed at the outset, paying the same amount every year throughout your life. Or they can escalate, either at a fixed percentage each year or in line with the Retail Price Index.

A fixed annuity pays a higher sum initially, as the table on page 166 shows, but over the years its purchasing power will decrease. Even if the rate of inflation stays modest, say 2% a year, in ten years' time you will need £1.22 to buy the £1-worth of goods and services you can buy today; after 20 years, you will need nearly £1.50.

This need not be too much of a concern if you expect to have other sources of income or capital in the future, such as an inheritance or proceeds from downsizing on your property. Remember also any state pensions you will receive are index-linked, so this will help.

But the big argument in favour of a level annuity is that payments start off so much higher. A man of 65 could get £736 a year from a level annuity compared to £349 from one increasing at 5% a year. It would take 12 years until payments on the increasing annuity started to exceed those from the level annuity and 20 years until the total amount received was bigger. And if you throw in the fact that the level annuity man gets his income immediately and can invest some of it and earn interest, you're talking of a cross-over point even further away. Not a lot of people are going to be that patient, or that confident of surviving, to bother.

Joint or single life

If you are married or have a long-term partner, a joint life annuity is the most sensible choice. It will provide an income for them if you die first – with a single life annuity, the income stops when you die. You can choose a joint life pension where payments remain at the same level after your death or one where they decline by, say, a third or a half. You get a better rate if you choose one where the payments drop, but against this, of course, you must consider whether there would be enough income for your partner to live on.

Occasionally, there might be circumstances where it is sensible to take a single life annuity even if you are married. The main one is if you have a guaranteed annuity rate attached to your pension policy only for a single life pension. These guaranteed rates are often much higher than you could obtain on the open market today, so it could be worth going for and making alternative arrangements for your partner (see page 167).

With or without a guaranteed period

All annuity payments are guaranteed to last as long as you do, but if you (and your partner) died tomorrow, that is a lot of money down the drain. An annuity with a guaranteed period promises to continue paying the income for a set term, typically five or ten years from the outset, whether you live or die during that time. As the table shows, a five-year guaranteed period for standard annuities costs practically nothing, even at older ages, and is probably always worth taking. A ten-year guarantee is more pricey and is a harder call to make. If you're confident of making old bones, don't choose it.

Value protected

This option is not available at present but should be for anyone buying an annuity after April 2006. A value protected annuity will probably return the balance of any unused capital, up to age 75. As with the current guaranteed period options, value protection will cost money in terms of a lower annuity rate.

Payment frequency

You can choose to have your annuity paid monthly in advance, monthly in arrears or quarterly, half-yearly or yearly – again, either in advance or in arrears. Most people go for monthly payments either in advance or arrears. The longer you are prepared to wait, the higher the annuity will be. As a rough guide, payments made quarterly in arrears will be around 1.5% to 2% higher than those made monthly in advance. All the figures in the table over the page are for payments made monthly in advance.

With or without proportion

This feature relates only to annuities which are paid in arrears. If you die just before a payment is made, an annuity without proportion makes no payment. An annuity with proportion makes a part-payment of the amount due. If you choose an annuity payable annually in arrears, for example, it could be worth choosing one with proportion, although this means a very slightly lower rate.

Pension annuity rates for a purchase price of £10,000

Single life	Level, no guarantee	Level, 5 yr guarantee	Increasing at 5% a year*	RPI linked*
Man 60	£637	£634	£349	£429
Man 65	£736	£726	£443	£521
Man 70	£872	£850	£575	£652
Woman 60	£600	£597	£310	£388
Woman 65	£671	£667	£381	£463
Woman 70	£780	£768	£488	£568
Joint lives, including two-thirds widow's pension				
Man 60/Woman 55	£532	£532	£244	£336
Man 65/Woman 60	£586	£584	£297	£391
Man 70/Woman 65	£661	£656	£370	£464

All figures based on payments made monthly in advance.

*Without guaranteed period

Source: Investment, Life & Pensions Moneyfacts

Annuities for people in bad health

If you are not in the best of health, you should take advantage of this by choosing what is still rather ghoulishly known as an impaired life annuity. You are likely to be able to get a higher rate, and it is definitely worth getting advice before you choose. Each case is usually underwritten individually and you may have to have a medical. Higher rates are usually available for people with diabetes, liver impairment, certain heart conditions and cancer.

If you opt for a joint life pension, your partner's state of health will also influence the rates available.

Smokers

Regular smokers may also get better rates. If you have smoked at least ten cigarettes a day for the last ten years, you could qualify for higher rates. If you give up smoking once the annuity has been set up, the rate won't be cut.

Other special rate annuities

Manual workers living in various parts of the UK can also get better than average rates, as statistics have shown that they are likely to have a lower than average life expectancy.

Guaranteed annuity rates

As mentioned above, some pension companies in the past offered annuity rates that were guaranteed at the time you started the plan. These are in general much better than current rates, as they were set when interest rates were much higher.

Pension companies have done all they can to wriggle out of their obligations here – it was this that led to the well-publicised problems of Equitable Life – and where they cannot escape them, they make sure they stick very closely to the small print of their contract. Most guaranteed rates only apply to a single life pension and if you want a joint life pension instead, there will be no guarantee at all.

If you are in this position, get professional advice. It could still be worth taking the single life option and making alternative arrangements for your partner, such as a life insurance policy which will pay out on your death.

Investment-linked annuities

These are riskier than fixed-rate annuities because the amount payable depends partly on the investment performance of an underlying fund. That means payments might go down. On the other hand, if investment performance is good, it means they should rise over the years.

They are not a sensible idea for anyone with limited funds, because the risk is too great. But they can be very useful in other circumstances – for instance, if you have an AVC fund and already have a secure pension from an employer's scheme.

One annuity or several?

If you have a clutch of pension plans – as many people do – there is no reason why you should stick with one annuity. You could, if you liked, build up a portfolio of annuities – a fixed rate, level annuity for the bulk of your income, perhaps, with some going into an index-linked annuity and maybe an investment-linked one on top. The only limiting factor is the amount of money going into each annuity. Few pension companies are interested if you have less than, say, £20,000 in the fund, and you may well get a better rate for a higher purchase price.

How about the tax-free cash?

All pension plans allow their holders to take a tax-free cash sum from their fund on retirement. The rules on exactly how much you can take are in a state of flux, but the likelihood is that, from April 2006, almost everyone will be able to take 25% of their fund in cash, rather than buying an annuity with it.

You don't have to take the cash, but should you? If you do, of course, your annuity will be that much lower. But most people choose to take the cash, though hardly for financial reasons. It represents their ticket on a world cruise, their trip to see the grandchildren in Australia or maybe their new dream kitchen.

Even if you wanted to make your decision on a strictly financial basis, you should probably take the cash. Die tomorrow and the money that has gone to buy your annuity is lost for ever. At least if you took the cash, there would be something to leave your heirs. Then again, the cash could be used to pay off debts – the rump of the mortgage, for instance, or credit card balances, saving you far more in interest than the loss of the extra annuity would represent.

But suppose you are going to need every penny from your pension fund to produce a reasonable income? Even in these circumstances, it's worth taking the cash and using it to buy an ordinary life annuity instead. The reason is to do with a little known tax wrinkle. With an ordinary annuity, part of each annual payment counts as 'return of capital' in the eyes of the taxman, which means it is tax-free. Pension annuities, on the other hand, are all taxed as earned income.

As the following example shows, you can be better off, after tax, by taking the cash and buying an ordinary annuity. This is the case even though the rates on ordinary annuities are usually lower than pension annuities – the reason for that is that they tend to be bought by longer-lived people.

> Robert has a pension fund of £100,000. He is 65 and single. The £100,000 would buy him a pension annuity paying £7,336 a year gross, £5,722 net of tax. If he takes £25,000 as cash, the remaining £75,000 buys a pension annuity paying £4,292 net, while the £25,000 buys an ordinary annuity paying £1,631 net. Overall, then, he will get £5,722 net per year if he uses the whole fund to buy a pension annuity, but £5,923 net per year if he takes the cash and buys an ordinary annuity.

Alternatives to annuities

As long as you are under 75 when you retire, you don't have to buy an annuity straight away. But if you need income from your fund, what are the options? There are basically two: a phased retirement arrangement or an income drawdown scheme. Or to be really sophisticated, you can do a combination of the two.

Phased retirement

This is the fancy name for something that plenty of self-employed people have been doing, in an informal way, for years. Instead of retiring overnight, and turning their pension fund into an annuity all in one go, they wind down gradually from work and phase in their various pension policies over a number of years, turning some into annuities, keeping some in reserve for later. As their income from work decreases, they gradually jack up the amount they get paid as pension.

This, of course, assumes they have more than one policy. In fact, nearly everyone does, whether they are aware of it or not. These days, single policies are segmented into hundreds of tiny parts, so you can fine-tune the phasing. One way of doing it is to use the tax-free cash entitlement from each segment as part of your 'income' for that year. The table shows how this could work.

Phased retirement in practice

Pension fund: £300,000. Target yearly income: £20,000

Age	Starting fund	Amount encashed	Tax-free cash	Annuity payment	Total income	Remaining fund
60	£300,000	£65,400	£16,350	£3,650	£20,000	£235,000
61	£235,000	£52,100	£13,000	£7,000	£20,000	£192,000
62	£192,000	£41,600	£10,400	£9,600	£20,000	£160,000
63	£160,000	£32,900	£8,230	£11,770	£20,000	£135,000
64	£135,000	£25,700	£6,440	£13,560	£20,000	£116,000
and so on until…						
73	£81,700	£2,510	£628	£19,370	£19,998	£84,300
74	£84,300	£1,330	£334	£19,600	£19,934	£88,300
75	£88,300*					

*This will provide tax-free cash of £22,075 plus an additional pension of £8,650 a year alongside the continuing pension of £19,600.

The table assumes level annuity payments and annual growth at 7% on investments remaining within the fund. If they grew more slowly, income would diminish with age. Remember, each year's annuity payments are added to those being made from the annuities started up in earlier years. Income payments are shown before tax.

Note: This particular scheme involves a big leap in income from age 75. It would be possible, by cashing in more segments in the earlier years, to have a smoother progression, but the thinking behind it is to build in a bit of a safety net in case investments do not grow steadily at the 7% forecast. This is a very sensible precaution, because there can be no guarantees.
Source: Clerical Medical

Why phased retirement is a good idea...

Phasing your retirement gets over one of the big investment risks connected with turning your pension fund into an annuity all in one go. Many pension funds are invested wholly, or largely, in equities. If you have the bad luck to retire at a time when stock markets have just crashed, your annuity income will likewise crash from what you were expecting, when your fund value was higher. But stock markets usually recover, in time, so if you can afford to wait until your fund value recovers, you will be better off.

There is another way round this problem, which is to switch your pension fund in the run up to retirement to something safe such as a cash fund. But realistically, to avoid investment risk successfully, you would have to do this in stages over the last five to ten years of your working life, and while it might be safe, you could well miss out on growth.

Phased retirement has another advantage, too, in that if you die in the middle of your phasing, the value of the pension fund which has not yet been turned into an annuity can be left to your heirs. With annuities, remember, there is no capital returned on death.

And why it isn't...

The disadvantages of phased retirement boil down to investment risk once again. Your pension fund might grow during the years while it stays invested, before it has been turned into an annuity – then again, it might not. In this respect, the table could lull you into a false sense of security. It blithely assumes your investments are going to grow at a steady 7% a year. So take it with a pinch of salt.

There are two other considerations that might put you off a phased retirement programme. The first is that, if you arrange it so you are using regular segments of tax-free cash to bump up your income each year, there may never be a point at which you get your hands on a big lump sum. So it may mean goodbye to the world trip you had promised yourself.

The second reason is the phenomenon of 'mortality drag' in relation to annuities, which is described in detail in the section on income drawdown. In essence, this means that, after a certain age, the longer you leave your pension fund invested, and put off buying an annuity, the faster your fund must grow in order to match the return you would otherwise get from buying an annuity.

And the conclusion is...

Some form of phased arrangement makes excellent sense if it dovetails into your working pattern: if you are phasing out work as you phase in retirement. But if you plan to retire completely and never earn a penny again, think carefully before going for this rather than a straightforward annuity. If you have plenty of money in your fund, and maybe capital elsewhere, you can probably afford to take the investment risk involved and it could well be to your benefit. But if you're on a tight budget, an annuity may be best all round.

Income drawdown plans

These schemes once again allow you to delay purchasing an annuity. Instead, you simply draw a regular income from your pension fund. There are rules on how much and how little you can withdraw, and you can vary it within these limits from year to year. If you want to take the cash lump sum allowed under your pension rules, you must do this as soon as your drawdown scheme comes into operation.

Minimum and maximum income limits

These limits are set by the Government Actuary currently at three yearly intervals. They are set with reference to your age and gender. The maximum is, roughly, equivalent to what a single life annuity would produce for someone of your age, given the value of your fund. The minimum is 35% of the maximum. Once you start the drawdown, you cannot suspend it – you must take at least the minimum each year.

From April 2006, these rules will change and provide more flexibility: limits will be set every five years rather than three, and the minimum and maximum will also be changed. The maximum will be 120% of a single life annuity for a person of your age, the minimum just £1 a year. It might seem pointless to start up your pension if you're only going to take £1 a year, but the point is you can access the 25% tax-free cash at this time.

Why income drawdown is a good idea...

There are two big pluses to the scheme. The first is that, during the period it is in operation, your pension fund can remain invested and so, hopefully, benefit from investment growth. The second – which makes the plans highly attractive to many people – is the fact that, as with phased retirement, you still have some control over the capital.

If you die before turning the fund into an annuity (which must be done by age 75) the balance remaining can be returned to your heirs, less a tax charge, currently 35%. If you have a surviving spouse, the income withdrawal can remain in place until he or she reaches 75 or you would have reached 75, if that is earlier. From April 2006 this rule will be amended slightly so it can always be put off until the survivor reaches 75, even if this is later than you would have done. Alternatively, the remaining fund can be turned into an annuity straight away.

And why it isn't...

Once again, there is the flip side of the coin: keeping your pension fund invested may mean investment growth, but it could also mean loss. If the fund has fallen in value at the reassessment point after three or five years, the maximum amount of income you can withdraw will fall, too. And there can be a 'double whammy' effect. Over the last few years, the trend has been for annuity rates to fall. This is partly down to the fact long-term interest rates have fallen, but it is also because people have been living longer. So when the Government Actuary's limits are revised, you may find you can only take out a lower percentage of a smaller fund.

This double whammy has hit quite a number of drawdown planholders over the last few years. It is fair to say they have been exceptionally unlucky, as their plans have had to cope not just with a falling stock market, but a period when annuity rates have dropped markedly.

Because the Government Actuary's limits are set with reference to your actual age every three years, you would normally expect them to rise as time goes by because annuity rates increase with age. But the overall drop in annuity rates in recent years has more than cancelled this out.

Is this likely to be the case in the future? The answer is probably not. Long-term interest rates are unlikely to fall much from current levels in the near future and we are probably nearing the end of big adjustments made to annuity rates because of increasing longevity. But just store that thought away at the back of your mind.

Then there is the effect of mortality drag. The later you put off buying an annuity, the more the level of income you get is cross-subsidised by people in your age group dying off. By age 70, this is quite significant, which means your pension fund would have to grow that much faster each year to be worthwhile delaying purchase of the annuity. In other words, the longer you keep income drawdown going, the bigger the investment risk you are taking, which for most people is not really sensible.

And the conclusion is...

Drawdown plans are not for someone on a tight budget. The administrative charges involved make it uneconomic for anyone with less than around £200,000 in their fund. And if this is all you've got to provide your income – if you have no earned income from other sources, and no other savings or investments – they are still probably not for you: you cannot take the risk.

So who do they suit? Richer people, for a start, and especially those who have other sources of income, perhaps from part-time consultancy work after retirement. The flexibility of being able to vary the amounts you withdraw each year can be extremely useful here. And if you are retiring early, in your mid to late 50s, for example, an income drawdown plan, like phased retirement, can give you many years of potential investment growth.

Finally, if you're going to kick the bucket well before age 75, income drawdown – like phased retirement – is a good idea, as you will be able to leave some capital behind to heirs. But bear in mind that, unless you have specific health problems, the likelihood is you will live longer. A man of 65 has, these days, a two-thirds chance of reaching age 81.

Post April 2006: one more option

There will be a new scheme which the government has called 'alternatively secured income' which allows people to continue with income drawdown after that all-important age of 75. But it is hardly attractive for most people. It has been devised, according to the government, to meet the objections of people who see annuities as a gamble and hence unacceptable to their religious beliefs.

Under the proposed rules, planholders will be able to withdraw a maximum of 70% of a single life annuity rate calculated at age 75 and this maximum will never be raised, however long you live. Once you die, if you have a dependant, they can either buy an annuity with the balance of the cash or continue income drawdown with the same limits. If you don't have a dependant, no cash is returned to your estate, but the Revenue is considering allowing you to leave it to charity rather than have it swell the pension company's coffers.

Getting advice

Phased retirement and income drawdown are neither very straightforward schemes. They may seem so but the implications of the way they work need some thought and reflection. Do, please, get independent professional advice before embarking on either.

There are further refinements – you can go for a drawdown scheme combined with a phased arrangement – and you may be advised to transfer the funds to a self-invested personal pension (Sipp) before embarking on the scheme. A Sipp basically gives you the ability to move your invested funds from one manager to another if the first is not performing well or to have a number of different managers looking after different parts of the fund.

Pre-retirement planning courses

There is more to retirement than finance, of course. A number of colleges and adult education centres run pre-retirement courses, and many large companies run their own or buy places for employees on commercially-run courses. Typically, they include advice on leisure, relationships and health as well as finance.

The Pre-Retirement Association, a charity, runs two-day courses for groups and individuals. The current cost is around £300 plus Vat for one person, £400 plus Vat for a couple. See Appendix for contact details.

Investing after retirement

There is no particular investment which comes with a neat tag attached saying 'retirees only'. Nevertheless, for most people retirement marks the biggest change to their lifestyle since they left school or university maybe 40 years before.

Their 'big picture' is going to change – and their investment outlook and strategy should adapt at the same time.

Don't rush it

Investing in haste has certainly led an awful lot of people to repent in their new-found leisure. In recent years there have been horror stories such as precipice bonds, marketed largely at retired people looking for a high fixed income to eke out their pensions. They turned out to be highly unsafe and succeeded in losing pensioners most of their capital.

Once they have retired, almost everyone needs to lower their risk tolerance a notch or two. When you have an earned income coming in regularly, you can afford to ride out ups and downs in the stock market. You are probably not spending the income produced from your investments and may, indeed, have deliberately gone for investments that produce little or no income, for the sake of tax efficiency. But after retirement, there is an about turn. You will be looking to your capital to start earning its keep by providing you regular, spendable income.

Asset allocation in retirement

So how should you spread your investments to meet your post-retirement needs? Take time to stand back and look at your new big picture. The first thing to do is consider your new sources of income. Your pension will be replacing your earnings as the mainstay of your financial life from now on.

Stocktaking for inflation

Inflation may be minimal but it can still pack a serious punch given enough time. Suppose you are retiring at 60 and it remains at the apparently negligible rate of 2% for the rest of your life. Every £100 you have now will be worth only £82.03 in real terms by the time you reach 70 and only £67.30 when you hit 80. And there are some unavoidable expenses – council tax springs to mind – which have shown a distinct tendency to rise by far in excess of inflation.

So the first thing to do in planning your new investment strategy is take a close look at your sources of income. All state pensions and civil service pensions are guaranteed to rise fully in line with the Retail Price Index. Many company schemes also provide index-linked pensions at least to some extent. People with money purchase pension schemes may have a mixture and employees may have part of their pension index-linked. However, if you have only personal pensions, the likelihood is you have opted for a level pension with no index linking.

Spreading the risk

The extent to which your pension income is inflation-proof is a key factor in how you should balance the rest of your investments. Broadly speaking, you have a choice, between financial assets, which pay interest on the capital invested, and real assets, such as company shares and property, where your money is invested in something tangible – bricks and mortar or factories, offices and people working at producing goods and services other people are going to buy.

Only real assets are capable of producing an income which has the potential to rise, long term, along with inflation and the growth in the economy generally. And it's worth remembering that the growth in earnings has, for most of the last century, outpaced the rise in prices. Even if your pension is fully index-linked, it is tied to prices. Although, in price terms, your income will remain at the same real level, so you won't actually get poorer as the years go by, you may feel poorer, as you lag behind the buying power of the majority of the population. It may only be a feeling, but going by the reactions of many pensioners, it's a very real one.

But what proportion of your money should you invest in real assets and how much in financial assets? This is the archetypal how long is a piece of string question. The answer will depend on your particular circumstances.

The great dilemma for the retiring investor is that while financial assets – cash deposits and fixed-rate securities – generally provide a higher starting yield and greater capital security, they cannot produce that all-important growth in income.

On the one hand, you may think: 'I'm retired now, so I cannot afford to risk my capital.' On the other hand, you should equally think: 'I'm retired so I cannot afford to risk my income.' Investing solely in cash, for example, while it means your capital is secure, also means you are risking your income. Interest rates can go up and down, and no one knows what the trend will be over the next ten or 20 years.

If base rates rise by 1% from their current level (4.25% at time of writing), that's great news: your deposit interest will also increase. If it rises in line with base rates, your gross income will go up by almost 25%. But if subsequently rates fall from 5.25% to 3.5%, your income will drop by a third. Investing in cash, in short, means tying your income levels to an unpredictable roller-coaster.

The only sensible thing to do is to have a mixture of financial and real assets in your post-retirement portfolio. But the balance must depend on your situation.

Real assets

Equities

Investing in shares is the classic way of getting a growing income over the years. In theory, share dividends should rise at least in line with inflation. It doesn't always work and your capital is not secure. The shares themselves may rise or fall in value along with the outlook for the stock market in general and its view of individual companies in particular. Nevertheless, at least in the past, company dividends have, over the long term, risen reasonably steadily.

Unless you have large amounts to invest, or a personal interest in managing your money, an equity income unit trust or its modern equivalent, an open-ended investment company (Oeic), is the simplest choice.

There are many funds which specialise in providing equity income. Most of them make income distributions twice yearly, although a few pay monthly. Alternatively, you can ask an adviser to put together a mini portfolio of income funds with different distribution dates, so you get payments made quarterly, for example.

The table below gives an example of the income and capital record of a typical UK equity income trust over the past ten years. This is clearly not an investment for someone who can't sleep at night unless their capital is 100% secure, but if the object is to provide a regular income which by and large should grow over the years, it may be you need not worry too much about what happens to the capital value.

As the table shows, investing in a deposit account with a building society, for example, is likely to produce a higher income immediately, but the level of income received is at the mercy of interest rates in general, which none of us can predict.

Investing for income

£1,000 invested on 31 December, 1993

Date	Equity income unit trust Capital value at end of year	Net income for year	Building society Net income for year
1994	£845	£32	£40
1995	£982	£34	£42
1996	£1,022	£37	£36
1997	£1,207	£42	£42
1998	£1,204	£44	£51
1999	£1,267	£47	£40
2000	£1,321	£48	£43
2001	£1,166	£46	£39
2002	£ 918	£46	£30
2003	£1,066	£44	£27

Capital value is shown after initial charges. Income figures are net of basic rate tax. If you had invested at the launch of the fund in 1964, income in 2003 would have amounted to £792 net of basic rate tax per £1,000 originally invested.
Source: M&G Dividend Fund

In any case, shares in companies which provide decent long-term dividends have shown themselves pretty resilient as regards their capital value. While there was a fashion for high growth companies in the boom years of the 1990s, which paid little or no income, there has been something of a return to basics in the past few years. Ultimately, investors value shares for the income they produce. And if the income rises, you can be pretty sure that, over the long term, the capital value will rise as well.

Most equity income funds pay a relatively low starting yield – probably around 3.5%. If yields are much greater than this, it may well be because the fund includes an element of fixed-interest investments, which offer a higher initial yield but no prospects for growth. Always look beyond the name of the fund to find out what it is invested in.

Buy-to-let property

Property is the only other real asset which can be expected to produce long-term growing income, as rental levels should rise along with earnings inflation. It is understandable many people see buy-to-let property as a good alternative to pensions for providing an income in retirement. But there are risks. See pages 57-58 on buy-to-let mortgages in Section Two for more details.

Financial assets

Fixed-interest securities

Gilts, corporate bonds and permanent interest bearing shares (Pibs) are all examples of fixed-interest securities which you can buy through a stockbroker, or in the case of gilts, direct from the Bank of England as well. They are all long-term debt, issued either by the government (gilts), commercial companies (corporate bonds) or building societies (Pibs). If you buy and hold them until their redemption date, their capital value is fixed – assuming, of course, the issuing institution does not go bust in the meantime.

But they can also be traded on the stock market, and their price varies according to the general outlook for interest rates. If rates are going up, the value of your holdings will fall, because the fixed rate of interest you are getting will look less attractive.

In the case of gilts and especially corporate bonds, you can buy through unit trusts and Oeics. The starting yield will be a good bit higher than on equity income funds – typically 4% to 7%, at present, depending on the average credit ratings of the companies whose bonds are in the portfolio. Many investment managers offer two bond funds, one investing in those issued by the best rated, most solid companies and one in more risky companies. The higher the yield, the riskier the fund and the more volatile its price is likely to be.

If you want to invest in corporate bonds, don't choose just according to the yield: higher does not necessarily mean better. Look also at the average credit rating of the bonds. Most managers have strict criteria. Their lower yielding bond fund, for example, may restrict investment to securities which are rated double A or above, while their higher yielding fund may go down to companies rated a single B – this information should be readily provided. The simplest way of making sure you are not taking too big a risk is to split your cash between at least one of each type of fund.

Permanent interest bearing shares

These are a relatively little known investment but could be extremely useful for someone trying to squeeze a bit extra from their retirement portfolio. They are fixed-interest securities issued by a number of building societies and ex-building societies such as the Halifax (those from the latter are now called 'permanent subordinated loans'). Because the issues are relatively small in size and few in number, they don't particularly interest the institutional market and there are no pooled funds investing solely in Pibs – you will have to buy them, through a stockbroker, individually.

Pibs and PSLs are currently yielding between about 6.5% and 7%, depending on the institution and the minimum investment size, as well as its credit rating. A few have a minimum investment of well over £50,000 but there are also a number with a minimum of little more than £1,000.

The interest rate looks excellent compared to cash deposits, but there is a catch: the capital is not secure. If the bank or building society goes bust, there is no safety net, as there is with cash deposits – you would simply lose all your money. It is an unlikely scenario but needs emphasising all the same.

The other point to bear in mind is that they are 'permanent' – there is no redemption date on which you are promised the full return of your capital. If you want to realise your investment, you must take pot luck in the market. If interest rates have risen since you invested, you are likely to get back less than you paid.

Using your old Peps and Isas

Many people coming up to retirement will have personal equity plans (Peps) and individual savings accounts (Isas) tucked away. They may well be in funds that no longer meet their needs, invested, say, in risky growth funds providing little income. But don't just cash them in. For the next few years, at any rate, these plans still offer a useful tax shelter. Since April 2004 there has been no income tax advantage for basic rate taxpayers in holding ordinary shares within a Pep or Isa. But until April 2009, at least, income from fixed-interest securities such as corporate bonds and Pibs will still be tax-free if held in a Pep or Isa.

There are limits on the amount of new money you can invest in an Isa each year – a maximum £7,000 in the 2004-5 tax year and £5,000 after that – but you can shift around the investments in your old Pep and Isa plans. If you have used your Pep and Isa allowances each year since they started, you might well have £50,000 or £100,000 within the plans, which is an extremely useful size of tax shelter. But you'll lose it if you simply ask to cash in your existing plans; you must request a transfer to another Pep and Isa fund or provider instead.

There's another tax plus if you have been using Peps and Isas regularly over the years. Normally, when you sell an investment, any capital gains must be calculated and, if they total more than the annual exempt allowance, be declared and taxed. Investments in Peps and Isas, however, are CGT-free.

Given the way the stock market has behaved over the past five years, you may think this is not much to write home about – most people who invested five years ago or so are still showing a loss. But if you've been a longer term investor, you would still have to do the calculation. And given the fiendish complexity of the CGT rules (explained in more detail in Section Six), the mere fact you won't have to bother with this is a big plus point.

Cash deposits

Everyone needs cash deposits for short-term spending and emergencies, and retired people are probably going to feel more comfortable if they have an extra layer of cash tucked away, producing regular income.

You should have two mottoes as an investor in cash. Number one: shop around. And number two: beware the taxman. We have all seen how building societies and banks launch new accounts with loud fanfares at great rates – and how, funnily enough, those great rates have become positively pathetic a few years down the line. If you don't watch it like a hawk, you could find yourself – not to put too fine a point on it – being well and truly done.

Section One in this book goes into detail about the various types of cash deposit on offer. If you cannot bear the thought of checking savings rates obsessively every week after your retirement do, at least, make a resolution to check out the competition once a year and move your money if you find better rates elsewhere.

Tax and your savings

The other major point to bear in mind is your tax position. You don't have to be super rich as a pensioner to be hit with an effective marginal income tax rate well above basic rate tax. This is because anyone over the age of 65 is entitled to a higher personal allowance (the amount of income you can get tax-free before income tax starts to bite). Basically, if your total income is somewhere between about £18,900 and about £27,000, this extra allowance is withdrawn at the rate of £1 for every £2 of taxable income you receive above the limit.

In this context, the order in which your various sources of income are taxed is very important. The basic state pension comes first, being set against your personal allowance; then come your other pensions, and last of all, the 'top slice' of your income, is investment income – interest and dividends. So it is the interest and dividends which will suffer this higher rate.

Avoiding the age allowance trap

If you are in this position, it is worth giving some thought to your investment plans. National Savings Certificates, for example, do not usually pay very attractive rates of interest but they are tax-free, so the interest will not affect your age allowance.

Guaranteed income bonds

These are another useful investment for retired people. Issued by life assurers, guaranteed income bonds (GIBs) are limited offers and have fixed terms of typically two to five years. They are not much good for non-taxpayers, as basic rate tax cannot be reclaimed, but they are good for basic and higher rate payers.

Rates are generally slightly ahead of what you can get on a normal bank or building society account. Because they are fixed, bear in mind you could win or lose over the term, depending on how interest rates move. Current bond issues may be quoted in the savings rates tables in national newspapers. Independent financial advisers sometimes offer special deals to attract custom by throwing in a portion of their commission.

The name's bond...

The key point about GIBs is they are guaranteed, both as regards capital and interest. But there are a lot of products out there which look like guaranteed income bonds but which are very different beasts. This is one of the bugbears of the whole financial market – the confusion of names. We have premium bonds, corporate bonds, guaranteed income bonds, managed bonds, with-profits bonds and high income bonds, to name a few. To people within the industry, it's obvious these represent completely different investments with very different risk profiles.

But how can an outsider be sure? It's not easy. If you're tempted to invest in anything called a bond, especially one which has a high figure followed by a % sign, be on your guard. You need to ask: is my capital guaranteed? Does its value depend in any way on the future performance of the stock market? Unless you can get an unequivocal yes to the first question and an equally plain no to the second, you are going to have to dive into the small print to find out exactly what's going on. And ideally, get independent advice before parting with your money.

Investing in the later years of retirement

When my father reached his early 80s, he decided that he could not be classed as a long-term investor any more. There does come a point at which talk of long-term growth potential ceases to have an appeal, while immediate rewards begin to appear a good deal more attractive and a rebalancing of your portfolio may be in order.

Little by little

Once again, there is no point rushing, which could lead to a capital gains tax bill if you decided to sell all your shares in one go. The principle of little by little makes a great deal of sense from two angles. First, investment: unless you are that mythical being who can accurately call the top of the stock market, dis-investing over a number of years will spread the risk that you get the timing wrong.

The second reason is tax. At this stage in life, there are two taxes that loom large in anyone's life: capital gains tax and, even more, inheritance tax. The nil-rate band for inheritance tax (IHT) is just £263,000 in the 2004-5 tax year – a figure which is easily swallowed up (and more) by the value of many people's houses. As the section on tax shows, there are some schemes that may succeed in mitigating IHT but they are expensive and fraught with difficulty, as no one can be certain they will still work at the time of your death.

The simplest way of cutting down IHT is to make use of the annual exemptions and the rules on lifetime gifts, just as the simplest way of escaping CGT is to use the annual exemption from that tax.

Giving away capital during your lifetime has one big drawback – how do you make sure you are leaving yourself enough to live on? This is where a shift from real assets to financial assets can help. The immediate returns from cash deposits and fixed-interest securities are higher than from equities, so making the switch should bring you in a greater amount of income, hence allowing you to give away some capital.

Two schemes in particular can push up your income and take a swipe at IHT at the same time. They may not necessarily appeal to you – but keep the thought in the back of your mind. The first is an annuity. The second is some form of equity release.

Ordinary annuities

These have been described earlier in this section. In brief, they provide a guaranteed income for life, however long that may be, in exchange for a capital payment up front. Unlike pension annuities, no one has to buy them and they are only partly taxed, as the remainder of each payment consists of 'return of capital' and so is tax-free.

They do, however, have the disadvantage that if you died shortly after taking one out, you would lose the capital, which cannot be returned to your estate. But looking at it from the angle of IHT, this is not quite as bad as it seems. After your death, assuming the value of your house uses up the nil-rate band, 40% of any remaining capital you leave would be swallowed by IHT anyway. The table over the page shows typical annuity rates at various ages.

Ordinary annuities

Typical annual rates for a purchase price of £10,000 with level payments, guaranteed five years, paid gross

Man 65	£692
Man 70	£816
Man 75	£978
Woman 65	£609
Woman 70	£718
Woman 75	£867
Man 65/Woman 60	£485
Man 70/Woman 65	£559
Man 75/Woman 70	£619

Source: Investment, Life & Pensions Moneyfacts

You can find out rates by looking at *Investment, Life & Pensions Moneyfacts*, a monthly publication, but it is worth getting independent advice to ensure you get the best rate on offer at the time you buy.

A variation on ordinary annuities is an immediate care annuity. These are designed specifically for people about to enter a residential home. Fees are currently between about £400 and £700 a week, and can eat up someone's remaining capital at an alarming rate.

The extra advantage of an immediate care annuity is that the income is paid direct to the home itself and, because of this, is not taxed. If you're thinking of buying one, either for yourself or for a parent or other elderly relative, get independent advice and be prepared to shop around. Only a few life companies provide them and the rate offered will depend on the individual's medical condition and on the assessment, by each company's underwriter, of those medical facts. As that is a matter of judgment, you could find one company offers a good bit more than another.

Equity release

Read pages 55-57 in the borrowing section to find out about equity release schemes, which allow you to take out some of the capital from your home while keeping the right to live there.

There's no doubt such schemes can be useful for older homeowners who want to get at the capital tied up in their property without the bother and maybe heartbreak of leaving their home. But they are not perfect. Although they may look as if they let you have your cake and eat it too, in reality, it doesn't work like that. Here's a basic calculation to illustrate the point.

> Anne, who is 75, has a house worth £200,000. She decides she wants to release the capital tied up in her home. But the most she can take, at her age, may be £80,000. If she dies ten years later, the debt, which is growing at a fixed interest rate of 7% a year, will have almost doubled, to £157,372. If she carries on until 90, it will have climbed to £220,723.

Presumably, the value of the house in this example will also have risen, but anyone taking out such a plan should not, in any case, have to worry about leaving a debt to their heirs, as such schemes generally include a guarantee that there will be no negative equity – in other words, the value of the loan plus rolled up interest will never exceed the current value of the property. But this calculation may make people think twice before taking one out.

On the other hand, looking on the bright side, if you release capital in this way it may mean you can carry out essential repairs to your house, thus protecting and probably enhancing its value – or perhaps it will allow you to adapt your home to allow wheelchair access, for instance, or to pay for care while staying there, saving on residential home fees.

As with many financial products, the key is to think it through before you decide. On the plus side, you get money when you need it and there could well be a saving in inheritance tax for your heirs. On the minus side, such schemes are quite costly and you may lose out on some means-tested state benefits you could otherwise claim.

Ultimately, your decision cannot be based purely on financial issues – there are simply too many imponderables. It's your life and your house – it all depends on what you want to do.

Trouble-shooting guide

Most of the potential problems facing people deciding how to invest in their retirement are no different from those for people at other stages in their lives. The main difference – although you may not welcome me saying so – is you have more time than the rest of us for sorting out your problems. This may not be how you planned to spend the longest holiday of your life but you might, perhaps, approach it by saying: 'I had a good income in exchange for a full working week before I retired. Now I've given up employment, it's not such a bad bargain to have to work, if only for an hour or two a week, to ensure my finances are in proper order.'

If you do have financial problems, the Financial Ombudsman Service is likely to be your main port of call. It covers the sale of all managed investments, including personal and stakeholder pensions and annuities. Problems with a company pension scheme will be dealt with initially by the Office for the Pensions Advisory Service (Opas) and failing resolution there, the Pensions Ombudsman. Opas may also cover the management, as opposed to the sale, of personal pension schemes. If you have a problem which seems to straddle the two, just ask and you will be directed to the right place. See Appendix for contact details.

6

Tax and Tax Planning

In this section we will look at

The ground rules for tax planning

Tax deadlines

Minimising the tax you pay

Tax-efficient investments

Capital gains tax

Inheritance tax

Wills

Tax allowances

6

Tax and Tax Planning

This section will take you on a quick tour of taxation. It's not the jolliest of subjects, but it is rather more cheerful than the consequences of ignoring it, either in your earning life or as regards your investments. It looks at:

◆ **The ground rules for tax planning** The dos and don'ts for a stress-free life.

◆ **Tax timing** When you have to cough up and the consequences if you don't.

◆ **The basic rules of income, capital gains and inheritance taxes** These are the big three for individuals.

◆ **How to plan your investments in the most tax-efficient manner** A must for everyone, even millionaires.

If you think the tax system has got a great deal more complicated in the past few years, it's not your imagination: it has. 'Stealth taxes', and for that matter 'stealth tax credits', have mushroomed over the years of the Labour government, although to be fair, the Tories in their day were not averse to a bit of stealth either.

But it was Labour's pledge not to increase income tax rates that has forced it to find other, more hidden, ways of increasing revenue, while its determination to help the poorer sections of the community has led to a proliferation of means-tested tax and savings credits so complicated even accountants sometimes find them hard to grasp, let alone old age pensioners trying to work out if they qualify for the pension credit.

This is not specifically a tax handbook, and if you want detailed information you will need one of those – or to read the appropriate leaflets and booklets from the Inland Revenue. They can be downloaded from www.inlandrevenue.gov.uk or you can get hard copies at local tax offices. If you are seriously rich and have complicated affairs, you would do best to employ a specialist firm of accountants.

Tax planning

There are some reasonably simple steps anyone can take to minimise their tax liability. Remember we're talking about tax avoidance – that is, sensible steps to cut down, quite legally, the amount you pay. Tax evasion is illegal. Sometimes it's quite blatant – some people don't declare all their income or conveniently forget their gains, work for cash or put their money in offshore accounts and don't mention the interest they earn. Sometimes it's not – people may enter into a tax-planning scheme, in good faith on the advice of an accountant, which subsequently turns out not to work the way it is supposed to.

There's no doubt something of a game goes on between accountants and the Revenue. Accountants spend their time finding loopholes and the taxmen scurry after them trying to plug each one as they discover it. The 2004 Budget took things a step further when it announced that in future, accountants will have to register new schemes with the Revenue, giving the taxmen a head start in plugging the gaps.

A few ground rules to get you started

◆ Try to keep your financial affairs in good order, so you won't miss tax paying deadlines and incur penalties and interest.

◆ Claim everything you're entitled to, but don't get caught out by forgetting to declare income received or gains made.

◆ Don't go to ridiculous lengths to avoid tax. Emigrating may save you tax, for instance, but if you're unhappy in your new home, there's not much point.

◆ Don't jeopardise your financial security by trying to save tax. For example, you may save inheritance tax by giving away most of your assets during your lifetime, but this is not necessarily a wise move.

◆ Don't let the tax tail wag the investment dog by choosing products solely because of their supposed tax efficiency. You might be better off at the end of the day choosing a product that involves paying a little tax. If you really want to save tax, keep all your money under the mattress and spend it bit by bit. There would be no income or capital gains tax to pay, but you'd be daft, all the same.

◆ Try to keep things flexible. Tax laws may change in ways we cannot currently imagine and so might your circumstances.

Tax deadlines

Thousands of people waste money every year by failing to get their tax return in on time and having to pay penalties and interest on late tax. These are the key dates:

Filing tax returns

◆ **30 September** Deadline for filing a completed paper tax return for the previous year, if you want the Revenue to calculate the tax due.

◆ **30 September** Deadline if you want any tax you owe (up to £2,000) included in next year's tax code.

◆ **5 October** Deadline for letting the Revenue know if you need a tax return for the previous year and have not been sent one. It is your responsibility to ask for one.

◆ **30 December** Deadline if you are filing online and want any tax you owe (up to £2,000) included in next year's tax code. Filing this way means the tax is automatically calculated for you.

◆ **31 January** Deadline for filing your tax return for the previous year, if you make the tax calculation yourself.

Paying tax

◆ **31 January** Deadline for paying 50% of previous year's income tax, less tax deducted at source.

◆ **Following 31 July** Deadline for paying the other 50% of income tax, less tax deducted at source.

Penalties for late filing and interest on late payments

There is a £100 penalty if the return is not received by 31 January and an additional £100 if it is still not received by 31 July. Interest on late payment of tax is charged at a variable rate, which (April 2004) is currently 6.5%. And there are extra surcharges: 5% of the relevant amount if payment due on 31 January is not received until 28 February and a further 5% if it is not made by 31 July.

Minimising tax on your investments

Investment income counts as the 'top slice' of your income, so it is taxed at your highest marginal rate. That means it is worth giving some thought to the type of investment products you go for. But do remember the tax planning rule mentioned above: don't choose a product simply because it is tax efficient; choose it because it suits your time horizon, risk profile and investment aims.

But if you can find a product that is more tax efficient than another in your situation, go for it. Here are some examples:

◆ **National Savings** Products such as income bonds pay out income gross so can be useful for non-taxpayers. But remember also you can register to receive gross interest from bank and building society accounts by filling in form R85.

◆ **Mini cash Isas** These pay interest tax-free as do Tessa-only Isas. It makes sense for taxpayers to choose an Isa for their cash savings in preference to taxed accounts, although there can be a dilemma here if you want to invest in equities as well. The maximum investment in an equity Isa is £7,000 (2004-5 tax year), but if you choose a mini cash Isa (maximum £3,000 in 2004-5), the most you can put into an equity Isa is £3,000. Isa investment limits will be cut from April 2005 – see page 102 for details.

◆ **Equity Isas** These are invested in shares and retain some income tax advantage, but only for higher rate taxpayers. Share dividends are taxed at 10% which satisfies basic rate payers' liability and, within an Isa, there is no more for higher rate payers to pay. However, if you choose an Isa investing in fixed-interest securities and corporate bonds, all the interest is tax-free. That's not in itself a good reason to choose a corporate bond Isa in preference to one investing in shares, but if your portfolio includes both types of investment, make sure you use the Isa for investing in the corporate bonds.

Planning between husband and wife

Everyone is taxed separately these days, so if one partner has a lower marginal income tax rate than the other, he or she should hold a couple's income producing investments. At most, this will result in a 40% tax saving, where one partner is a high earner subject to 40% tax and the other is not earning and can get interest free of tax. Investments held jointly are treated by the Revenue as if each partner owned 50% and taxed accordingly.

Married couples can also limit their capital gains liability. Everyone has an annual exemption from capital gains tax (CGT), which for 2004-5 is £8,200. If you want to sell shares which will take you over the exempt amount, consider giving some to your spouse first as this gift will not in itself give rise to a CGT liability. (This does not apply to gifts made to anyone else.) The two of you can then sell the shares and each benefit from an annual exemption.

In addition, the rate at which CGT is charged depends on your income for the year in question: the gain is added on top of your income and taxed at the appropriate rate. So it can still be worth doing this even if you have both used up your exemption for the year, if one partner pays at a lower rate than the other.

Timing

Generally speaking, for UK residents, income tax is payable either during the year in which the income arises or at some point during the following tax year. Capital gains tax is only payable once a profit is realised.

Some financial products provide exceptions to the income tax rule and there is room for manoeuvre if, for example, you are a higher rate taxpayer but are pretty certain you are going to drop down to the basic rate band in a few years. You might be a higher rate taxpayer a few years away from retirement and know your pension income is going to be a lot lower. Here are a few examples of investments which can take advantage of this situation:

◆ **Guaranteed growth bonds** These typically last for three to five years and returns are net of basic rate tax. A liability to higher rate tax arises only in the year in which they mature, so if you have dropped a tax band by then, there may be no extra to pay.

◆ **Offshore roll-up funds** Most offshore funds distribute income yearly, but some roll it up and it is taxable only in the year you encash the fund. This structure is not suitable for equity investments, because all profits from roll-up funds, whether arising from income or capital gains, are taxed as income. But a sterling deposit fund has no possibility of gains, so this allows higher rate taxpayers to delay paying tax on their interest until they cash in the fund after their marginal rate has fallen.

◆ **Qualifying life assurance policies** The underlying investments are taxed as they go at the basic rate, but as long as you obey the qualifying rules, there should be no higher rate tax to pay on maturity. The rules are complex, but basically they cover regular savings life policies kept in force either until maturity or for at least ten years.

◆ **Pensions** See the section below. These are especially tax efficient if the rate you pay when you make the investment is higher than the one you will pay once you start receiving the income.

Three tax-efficient investments

Peps and Isas

Until April 2009, investments held within personal equity plans (Peps) and individual savings accounts (Isas) are free of capital gains tax. As mentioned above, the situation with regard to income tax is more complicated. Peps and Isas which hold interest producing investments such as cash deposits, fixed-interest securities and corporate bonds are free of income tax. But equity funds, defined as those with 40% or more in equities, are subject to tax on dividends at 10% which cannot be reclaimed.

Many investors feel there is no point using Isas for investment any more, as they offer no income tax saving for basic rate taxpayers, while their annual capital gains tax exemption is more than sufficient to cover any gains they make. But it is no more expensive investing in managed funds via an Isa than investing directly, so the question should really be: why not? In any case, you may wish at some point to switch from equities to fixed-interest investments, where the tax advantages are greater.

No one knows what will happen after April 2009, which is after all less than five years away. The government has only pledged to keep the Isa and Pep tax advantages until then, which is hardly helpful for long-term planning. We can only hope whichever party is in power will be convinced of the need to encourage people to save by keeping the tax breaks going.

Pensions

Pensions are one of the most tax-efficient forms of saving. You get income tax relief at your highest rate on money paid into their plan and even non-taxpayers get relief equivalent to the basic rate of tax (22%).

The investments themselves are treated in the same way as investments in Peps and Isas, with no capital gains tax and share dividends subject to tax at 10% only, while interest from cash and fixed-interest investments is tax-free. The drawback with saving through a pension is that your money is tied up until age 50 (and from 2010, 55). Even when you can access it, only 25% can be taken as cash and the rest must be used to provide an income, usually through an annuity.

Nevertheless, most people are looking for a reliable income in retirement to replace their earnings, so the obligation to turn most of the fund into an annuity by age 75 suits their requirements. Pensions, once in payment, are taxed as earned income.

As the tax relief is given up front, pension schemes are particularly tax efficient for people who expect to drop a tax band on retirement. A higher rate taxpayer will get 40% relief on the money going into the plan but may pay tax at only 22% on the income it produces. This also works for non-taxpayers, as they are automatically entitled to basic rate relief on pension savings. A non-earner can save up to £3,600 gross (£2,808 net) into a stakeholder pension and if they have no other income, the resulting pension could well be completely tax-free.

Venture capital trusts and enterprise investment schemes

There are big tax breaks with these schemes, designed to encourage people to take the risk of investing in small companies. In both cases, the companies must have no more than £15m of assets at the time of investment and they can either be unlisted or new issues coming to the Alternative Investment Market (Aim).

An investment in a venture capital trust qualifies for full tax relief up to 40%. The maximum investment is £200,000 and you get the relief (which is limited to the amount of income tax you have actually paid during the year you invest) as long as you hold the trust for at least three years. Disposals are free of capital gains tax and any dividends paid by the underlying companies are tax-free.

Whereas a venture capital trust holds a portfolio of shares, an enterprise investment scheme relates to a single company. Once again, the maximum investment is £200,000 and this attracts 20% income tax relief up front, with the additional attraction that if you have made gains elsewhere, you can 'roll these over' into an EIS without paying CGT. As long as you keep the EIS for at least two years, the investment falls outside your estate for inheritance tax purposes. Disposal of the shares is free of CGT as long as they have been held for three years.

The tax breaks are there, of course, purely because the investments are risky. This is a classic case of needing to be wary of investing just for the tax attraction. Many investors in the past have found the schemes were indeed tax efficient but have still ended up with a loss.

Capital gains tax

Sadly, not many investors in the stock market have had cause to complain of capital gains tax in the past few years. The reason, of course, is that gains have been very hard to come by thanks to the stock market fall of 2000-3. Those selling second homes or buy-to-let properties, however, have come up against the tax with a vengeance.

The CGT rules are complicated and doubly so for anyone who has held assets since before 31 March, 1998, when a different system of calculating taxable gains was in force. Those selling such assets now must use the two methods, one up until that date and the new one thereafter.

The nuts and bolts of the system can all be found in the leaflet CGT1 *Capital Gains Tax, An Introduction* which is free from local tax offices or on www.inlandrevenue.gov.uk. Briefly, taxable gains to 31 March, 1998 are calculated after indexation relief; thereafter they take no account of inflation, but are reduced according to the number of years you have held the asset, a system known as taper relief. Details of taper relief are at the end of this chapter.

Under both systems, you are allowed to deduct the costs of purchase and the subsequent sale from your gain. Under the indexation rules, you can index up the cost of purchase (up to March 1998) and hence reduce the gain.

For property, costs of purchase include survey or valuation and legal fees, the cost of advertising for a buyer and stamp duty, so keep a careful note of all these. Costs of sale would include estate agents' commission. You can also deduct costs of 'enhancing' the property, so once again, keep a careful note of the costs of any improvements you have made.

The annual exemption generally rises each year in line with inflation. For the 2004-5 tax year, it is £8,200. The rate at which CGT is charged, as noted above, depends on your taxable income for the year.

◆ Below the basic rate (22%) starting limit, you are charged at 10%.
◆ Between the basic rate and top rate starting limits, you are charged at 20%.
◆ Above the top rate limit, you are charged at 40%.

Capital losses can be set against capital gains when they are both realised in the same year. So if you know you have a large capital gain coming up – perhaps from the sale of a second property – this would be a good time to go through your investment portfolio. If you have shares or unit trusts which are showing a loss, and which you have wanted to get rid of in any case, this is the time to do it. Finally, note there is no capital gains tax payable on the following:

◆ Your principal private residence;
◆ Private cars;
◆ Personal belongings, such as paintings or furniture, if sold for £6,000 or less;
◆ Foreign currency bought for personal spending abroad;
◆ Gilts;
◆ Peps, Isas, National Savings Certificates, most pension plans;
◆ Shares in qualifying venture capital trusts, enterprise investment schemes and business expansion schemes bought after 18 March, 1986.

Inheritance tax

The first step in sensible planning for inheritance tax (IHT) is to make a will. If you do not, your assets will be divided according to the intestacy rules, which may not reflect your wishes. In England and Wales (but not in Scotland) getting married automatically revokes any will you have made previously, unless the will expressly states it is being made in contemplation of marriage.

The intestacy rules are complicated, but the table opposite gives a summary of what will happen to your assets if you die intestate in England and Wales. The rules in Scotland are slightly different. Under both systems, if you do not have any relatives within the rules' definitions, your estate will pass to the Crown.

Making a will

Quite apart from the tax issue, it makes sense to have a will, as clearing up your estate after death will be much easier. And if you want to leave personal bequests, either particular items or monetary gifts, to friends, godchildren or charities, it is the only way of doing so.

There is no need to use a solicitor, although most people do. You could do it entirely yourself with a will form from stationers or some charities or use a specialist will writing agency.

First, you need to state that this will revokes all others. Then, you must decide who is to be executor. Most people name two, in case one dies before you, and usually appoint relatives. You can also appoint a professional executor such as a solicitor, accountant or bank, but their fees will be charged to your estate, and if relatives are unhappy about this, they may not be able to change it.

The usual practice is to choose someone as the main beneficiary who will receive the residue of the estate after any other specific bequests. Don't leave so much in specific bequests that they are not left with enough after IHT has been paid on the estate.

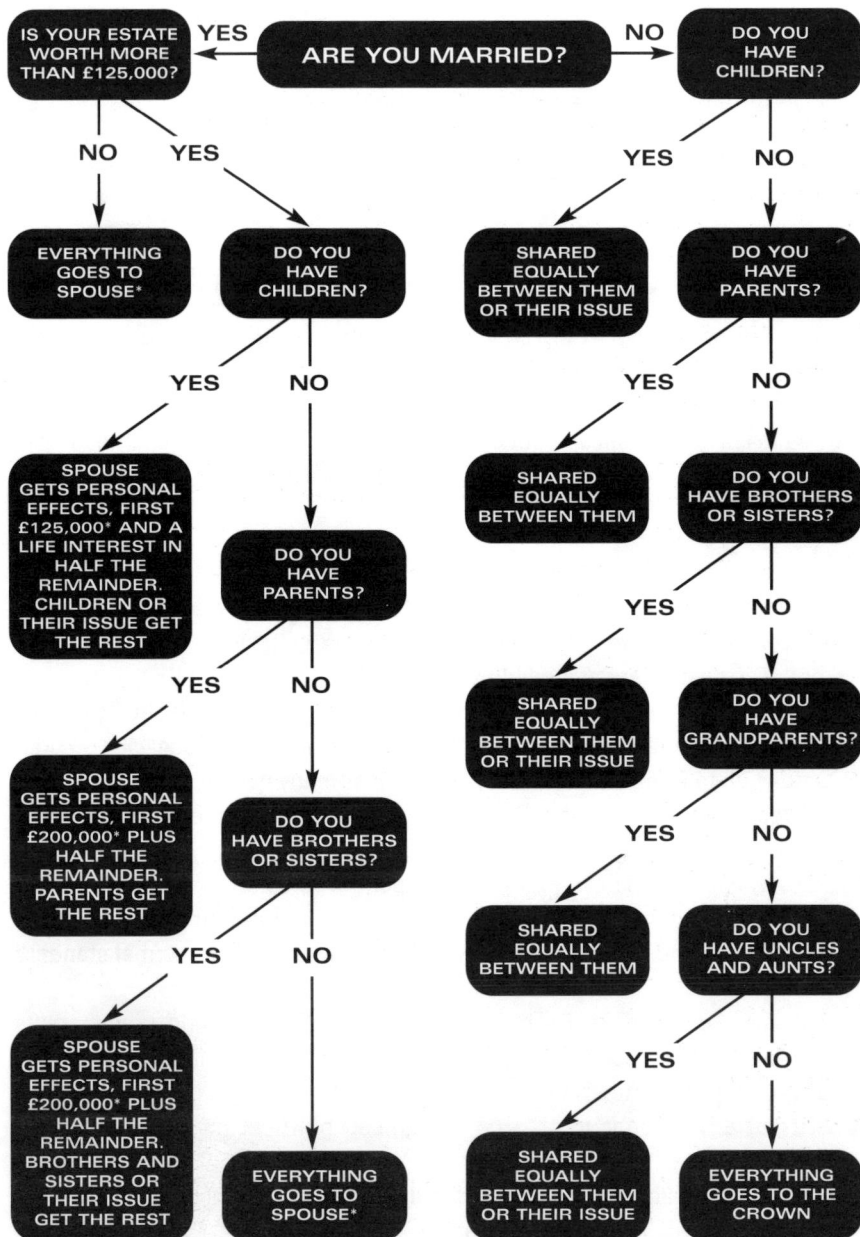

ARE YOU MARRIED?

YES → IS YOUR ESTATE WORTH MORE THAN £125,000?

- **NO** → EVERYTHING GOES TO SPOUSE*
- **YES** → DO YOU HAVE CHILDREN?
  - **YES** → SPOUSE GETS PERSONAL EFFECTS, FIRST £125,000* AND A LIFE INTEREST IN HALF THE REMAINDER. CHILDREN OR THEIR ISSUE GET THE REST
  - **NO** → DO YOU HAVE PARENTS?
    - **YES** → SPOUSE GETS PERSONAL EFFECTS, FIRST £200,000* PLUS HALF THE REMAINDER. PARENTS GET THE REST
    - **NO** → DO YOU HAVE BROTHERS OR SISTERS?
      - **YES** → SPOUSE GETS PERSONAL EFFECTS, FIRST £200,000* PLUS HALF THE REMAINDER. BROTHERS AND SISTERS OR THEIR ISSUE GET THE REST
      - **NO** → EVERYTHING GOES TO SPOUSE*

NO → DO YOU HAVE CHILDREN?

- **YES** → SHARED EQUALLY BETWEEN THEM OR THEIR ISSUE
- **NO** → DO YOU HAVE PARENTS?
  - **YES** → SHARED EQUALLY BETWEEN THEM
  - **NO** → DO YOU HAVE BROTHERS OR SISTERS?
    - **YES** → SHARED EQUALLY BETWEEN THEM OR THEIR ISSUE
    - **NO** → DO YOU HAVE GRANDPARENTS?
      - **YES** → SHARED EQUALLY BETWEEN THEM
      - **NO** → DO YOU HAVE UNCLES AND AUNTS?
        - **YES** → SHARED EQUALLY BETWEEN THEM OR THEIR ISSUE
        - **NO** → EVERYTHING GOES TO THE CROWN

* The spouse will benefit only if he or she survives the intestate by 28 days. Where the spouse does not survive, the intestate estate will be dealt with as if there had been no spouse.

Issue means children (including illegitimate and adopted), grandchildren, great grandchildren, etc.

Brothers and sisters of whole blood come before brothers and sisters of half blood. Uncles and aunts of whole blood come before uncles and aunts of half blood.

Deeds of variation

A will is not necessarily the final word on how your assets will be distributed. It is possible for a deed of variation to be executed after your death. This must be signed by all beneficiaries who will be disadvantaged by the new arrangement and it must be done within two years of your death. One of the most common reasons for such a deed is to avoid or reduce inheritance tax.

Inheritance tax planning

IHT is potentially payable both on gifts made during your lifetime and on assets passing after death. The big exception is assets passing between husband and wife: whether during life or after death, they are exempt from IHT. Everyone is entitled to leave a certain amount of assets free of IHT. This is called the nil-rate band and is £263,000 for the 2004-5 tax year. The tax rate for IHT is 40%.

Lifetime gifts

If you give assets away during your lifetime, they do not immediately attract tax. Depending on how much they are, and to whom they are made, they may be completely and immediately exempt from the tax or they may be 'potentially exempt'. Gifts which are immediately exempt:

◆ Up to £3,000 a year, to anyone. If this allowance is unused, it can be carried forward for one year but the current tax year's allowance must be used up first.

◆ Gifts of up to £250 per recipient per year to as many people as you like. But if the recipient receives more than £250, you cannot claim exemption for the first £250.

◆ Gifts which form 'part of your normal expenditure out of income'. This is not strictly defined but broadly it means they must be made out of income rather than capital and should not be so great as to diminish your normal standard of living.

◆ Gifts made on marriage. Each parent can give £5,000 per child, grandparents can give £2,500 each, and any other relative or friend, £1,000.

◆ Gifts of any amount between husband and wife.

◆ Gifts of any amount to charity, recognised political parties and certain institutions such as the British Museum.

◆ Gifts for the maintenance of your family including, for example, to children under 18 or still in full-time education.

Any other gifts made during your lifetime are potentially exempt. If you live for seven years after making them, they become wholly exempt and fall out of the reckoning. If you die in the meantime, they are set against your nil-rate band. If the total of your potentially exempt lifetime gifts exceeds the nil-rate band, there is some taper relief on the excess, depending on how long you lived after making the gift, as the table opposite shows.

Years between gift and death	% of full IHT rate payable
0-3	100%
3-4	80%
4-5	60%
5-6	40%
6-7	20%

In practice, taper relief is rarely used, because most people are not able to give away enough during their lifetimes to use up the nil-rate band and more.

Simple planning

From the rules described above, it is easy to see what steps can be taken to whittle down IHT at death.

◆ Give away as much money as you can, as early as you can, using both the annual allowances for exempt gifts and making use of the rules on potentially exempt gifts.

◆ Try to use up at least part of your nil-rate band on death. In other words, don't leave everything to your husband or wife, with nothing to the following generations. If, for example, your husband inherited everything, there would be no tax to pay on your estate, but his would be that much greater, increasing the eventual bill.

◆ Consider starting a whole-of-life or term assurance policy which will pay out on your death. The money can be used to pay at least some of the IHT bill.

◆ If you feel uncomfortable making a will that leaves significant sums to people other than your spouse, as you don't know what your joint financial situation will be by then, make sure your family are aware of the deed of variation rules. Make it plain you would be happy for the terms of your will to be altered, if it is sensible and feasible to do so.

Gifts with reservation

The Inland Revenue insists that gifts for IHT purposes are genuinely that and have no strings attached. It has a special category of 'gifts with reservation', where you effectively pretend to give something away but keep some rights over it. For instance, if you give your home to your children but keep the right to live in it rent-free for the rest of your life, as far as the taxman is concerned, it is not a gift at all. You would have to pay the full market rent for the property to escape the gifts with reservation rule.

IHT and your home

One of the most problematic areas with IHT planning is the family home. Thanks to the rise in property values even modest homes in many parts of the UK are well above the current nil-rate band. And unless, before we die, there's a massive hike in the band or a big crash in property prices, they are likely to remain so.

One relatively simple solution sometimes advocated for couples is to hold the property as 'tenants in common' rather than as 'joint tenants'. This means that each partner owns 50% of the property and can give it away to whoever they wish on death. With joint tenancy, the surviving partner automatically inherits the other half.

With tenancy in common you could, for example, leave part of your half to your children. Your widow or widower keeps the rest so has a right to stay in the property but you, meanwhile, have used up some or even all of your nil-rate band on death.

But there are problems. It is always possible relations between the surviving parent and the children could deteriorate after the first death. Or a child could get divorced and his or her share of the home could count as part of their assets in any settlement. Or then again, the survivor might decide to move house and when the house is sold, the children (assuming they are not living there) could face a CGT bill on the increase in the value of their share since your death.

Until the 2004 Budget there were a number of schemes which claimed to avoid IHT on the home by means of trusts. Some have now been made ineffective. It is a hugely complicated area and it is impossible to be certain any scheme will still work at the time of your death. If you are interested in pursuing this, get specialist advice and be prepared to pay significant fees. And remember, you will need ongoing advice to ensure any scheme you choose is still appropriate against a backdrop of changing legislation.

IHT-friendly investments

The Queen Mother's IHT planning could not be faulted, if the stories were true that she had a big overdraft at the time of her death. Dying in debt is maybe an extreme (although guaranteed successful) way of avoiding IHT. However, ironically, you may have to be rich to afford to die in debt. Banks won't be happy extending a huge overdraft to people whose children do not have the assets or income a reigning monarch can command.

But two schemes can produce extra income while allowing people to cut the assets they leave on death. The first is an annuity, the second some form of equity release. You can read about these on pages 162-168 and 55-57. They both, in effect, cut down your capital assets in return for giving you an income. That may mean you can afford to make full use of the rules on IHT exempt gifts. If you are considering either of these schemes, remember there may be an effective 40% saving of the capital cost, thanks to the IHT your estate will be saved.

Biting the bullet

There comes a point at which tax planning can be taken too far. It may not be especially welcome to think part of your estate will be subject to 40% tax, but it's important to keep a sense of perspective. It is far more important to leave your widow or widower with enough to live on comfortably without worry, than to use the whole of your nil-rate band on gifting assets to children or grandchildren.

A little bit of planning – using the annual exemptions, for instance, and bequeathing even modest sums outside these limits to children on your death to make at least partial use of your nil-rate band – will certainly save some tax. For many people, this will be quite enough. After all, if you've got to pay tax, paying it when you're dead is probably the least painful time to do so.

Income tax

Personal allowances for 2004-5

Personal allowance (basic)	£4,745
Personal allowance (age 65-75)	£6,830
Personal allowance (age 75 & over)	£6,950
Married couple's allowance (age under 75*)	£5,725
Married couple's allowance (age 75 & over)	£5,795
Married couple's allowance (minimum amount)	£2,210
Income limit for full age-related allowances	£18,900

*Only those born before 6 April, 1935 qualify

Tax on earned income

Rate	Taxable income
10% on	£0-£2,020
22% on	£2,021-£31,400
40% on	the balance

Savings income

◆ **Interest** Taxpayers below the 40% threshold pay 20% on interest. Taxpayers whose marginal rate is 10% can reclaim 10%.
◆ **Dividends** Share dividends are paid net of a 10% tax credit which satisfies basic rate taxpayers' liability. Non-taxpayers and 10% taxpayers can't reclaim the tax, while 40% taxpayers must pay extra, equivalent to a total of 32.5%.

Capital gains tax

Annual exemptions

£8,200 for individuals
£4,100 for trusts
Tax rate depends on the individual's income for the year.

Taper relief

The percentage of the gain that is taxable (after the annual exemption) falls the longer an asset has been held.

Years owned after 5 April, 1998	% of gain taxable Personal assets	Business assets
1	100%	50%
2	100%	25%
3	95%	25%
4	90%	25%
5	85%	25%
6	80%	25%
7	75%	25%
8	70%	25%
9	65%	25%
10	60%	25%

Assets held before 17 March, 1998 qualify for one year's extra taper relief.

Inheritance tax

Nil-rate band	£263,000
Rate of tax on excess	40%

Trouble-shooting guide

As the earlier parts of this section have made clear, there is not much fun to be had from getting into a mess over your tax and missing the deadlines for payment.

As far as income tax is concerned, there is little excuse for most people to miss the self-assessment deadlines. Keeping your paperwork in reasonable order is the first step to a stress-free life. Taxpayers can justifiably complain the complications of the tax system make their life harder than it might be. The steps required to work out taxable capital gains on, for example, a regular savings unit trust plan which you started contributing to 20 years ago would put off almost everyone. But you can always ask the Inland Revenue for help.

Many people don't like to approach the Revenue direct, even with straightforward questions. But the local enquiry offices are – allegedly – used to dealing with questions from members of the public which start: 'I have a friend who...'

The Revenue website (www.inlandrevenue.gov.uk) is not the most user-friendly but it does contain heaps of information and the introductory leaflets on, for example, capital gains and inheritance tax on the whole succeed in turning highly complex sets of rules into relatively plain English. If you don't have access to the net, you can order most Inland Revenue booklets and leaflets by calling 0845 900 0404.

Appeals

What if you don't agree with a tax demand? You can appeal but there are time limits. You may appeal to one of two independent tribunals: the General Commissioners of Income Tax or the Special Commissioners. Unless your affairs are highly complicated, the General Commissioners are likely to be the most appropriate. They are independent laymen and women, appointed by the Lord Chancellor, who are 'fair, open and impartial and representative of the area for which they are appointed' according to the Revenue.

Special Commissioners are full-time and tend to deal with more complex issues. There are also certain issues which only they can decide upon. For example, any appeal on the value of UK unquoted shares for capital gains tax purposes can only be made to the Special Commissioners. In addition, they alone can make awards of costs, but only if they judge one of the parties has acted 'wholly unreasonably'.

Appeals are free but you have to tell the Revenue in writing that you want to make one within 30 days of receiving the assessment. Later appeals are only allowed if you can demonstrate you have a good reason for the delay.

Complaints

If you want to complain about the way the Revenue has treated you, rather than the amount of tax you have been asked to pay, contact the Inland Revenue Adjudicator. The Adjudicator – who is independent of the Revenue – can look into issues such as:

◆ Mistakes;
◆ Delays;
◆ Misleading advice;
◆ Staff behaviour;
◆ The use of discretion.

Like other ombudsman schemes, you have to try to get your complaint sorted out internally first by contacting the complaints manager of your tax office or, if this does not produce a result, the Inland Revenue director responsible for your office.

If the director does not uphold your complaint, you can then appeal to the Adjudicator, with a six-month time limit for doing so from the director's final reply. You can make your complaint by phone or in writing (see Appendix).

The Adjudicator can only make recommendations in its decisions, but since it was set up in 1993, the Revenue has always accepted these. It can recommend the Revenue apologises, pays you appropriate costs (for telephone calls you have had to make, for instance) and it can also suggest awards for worry and distress, which are typically between £25 and £500.

Still not satisfied?

There's one final option for a determined complainer. If the Adjudicator does not uphold your complaint and you want to take it further, you can ask your MP to put it to the Parliamentary Ombudsman.

7

Getting Advice and Making Complaints

In this section we will look at

The pros and cons of taking advice

Ways to pay for advice

Tied and multi-tied advisers

Independent advisers

How to choose an adviser

Getting specialist advice

How to make a complaint

Protection schemes

7

Getting Advice and Making Complaints

Do-it-yourself financial planning has become much easier nowadays. The press provides plenty of advice, the internet is a mine of information and, of course, there are books such as this one to guide you through the maze. But it often makes sense to get outside help. No matter how much you would like to control your own affairs, you may not have the time or the expertise to do so. And if a real problem arises, it may be that only the intervention of an ombudsman will sort things out. This section is therefore designed to assist you to get help from the right place when you need it. It covers:

◆ **Why seeking advice makes sense** Good advice can often help you organise your financial affairs better and more tax efficiently, and if you receive bad advice you may be able to claim compensation.

◆ **Deciding how to pay for advice** If you want to call the tune, you may need to pay the piper.

◆ **The difference between the types of advisers you may encounter** Some can give you more advice than others.

◆ **Finding an adviser to suit you** How you can narrow down your search.

◆ **Complaining effectively** Don't suffer from bad products or poor service – find out how to get redress.

The pros and cons of taking advice

Many people would like to seek financial advice but are worried they will not be able to find the right sort of adviser. They are often suspicious advisers will put their own interests ahead of those of their customers. This has happened in the past but you can avoid it by picking the right adviser. There are many good ones who are keen to give the best service they can to keep you as a long-term client.

The benefits of taking good professional financial advice are considerable. Advisers can help you plan more effectively for the future. They can help you find the best value products, build up your investments and organise your financial affairs tax efficiently. If they don't and their advice proves unsuitable, you may be able to claim compensation. If, on the other hand, you make your own decisions and something goes wrong, unless you can prove you based your decisions on incorrect and misleading information, you will have no one to blame but yourself and no prospect of compensation.

Paying for advice

If you want advice on personal finance matters, one of your first considerations must be how to pay for it. Some professional advisers such as accountants, solicitors and stockbrokers automatically charge fees. But with financial advisers you have a choice of paying the adviser yourself or letting the company, whose products the adviser has recommended, pay him or her through commission. Either way, you foot the bill.

In future, probably from early 2005, financial advisers will have to provide you with a 'menu' of charging options so you can see exactly how much each one is likely to cost.

Fee-based advice

Fees can seem expensive. You may have to pay £100 an hour or more for an adviser's time. But there can be considerable advantages. It will give you the certainty you are not being recommended certain products just because they pay a high commission. A fee-based adviser can also spend time helping you reorganise or plan your finances without selling you any products at all. Similarly, he or she can recommend investments which pay no commission or where the commission can be stripped out. All this can save you more money in the long run than you pay in fees. On the other hand, there is no guarantee an adviser who charges fees will give you the best advice.

Commission and salary-based advice

If you opt for commission-based advice or go to a salaried adviser, an initial and ongoing annual percentage of the money you pay for the products you buy, such as pensions, insurance policies, investment bonds, individual savings accounts (Isas) and unit trusts, will be deducted to pay the adviser. The amount he or she receives is currently shown in the 'key features' documents when you take out these products. Commission is also paid to advisers by some banks and building societies on savings accounts, and most mortgage providers give commission to advisers who put business their way.

Many who are paid commission give good advice but there is always a suspicion they will not recommend products, such as those from National Savings, which pay no commission and will focus on the products and companies that pay the most. But some advisers will offer to share their commission with you if they feel they are adequately remunerated.

Which is best?

If you can afford it, fees are undoubtedly preferable. They help remove any doubt about an adviser's motives for recommending a certain type of product. But if you don't like having to pay for advice, make sure you shop around among commission-based advisers until you find someone you feel you can trust. Ask them about the interaction between their advice and commission and only go ahead if you are happy with their answers.

Types of adviser

There are plenty of people and companies offering advice, from one-person firms to international organisations. The scope of the guidance they provide will partly depend on the qualifications of the individual advisers and also on the type they are.

Qualifications

All financial advisers must be qualified nowadays. Before they can give advice they must have passed all three levels of the Financial Planning Certificate (FPC) or equivalent. This is a basic qualification which means they have reasonable all-round knowledge of personal finance.

If you want a better qualified adviser, look for one with the Advanced Financial Planning Certificate (AFPC). Advisers with this qualification must have a minimum of five years experience and have passed three exams covering specialist areas. One must be on taxation and trusts, others include pensions, investment portfolio management and long-term care, life and health insurance. When you are seeking specialist advice, it is sensible to look for an adviser with expertise in the area that interests you.

Specialist advisers may also have other qualifications or be members of professional bodies which require them to take other exams. This does not guarantee the advice you will get is any better but it can indicate the adviser cares about his or her professional standing.

Finding out what type of adviser you are dealing with is important as it will influence the extent of the help he or she can provide. Although all advisers are required by regulation only to recommend products that are suitable for your needs, some deal with just one company and others with the whole market. In future, there will also be a halfway house – some advisers will deal with a limited range of companies.

Tied advisers

These are bound to one company so they can only recommend and discuss its products. This means the advice they give will be limited because if their company does not offer certain products, they won't be able to give guidance on them. If you have done your homework and know this company can offer what you want, it may not be a problem. However, it will be up to you to find out whether you could get a more competitive deal elsewhere.

Most banks and building societies fall into this category as they are tied to insurance and investment providers within their own groups or are in partnership with outside companies which pay them commission. The banks and building societies have their own in-house teams of 'financial consultants' (sales staff) based in branches who are trained to advise on these products. They are normally paid a basic salary but targets may be given to encourage them to sell certain products to customers.

In the past many insurance companies also sold their insurance and pension policies through their own sales teams or self-employed consultants. Some, including the Co-operative and Zurich (formerly Allied Dunbar), still do, but many have slimmed down their sales teams and are selling direct over the phone or internet or via banks or independent advisers.

Multi-tied advisers

Rules likely to be introduced around the start of 2005 will permit advisers to have marketing arrangements with several companies instead of just one. Customers will need to be aware these arrangements are commercial ones. There will be no obligation on advisers to choose companies offering the best range of products for consumers; it is more likely to be those that offer the adviser the best deals.

Many banks and building societies are expected to go multi-tied in future to provide customers with some choice. Some self-employed advisers or firms that have operated independently in the past may also convert to multi-tied status as it will be easier for them to deal with a limited number of companies than with the whole market.

Independent advisers

As their name suggests, independent advisers are not linked to particular product providers. This gives them an advantage over tied or multi-tied advisers as they can shop around to find the companies that offer the best products or that have the best investment performance in each area. This does not mean they will necessarily recommend the cheapest products on the market if they can show there are good reasons why others may be more appropriate. Another advantage of this approach is that you will have a greater spread of risk instead of trusting all your finances to one company.

There are a wide variety of independent advisers and the services they offer differ. Some are small firms, some belong to national networks, some are nationwide companies, and some are part of other organisations such as banks or firms of accountants or solicitors. Many are 'general practitioners', dealing mainly with packaged products, such as life insurance, pensions and unit trusts. Some specialise in certain areas, such as investment advice or mortgages. Others offer more extensive financial planning services.

Finding an adviser

Finding an adviser on your local high street is not difficult but most will be tied and work in banks and building societies. Tracking down a good independent one may take more time but could pay dividends in the long run. The best way to find one is through personal recommendation, but if this does not work there are several organisations which can provide details of advisers close to your home or work.

One of the most active is IFA Promotion. Through its helpline (0800 085 3250) or website (www.unbiased.co.uk), you can narrow down the type of adviser you would like by specifying the areas on which you want advice, whether he or she should have advanced qualifications, whether you want to pay by fees or commission and whether you would prefer a male or female adviser.

Other organisations you can contact for details of fee-based independent advisers in your area include the Society of Financial Advisers (020 7417 4442, www.sofa.org) and the Institute of Financial Planning (0117 945 2470, www.financialplanning.org.uk). Both encourage members to gain additional qualifications and have codes of practice by which they must abide. If you would prefer advice with an ethical slant, contact the Ethical Investment Research Service (020 7840 5700, www.eiris.org). See Appendix for addresses.

Once you have a list of advisers, take the time to visit at least two or three before going ahead. It is very important you feel completely happy with the one you choose on a personal as well as a professional level, as you will need to reveal a lot of personal and financial details about yourself. Even though you may only want advice about a specific problem, a long-term relationship could be even better for your finances.

Arrange an introductory chat with as many as you feel you can manage. Even advisers who charge fees will normally be prepared to give you an initial interview free of charge. This is an opportunity for you to find out more about the adviser and the services he or she provides. Don't be shy about asking questions; it's what they expect. Here are some you could ask at your first meeting:

◆ How long has the firm been in existence?
◆ How long have you been an independent financial adviser?
◆ What qualifications do you have over and above the minimum that might be relevant to me?

- Will you be dealing with my affairs or will it be another member of staff? If so, what are his or her qualifications?
- What is my choice of payment options?
- If I decide to pay a fee, can I have an estimate of initial and annual charges, and will there be any charge if I wish to take my business elsewhere in future?
- What ongoing services do you provide?
- Explain what sets your firm apart from the advisers at my bank or building society and from other independent advisers.
- Can I speak to two or three of your other customers about your service?

What an adviser will ask you

Once you have decided to seek the help of a particular adviser, expect to be quizzed in considerable detail about your financial affairs. It is a legal requirement for advisers to carry out a full 'fact find' so they know all about your circumstances before giving you guidance. Even if you only want advice on a specific problem, they will need to know about your overall situation so they can put this in the right context.

They will ask about your income, any pension provision, your mortgage, debts, insurance, savings and so on, as well as discussing your family commitments and what you want to achieve in the future. Your attitude to risk will be another key consideration if you need advice about savings and investment. Be prepared to provide paperwork and details of your current arrangements.

After you have supplied all this information, you will normally receive a report outlining the adviser's understanding of your present circumstances and needs and setting out his or her recommendations. You can then decide if you want to go ahead. If you don't understand something, ask for a further explanation. If you are still unsure seek a second opinion.

Don't be rushed into decisions and don't sign any blank forms. Be wary if an adviser suggests you sell all your existing investments and buy a complete set of new ones. There may be a good reason for suggesting changes if your present investments are unsuitable or poor performers or if your needs have changed. However, switching can be expensive and should only be undertaken if it is absolutely necessary.

Other advisers

If you need help on specialist subjects, it may be better to use a specialist adviser.

Legal matters

If there are legal matters on which you need advice, such as divorce or drawing up a will, you will need to consult a solicitor. To find one locally that specialises in the area that you require, contact the Law Society (020 7242 1222, www.lawsoc.org.uk). Some solicitors also offer financial planning and investment advice on a fee basis. For names, contact the Association of Solicitor Investment Managers (01732 783548, www.asim.org.uk) or Solicitors for Independent Financial Advice (01372 721172, www.sifa.co.uk).

Pensions

If you need advice about complex pension matters, such as a transfer from a company scheme, you may need to see an actuary. The Association of Consulting Actuaries (020 7248 3163, www.aca.org.uk) can provide names of firms in your area.

Shares

For advice on which shares to buy, or share portfolio management services, you will need to go to a stockbroker. Many will also provide advice on unit and investment trusts, venture capital trusts, enterprise investment schemes and other investment areas. To find out which stockbrokers offer these services, contact the Association of Private Client Investment Managers and Stockbrokers (020 7247 7080, www.apcims.co.uk).

Tax

Accountants are the best source of advice of tax matters. Some also provide independent advice on a range of financial matters. For names of local accountants, contact the Institute of Chartered Accountants (England and Wales: 020 7920 8100, www.icaew.co.uk; Scotland: 0131 347 0100, www.icas.org.uk), the Association of Chartered Certified Accountants (020 7396 7000, www.accaglobal.com) or the Chartered Institute of Taxation and the Association of Tax Technicians (020 7235 9381, www.tax.org.uk).

Trusts

There are a variety of professionals who can provide advice on how to set up and manage trusts. For a list of specialists with practical expertise from the legal, accountancy, insurance and other professions, contact the Society of Trust and Estate Practitioners (020 7763 7152, www.step.org).

Complaints

This book is designed to arm you with the information you need to make the right financial decisions and avoid the pitfalls that might prevent you making the most of your money. But even the best laid plans can go wrong. The trouble-shooting guides in each section have dealt with some of the most common problems. Here we look at how to tackle complaints generally.

As a consumer, remember it is vital to exercise your rights. Too many people are apathetic and this gives businesses the upper hand. Making the most of your money means not putting up with unsatisfactory goods and services. It is important to complain if you are unhappy with items that take up a large part of your budget, be they financial products or regular household bills.

You must always give the organisation which provided the goods or services a chance to put things right, but if you are dissatisfied with the response there are a number of ombudsmen schemes and other complaints bodies which will take up your case. They may not rule in your favour, but if they do you may be awarded compensation or at least put into a position where you haven't lost out.

A step-by-step guide to making a complaint

- Contact the organisation concerned, preferably by letter, to explain your problem. If it is no longer in existence, a regulatory body such as the Financial Services Authority (FSA) or your local trading standards agency should be able to advise you what to do.
- Send the letter to the person you first dealt with, or if they are no longer employed, to the head of the relevant department.
- You may prefer to outline your complaint over the phone but always keep a note of the conversation and the full name of the person you spoke to, and send a follow-up letter.
- Write 'complaint' at the top of your letter, include any reference or account numbers, explain your case as clearly and as briefly as you can and what you would like the company to do about it. You might request an apology, for matters to be put right or compensation. Remember to keep a copy of your letter.
- If you are not happy with the reply, ask for details of the company's formal complaints procedure. If it does not have one, write to the chief executive, stating your case again and why you are dissatisfied.
- If your complaint is still unresolved, take the matter to an independent complaints scheme. If you are not sure which to contact, call the FSA (0845 606 1234) or the Office of Fair Trading (0845 722 4499).
- Ask for the scheme's guide to making a complaint. This will explain exactly what information you need to provide and may supply a form on which you can give the details of your case.
- The scheme will examine what has happened and decide if your complaint should be upheld. If it rules in your favour, it will tell the firm what it needs to do to resolve the matter. The firm may also be ordered to compensate you. Some schemes can make financial awards of up to £100,000.
- Don't leave it too long to complain. Many schemes have strict time limits within which you must act once you become aware of a problem.

Independent complaints schemes

◆ **Financial Ombudsman Service** This provides a single complaints scheme which covers most types of financial firms including banks, building societies, financial advisers, friendly societies, investment managers, life insurance companies, pension companies and stockbrokers. From the end of October 2004 it will also deal with complaints about mortgage intermediaries, including brokers and estate agents, and from January 2005 it will cover general insurance brokers such as those selling motor and household policies. Contact: www.financial-ombudsman.org.uk.

◆ **Office for the Pensions Advisory Service** Opas provides initial advice and conciliation for complaints about employers' pension schemes. Contact: www.opas.org.uk.

◆ **Pensions Ombudsman** This ombudsman decides on complaints relating to company pension schemes which Opas has been unable to resolve. It also handles complaints relating to the management of personal and stakeholder pensions. The Financial Ombudsman deals with complaints about the mis-selling of these two schemes. Contact: www.pensions-ombudsman.org.uk.

◆ **Ombudsman for Estate Agents** This is a voluntary scheme dealing with complaints about estate agents from both buyers and sellers but not all estate agents are members. Contact: www.oea.co.uk.

◆ **Legal Services Ombudsman** Complaints should go to the lawyers' own professional body, the Law Society, in the first instance. The Legal Services Ombudsman oversees how these are handled in England and Wales. Contact: www.olso.org. The Scottish Legal Services Ombudsman does the same for Scotland. Contact: www.slso.org.uk.

◆ **Energywatch** This deals with complaints about gas and electricity companies. Contact: www.energywatch.org.uk.

◆ **Office of Telecommunications** Take your complaint to your telephone company first. If still unhappy, go to Oftel. Contact: www.oftel.gov.uk.

◆ **Office of Water Services** Complain to your local water company first but if you are dissatisfied and want to take the matter further, go to Ofwat. Contact: www.ofwat.gov.uk.

◆ **Inland Revenue Adjudicator's Office** This deals with complaints about the way Revenue staff have treated you. Contact: www.adjudicatorsoffice.gov.uk.

◆ **British and Irish Ombudsman Association** This provides a list of ombudsmen and other complaint handling bodies in the UK and Ireland, together with contact details. Contact: www.bioa.org.uk.

◆ **Office of Fair Trading** The consumer information section of its website contains lots of useful advice about your rights and where to go for help, with contact details of many other bodies from trading standards departments for shopping problems to the Society of Motor Manufacturers and Traders for complaints about cars. There are also details of organisations for holiday complaints and information on the court service including details of the small claims procedure. Contact: www.oft.gov.uk.

Protection

If you lose money due to maladministration or mis-selling or an organisation fails to honour its side of a bargain, an ombudsman can order the company concerned to put matters right. If the firm has gone bust or fraud has occurred, this may not be possible. However, a compensation scheme may be able to bail you out.

The Financial Services Compensation Scheme

You won't necessarily receive 100% compensation, so if you are worried about firms going bust you will be better protected if you spread your money around. The maximum amounts of compensation are:

◆ **Bank and building society deposits** 100% of the first £2,000 and 90% of the next £33,000 per individual (maximum £31,700).
◆ **General insurance** Compulsory insurance, such as third-party motor cover: 100%; non-compulsory insurance, such as home contents cover: 100% of the first £2,000 and 90% of the rest.
◆ **Long-term insurance** 100% of the first £2,000 and 90% of the remaining value of the policy.
◆ **Investments** 100% of the first £30,000 and 90% of the next £20,000 (maximum £48,000).

Contact: www.financial-ombudsman.org.uk.

Pension Protection Fund

Due to start in 2005, this will cover the pensions of members of insolvent final salary schemes when companies have collapsed. It will provide 100% of the pensions of those members who have already retired and 90% of those yet to retire up to a certain cap. The fund will also take over the responsibilities of the Pensions Compensation Board covering the liabilities of schemes where fraud or dishonesty has occurred.

Appendix

Regulation

The Financial Services Authority
25 The North Colonnade
Canary Wharf
London E14 5HS
Consumer helpline: 0845 606 1234
Website: www.fsa.gov.uk
Consumer helpline email: consumerhelp@fsa.gov.uk

Ombudsmen, complaints and advisory schemes

The Financial Ombudsman Service
South Quay Plaza
183 Marsh Wall
London E14 9SR
Tel: 0845 080 1800
Website: www.financial-ombudsman.org.uk
For complaints about individual pensions and free-standing AVCs, life
insurance, general insurance, mortgage, savings and investment products.

The Pensions Ombudsman
11 Belgrave Road
London SW1V 1RB
Tel: 020 7834 9144
Website: www.pensions-ombudsman.org.uk
For complaints about occupational pension schemes.

The Inland Revenue Adjudicator's Office
Haymarket House
Haymarket
London SW1Y 4SP
Tel: 020 7930 2292
Website: www.adjudicatorsoffice.gov.uk

The Office for the Pensions Advisory Service (Opas)
11 Belgrave Road
London SW1V 1RB
Tel: 0845 601 2923
Website: www.opas.org.uk
Email: enquiries@opas.org.uk
For advice about occupational pension schemes.

The Occupational Pensions Regulatory Authority (Opra)
Invicta House
Trafalgar Place
Brighton BN1 4DW
Tel: 01273 627600
Websites:
www.opra.gov.uk
www.stakeholder.opra.gov.uk
For general complaints about the running of company pension schemes. Opra does not handle individual complaints.

The Law Society's Consumer Complaints Service
Victoria Court
8 Dormer Place
Leamington Spa
Warks CV32 5AE
Tel: 01926 822007/8/9

The Ombudsman for Estate Agents
Beckett House
4 Bridge Street
Salisbury
Wilts SP1 2LX
Tel: 01722 333306
Website: www.oea.co.uk

The Mortgage Code Arbitration Scheme
12 Bloomsbury Square
London WC1A 2LT
Tel: 020 7421 7444
For complaints about mortgage brokers until October 2004; thereafter they will be dealt with by the Financial Ombudsman Service.

The General Insurance Standards Council
110 Cannon Street
London EC4N 6EU
Tel: 0845 601 2857
Website: www.gisc.co.uk

Pensions and retirement

The Pension Service
Your local DWP office or Jobcentre
See phone book for details
Tel: 0845 731 3233
Website: www.thepensionservice.gov.uk
For information on all aspects of state pensions.

The Pension Schemes Registry
PO Box 1NN
Newcastle upon Tyne NE99 1NN
Tel: 0191 225 6316
Website: www.opra.gov.uk
To track down old company pension schemes.

The Pre-Retirement Association
9 Chesham Road
Guildford
Surrey GU1 3LS
Tel: 01483 301170
Website: www.pra.uk.com

The Pensions Compensation Board
11 Belgrave Road
London SW1V 1RB
Tel: 020 7828 9794

Retirement Pension Forecasting Team
Department for Work and Pensions
Newcastle upon Tyne NE98 1WB
Tel: 0845 300 0168
Website: www.dwp.gov.uk

Annuity advisers

Many IFAs advise on annuities. The following are a selection of specialist advisers.

The Annuity Bureau

The Tower
11 York Road
London SE1 7NX
Tel: 020 7902 2300
Website: www.annuity-bureau.co.uk

Annuity Direct

32 Scrutton Street
London EC2A 4RQ
Tel: 020 7684 5000
Website: www.annuitydirect.co.uk

Wentworth Rose

Central House
75-79 Park Street
Camberley
Surrey GU15 3PE
Tel: 0127 626111
Website: www.retirement-advice.co.uk

Home income plans

Safe Home Income Plans (Ship)

PO Box 516
Preston Central PR2 2XQ
Tel: 0870 241 6060
Website: www.ship-ltd.org

Freeholds and leases

The Leasehold Advisory Service

70-74 City Road
London EC1Y 2BJ
Tel: 020 7490 9580
Website: www.lease-advice.org

Financial advisers

Fee-Based Advice
FBA House
PO Box 59
Droitwich
Worcs WR9 8YE
Tel: 0870 201 0111
Website: www.fba.co.uk

IFA Promotion
117 Farringdon Road
London EC1R 3BX
Tel: 0800 085 3250
Website: www.unbiased.co.uk

The Institute of Financial Planning
Whitefriars Centre
Lewins Mead
Bristol BS1 2NT
Tel: 0117 945 2470
Website: www.financialplanning.org.uk

The Association of Private Client Investment Managers and Stockbrokers (APCIMS)
114 Middlesex Street
London E1 7JH
Tel: 020 7247 7080
Website: www.apcims.co.uk

The Society of Financial Advisers (Sofa)
20 Aldermanbury
London EC2V 7HY
Tel: 020 7417 4442
Website: www.sofa.org
All members of Sofa have the advanced financial planning certificate.

The Association of Solicitor Investment Managers (ASIM)
Riverside House
River Lawn Road
Tonbridge
Kent TN9 1EP
Tel: 01732 783548
Website: www.asim.org.uk

Solicitors for Independent Financial Advice
10 East Street
Epsom
Surrey KT17 1HH
Tel: 01372 721172
Website: www.sifa.co.uk

The Association of Pension Lawyers
c/o Chris Webber
Charles Russell
8-10 New Fetter Lane
London EC4A 1RS
Tel: 020 7203 5000
Website: www.apl.org.uk

The Ethical Investment Research Service
80-84 Bondway
London SW8 1SF
Tel: 020 7840 5700
Website: www.eiris.org
Email: ethics@eiris.org

Accountants

The Institute of Chartered Accountants in England and Wales
Moorgate Place
London EC2P 2BJ
Tel: 020 7920 8100
Website: www.icaew.co.uk

The Institute of Chartered Accountants of Scotland
21 Haymarket Yards
Edinburgh EH12 5BH
Tel: 0131 347 0100
Website: www.icas.org.uk

The Association of Chartered Certified Accountants
29 Lincoln's Inn Fields
London WC2A 3EE
Tel: 020 7396 7000
Website: www.accaglobal.com

The Chartered Institute of Taxation and the Association of Tax Technicians
12 Upper Belgrave Street
London SW1X 8BB
Tel: 020 7235 9381
Website: www.tax.org.uk

Actuaries

The Association of Consulting Actuaries
1 Wardrobe Place
London EC4V 5AG
Tel: 020 7248 3163
Website: www.aca.org.uk
Email: acahelp@aca.org.uk

Legal matters

The Law Society
113 Chancery Lane
London WC2A 1PL
Tel: 020 7242 1222
Website: www.lawsoc.org.uk

The Law Society of Northern Ireland
Law Society House
98 Victoria Street
Belfast BT1 3JZ
Tel: 02890 231614
Website: www.lawsoc-ni.org

The Law Society of Scotland
26 Drumsheugh Gardens
Edinburgh EH3 7YR
Tel: 0131 226 7411
Website: www.lawscot.org.uk
Email: lawscot@lawscot.org.uk

Specialist magazines

Moneyfacts / Investment, Life & Pensions Moneyfacts
Moneyfacts House
66-70 Thorpe Road
Norwich
Norfolk NR1 1BJ
Tel: 0870 2250 476
Subscriptions: 0870 2250 1000
Website: www.moneyfacts.co.uk
Moneyfacts magazine publishes a monthly round-up of all savings account rates. For more up-to-date listings, see its website. *Investment, Life & Pensions Moneyfacts* gives details of a wide range of insurance and investment products, including annuity rates and performance statistics.

Money Management
FT Business
Tabernacle Court
16-28 Tabernacle Street
London EC2A 4DD
Subscriptions: 020 8606 7545
Money Management is aimed at professional advisers, with performance statistics and articles on aspects of financial planning.

Trade bodies

The Association of Investment Trust Companies
Durrant House
8-13 Chiswell Street
London EC1Y 4YY
Tel: 0800 085 8520
Website: www.aitc.co.uk
Provides information on aspects of investing in investment trust companies.

The Investment Management Association
65 Kingsway
London WC2B 6TD
Tel: 020 8207 1361
Website: www.investmentuk.org
Provides information on investing in unit trusts and Oeics.

Proshare
Centurion House
24 Monument Street
London EC3R 8AQ
Tel: 020 7220 1730
Website: www.proshare.org
Advises on setting up investment clubs and runs education programme.

The Association of British Insurers
51 Gresham Street
London EC2V 7HQ
Tel: 020 7600 3333
Website: www.abi.org.uk
Publishes information sheets on all aspects of insurance.

The British Insurance Brokers Association
14 Bevis Marks
London EC3A 7NT
Tel: 020 7623 9043
Website: www.biba.org.uk

The Building Societies Association
3 Savile Row
London W1S 3PB
Tel: 020 7437 0655
Website: www.bsa.org.uk

The Council of Mortgage Lenders
3 Savile Row
London W1S 3PB
Tel: 020 7437 0075
Website: www.cml.org.uk

The National Association of Estate Agents
Arbon House
21 Jury Street
Warwick
Warks CV34 4EH
Tel: 01926 496800
Website: www.naea.co.uk

The Royal Institution of Chartered Surveyors
12 Great George Street
Parliament Square
London SW1P 3AD
Tel: 020 7222 7000
Website: www.rics.org.uk

The Association of Residential Letting Agents (Arla)
Maple House
53-55 Woodside Road
Amersham
Bucks HP6 6AA
Tel: 0845 345 5752
Website: www.arla.co.uk

The Association of Policy Market Makers
Holywell Centre
1 Phipp Street
London EC2A 4PS
Tel: 020 7739 3949
Email: enquiries@apmm.org
Trade body for dealers in second-hand endowments. Has directory of members.

The Society of Trust and Estate Practitioners
26 Dover Street
London W1S 4LY
Tel: 020 7763 7152
Website: www.step.org

Charities

Age Concern England
Astral House
1268 London Road
London SW16 4ER
Tel: 020 8765 7200
Information line: 0800 009966
Website: www.ageconcern.org.uk

Age Concern Cymru
4th floor
1 Cathedral Road
Cardiff CF11 9SD
Tel: 0292 037 1566

Age Concern Scotland
113 Rose Street
Edinburgh EH2 3DT
Tel: 0131 220 3345

Age Concern Northern Ireland
3 Lower Crescent
Belfast BT7 1NR
Tel: 0289 024 5729

Help the Aged
207-221 Pentonville Road
London N1 9UZ
Tel: 020 7278 1114
Senior Line (information service): 0800 800 6565
Website: www.helptheaged.org.uk
Email: info@helptheaged.org.uk

Age Concern and Help The Aged can provide advice and information on many financial matters for retired people.

Borrowing

The Office of Fair Trading
Fleetbank House
2-6 Salisbury Square
London EC4Y 8JX
Tel: 0845 722 4499
Website: www.oft.gov.uk

The National Debtline
Tel: 0808 808 4000
Website: www.nationaldebtline.co.uk

The Consumer Credit Counselling Service
Tel: 0808 138 1111
Website: www.cccs.co.uk

The Association of British Credit Unions
Holyoake House
Hanover Street
Manchester M60 0AS
Tel: 0161 832 3694
Website: www.abcul.org

Experian
Consumer help service
PO Box 8000
Nottingham NG80 7WF
Tel: 0870 241 6212
Website: www.experian.co.uk

Equifax
Credit file advice centre
PO Box 1140
Bradford BD1 5US
Tel: 0870 010 0583
Website: www.equifax.co.uk

Call Credit
1 Park Lane
Leeds LS3 1EP
Tel: 0870 060 1414
Website: www.callcredit.co.uk

More websites

There are a huge number of websites offering information aimed at savers, investors and borrowers. The following are, necessarily, only a small selection of those available in May 2004.

Buying or selling a home

www.rightmove.co.uk
www.primelocation.com
www.assertahome.com
www.fish4homes.co.uk
www.huntahome.com
www.vebra.com
www.easier.co.uk
For buying and selling without an estate agent:
www.houseweb.com

Investment information and advice

www.investment-gateway.com
www.find.co.uk
www.moneyfacts.co.uk
www.funds-sp.com
www.trust-net.com
www.citywire.co.uk
www.everyinvestor.co.uk
www.morningstar.co.uk

Fund supermarkets

www.hargreaveslansdown.co.uk
www.fidelity.co.uk/direct/select/fidelity/

Offers of free financial newsletters and guides

www.financial-freebies.com

Online bookstore for investment books

www.global-investor.com

Books on investment

Beginners Guide to Investment, Bernard Gray, Random House
The Wealth Guide, Financial Times, Penguin
The New Online Investor, Peter Temple, J Wiley
The Motley Fool Investment Workbook, T Gardner, Simon & Schuster
One up on Wall Street, Peter Lynch, Penguin

Index

accident, sickness and unemployment cover 120–21
added years, pension contributions 151
additional mortgage security fee 46
additional voluntary contributions 150–51
advice 203–14
  commission-based 206–7
  fee-based 206
  salary-based 206–7
advisers 207–11
  independent 208–9
  multi-tied 208
  tied 208
  what to look for 209–10
AER *see* annual effective rate
all risks insurance 128
Alternative Investment Market 75
alternatively secured income 173
annual effective rate 12
annual percentage rate 34
annuities 162–7, 181–2
  and mortality drag 172
  for those in bad health 166
  how they work 162–3
  investment linked 167
  types of 164–5
annuity rates 150
  guaranteed 167
APR *see* annual percentage rate
assurance 110
assured shorthold tenancy 57
ASU *see* accident, sickness and unemployment cover
AVC *see* additional voluntary contributions
avoidance, tax 4
bank 1–2
  compensation scheme 17
bank accounts
  opening 12
  types of 11–15
Bank of England's Base Rate 10–11
bank statements 1
Banking Code 12
bankruptcy 40
base rate 10
boats, insurance of 133
BoEBR *see* Bank of England's Base Rate

boiler-room scams 105–6
borrowing 29–63
British and Irish Ombudsman Association 213
building societies, compensation schemes 17
buildings insurance 125–7
business, performance of 78–80
buying a house, costs of 51–3
buy-to-let, as an investment 58, 73–4
buy-to-let mortgages 57–8
capital gains tax 193–4, 200
  and Isas 23
capped rate mortgage 42
car loans 38
caravan insurance 132
cashbacks, and mortgages 43
Child Trust Fund 24, 104
children's accounts 13
Children's Bonus Bonds 16
CIF *see* collective investment funds
club accounts 13
collective investment funds 74–5
collective investments 89–106
  performance over time 97–8
  proposition to investors 90
  selecting 95–7
company pensions 148–53
  and retirement 161–2
  problems with 159–60
  topping up 150–51
company research, on the internet 87
complaints 211–13
  endowment mortgages 58–61
  making 203–14
compound interest 17–18
contents insurance 127–8
contrarianism, as an investment style 84
credit 31–9
  turned down 32–3
credit cards 2, 36–7
credit reference agencies 32, 33
credit scoring 32
credit unions 38–9
critical illness cover 115–16
CTF *see* Child Trust Fund
current accounts 2

debt, getting out of 39–40
decreasing term insurance 111
deed of variation, will 196
deferred car purchase loans 38
deferred retirement 161
defined benefit schemes, pensions 148–9
defined contribution schemes, pensions
    149–50
dental health insurance 123–4
dental treatment, cost of NHS 124
deposits 66–7
    and house purchase 48–9
discounted variable rate mortgage 43
discounts, and insurance policies 131
distribution funds 92, 100
dividend yield 77
dynamic asset allocation 101
early retirement 161
earnings, of a business 77
EBITDA 78
emergency money 9–11
endowment mortgage 3
    compensation for mis-selling 61
    mis-selling 3, 20
    time limits for complaints 60–61
    trouble shooting guide 58–61
    why they went wrong 50
endowment policies 114
    problems with 19–20
Energywatch 213
enterprise investment schemes 192
enterprise value, of a business 77
Equitable Life 19
equity 68
    of a business 77
equity income trusts, performance of 176
equity Isas 190
equity release 55, 182–3
escalator bonds 16
ETF see exchange traded funds
evasion, tax 4
excesses, and insurance policies 131
exchange traded funds 93
execution only stockbroker 88
family income benefit insurance 111
fast-track mortgages 47
final salary schemes 148–9

financial advisers 207–11
Financial Ombudsman Service 59, 60,
    136, 213
financial planning, the basics 1–5
Financial Services Authority 105
Financial Services Compensation Scheme
    214
first-time buyers 48–9
fixed-interest securities 177–8
fixed-rate accounts 15–16
fixed-rate bonds 16
fixed-rate investments 67, 72
    short-term 16–17
fixed-rate mortgage 42
fixed-returns saving plans 18
flexible mortgage 44–5
flooding, and insurance 126–7
FOS see Financial Ombudsman Service
freehold and leasehold 54–55
free-standing AVC 150–51
friendly society plans 23–4
FSAVC see free-standing AVC
fund supermarket 93–4
fundamental analysis of a business 78
funeral plans 114–15
gearing 22, 67–8
    and house purchase 50–51
general insurance 124–37
GIBs see guaranteed income bonds
greater fool theory of investment 84
group personal pension 157
growth investing 83–4
guaranteed credit, pensions 145
guaranteed growth bonds 16, 191
guaranteed income and growth funds 99
guaranteed income bonds 16, 180
higher loan to value fee 46
high-income funds 99
home, and inheritance tax 198
home improvements, borrowing for 48
home income plans 56
home insurance 125–9
home responsibilities protection 144
home reversion schemes 56–7
home security 128–9
home working, and insurance 128
house insurance 125–9

and flooding 126–7
and subsidence 126
HRP *see* home responsibilities protection
identity theft 33
IHT *see* inheritance tax
impaired credit loans 47–8
impaired life annuity 166
Incapacity Benefit 119
income drawdown plans 171–2
income replacement insurance 116–20
Income Support, and mortgage payments 121
income tax 199
income, and size of mortgage 42
independent advisers 208–9
index tracker fund 22, 92
individual investment account 102
individual savings accounts 14, 16, 191–2
  and emergency funds 11
  annual allowance 23
  self select 89
individual voluntary arrangement 40
inheritance tax 181, 194–8, 200
inheritance tax planning 196–8
initial public offering 80
instant access accounts 11, 14
insurance 3, 107–138
  accident, sickness and unemployment 120–21
  boats 133
  caravans 132
  compared with assurance 110
  cost of term 111, 113
  critical illness cover 115–16
  dental 123–4
  discounts 131
  endowment policies 114
  excesses 131
  funeral plans 114–15
  getting the most from your policies 137
  home 53, 125–9
  income replacement 116–20
  life 110–14
  medical 121–3
  motor 129–31
  motorbikes 132
  outdoor events 135
  paying by instalments 131
  pets 133–4
  problems with claims 135–7
  term 110–13
  travel 134–5
  weddings 135
  whole of life policies 114
interest, tax on 13
interest cover 78
interest-only mortgage 50–51, 56
interest rates 12
internet accounts 14
internet, use for company research 88–9
investing 3, 63–106
  after retirement 173–84
  for children 104
  for growth or income 103
  for retirement 104–5
  styles of 81–6
investment 63–106
  advice 104
  asset split 71–2
  club 89
  planning 4
  returns 69
  risk 65–6, 69–71
  trusts 94–5
  trusts, international 22
investments, minimising tax 189–99
IPO *see* initial public offering
Isa *see* individual savings account
job, changing, and pensions 152–3
joint policy, insurance 111
Key Homebuy scheme 49
Land Registry charges 52
Leasehold Advisory Service 55
leasehold homes 54–5
legal fees, house purchase 52
Legal Services Ombudsman 213
level-term insurance 111
life insurance 110–14
life insurance funds 98–9
life policies, selling 20–21
life policies, surrendering 20–21
lifestyle funds 100
lifestyle savings plans 21–2

limited risk funds 92, 101
loan, cost of 35
London Stock Exchange 75
long-term savings 20
managed funds 92
managed savings plans 18–19
managed unit-linked savings plans 21–2
market capitalisation 77
market-maker 76
maxi Isas 14
MIG see mortgage indemnity guarantee
mini cash Isas 14, 190
mis-selling endowment mortgages 59
money purchase schemes, pensions
  149–50
monthly income accounts 14
mortgage 2–3, 41–61
    and cashbacks 43
    but to let 57–8
    cost of 41
    flexible 44–5
    high percentage loan 46–7
    impaired credit loans 47–8
    indemnity guarantee 46, 47
    payment protection insurance 54,
      120–21
    payments, and Income Support 121
    repaying 49–50
    repayment, and government help 121
    size of 41–2
    term 43–4
motor insurance 129–31
motorbike insurance 132
MPPI see mortgage payment protection
  insurance
multi-tied advisers 208
National Insurance contributions 143–4
    home responsibilities protection 144
    gaps on contribution 143
    voluntary contributions 143
National Savings 17, 189–90
National Savings Pensioners' Guaranteed
  Income Bonds 17
Nav see net asset value
nest egg 2
net asset value 77, 94
no-claims discount 130

nominal rate 12
nominee accounts, with stockbrokers 87
notice accounts 11, 14
occupational pensions 148–53
Oeics see open-ended investment
  companies
Ofex 75
Office for the Pensions Advisory Service
  213
Office of Fair Trading 213
Office of Telecommunications 213
Office of Water Services 213
offshore roll-up funds 191
Ombudsman for Estate Agents 213
open-ended investment companies 92–3
    charges 93
outdoor event insurance 135
overdraft 35–6
own job, any job, and income replacement
  insurance 117–18
paid up life policies 20
penny shares 81
pension contributions, changes in 147
pension credit 145–6
pension forecast 142
Pension Protection Fund 214, 147
Pensions Ombudsman 213
pensions 3–4, 142–60, 191, 192
    advice 211
    alternatively secured income 173
    and changing companies 151–3
    and tax-free lump sums 167–8
    company 148–53
    deferred 142–3
    final salary schemes 148–9
    income drawdown plans 171–2
    money purchase schemes 149–50
    occupational 148–53
    personal 156–8
    phased retirement arrangement
      168–70
    reviewing provisions 158–9
    stakeholder 151, 153–6
    state 142–7
Pep see personal equity plan
PER see price/earnings ratio
permanent interest bearing shares 178

personal equity plan 178–9, 191–2
personal loans 37–8
personal pensions 156–8
    and retirement 161–2
    group 157
pet insurance 133–4
phased retirement arrangement 168–70
Pibs *see* permanent interest bearing
  shares
plc *see* publicly limited company
PMI *see* private medical insurance
policy in trust 112
postal accounts 12, 14
precipice bonds 101
Premium Bonds 14–15
price to book 77
price to sales 77
price/earnings ratio 77
private medical insurance 121–3
profit margins 78
property, as investment 67–8, 72–3
publicly limited company 76
qualifying life assurance policies 191
rainy day money 9–11
rate tarts 46
remortgaging 46
repayment mortgage 49–50
retirement 139–184, 160–62
    age, changes for women 142
    and tax 179–80
    early 161
    investing after 173–84
    investing in later years 180–83
    late 161
    phased arrangement 168–70
retirement planning course 173
return on capital employed 78
S2P 144, 145
salary sacrifice, and pensions 151
Sandler Report 20, 146–7
savings 7–28
savings credit, pensions 145
savings plans 18–23
savings plans, performance of 26
savings strategy 25
Scarps *see* structured capital at risk
  products

sector rotation 86
secured loans 37
self-certified mortgages 47
self-employed, and stakeholder pensions
  154
self-invested personal pension 157–8
    and changing job 153
self-select Isas 89
selling a house, costs of 51–3
Serps *see* state earnings-related pension
  scheme
share certificate 88
share issue, new 80–81
shared ownership 49
shareholders 76–7
shares, advice on investing in 86–7, 211
shortfalls on endowment policies 19–20
sick pay 118–19
Sipp *see* self-invested personal pension
split-capital investment trusts 95
spread betting 89
stakeholder pensions 151, 153–6
    and investing for children 104
stamp duty, and house purchase 52
standard variable rate mortgage 43
state earnings-related pension scheme 144
state pensions 142–7
    additional 144–6
state second pension *see* S2P
stock market 75–89
stock-market savings plans 22
stockbrokers 76, 88
stock-market investment 18
store cards 37
structured capital at risk products 101
subsidence, and insurance 126
survey, house 53
tax 4, 185–202
    advice 211
    appeals 201
    avoidance 4
    capital gains 193–4, 200
    complaints 201–2
    income 199
    inheritance 194–8
    minimising on investments 189–99
    on interest 13

payments deadlines 189
penalties for late payment 189
planning 185–202, 188
returns, dates for filing 189
technical analysis of a business 78
telephone accounts 12, 15
term insurance 110–13
   and pension schemes 112
   cost of 111, 113
tied advisers 208
travel insurance 134–5
treasurer accounts 13
trusts, advice on 211
unit trusts 90–91, 92–3

charges 92–3
unit-linked funds 21–2, 99
unsecured loans 37–8
valuation, house 53
value investing 82–3
value of a business 77
variable interest accounts 13–15
venture capital trusts 192
wedding insurance 135
whole-of-life policies 114
will, making 194, 196
with-profits bonds 99–100
with-profits funds 99
with-profits savings plans 19–21